Joomla! 4 Masterclass

A practitioner's guide to building rich and modern websites using the brand-new features of Joomla 4

Luca Marzo

BIRMINGHAM—MUMBAI

Joomla! 4 Masterclass

Group Product Manager: Alok Dhuri
Publishing Product Manager: Harshal Gundetty
Book Project Manager: Prajakta Naik
Senior Editor: Rounak Kulkarni
Technical Editor: Jubit Pincy
Copy Editor: Safis Editing
Project Coordinator: Manisha Singh
Proofreader: Safis Editing
Indexer: Tejal Daruwale Soni
Production Designer: Alishon Mendonca / Ponraj Dhandapani
Developer Relations Marketing Executive: Deepak Kumar and Rayyan Khan
Business Development Executive: Puneet Kaur

First published: January 2023

Production reference:1221222

Published by Packt Publishing Ltd.
Livery Place
35 Livery Street
Birmingham
B3 2PB, UK.

ISBN 978-1-80323-897-5

www.packt.com

To my grandmother, Gina, for her love and support.

Special thanks to my friends Eugenia and Giovanni, and my sister Erica, for their support on this writing adventure.

– Luca Marzo

Foreword

Powering millions of websites worldwide, Joomla has proven to be one of the major **content management systems (CMSes)**. It's flexible, versatile, secure, and very stable, and it's packed with possibilities, right inside the core. Whether you're a first-time hobby user or a web developer by profession, Joomla 4 (the latest version) offers you a platform you can use to build almost everything you can imagine… if you know how and where to start.

And that is exactly what this book is about. In *Joomla! 4 Masterclass*, Luca Marzo explains everything you need to know to create any – and by any, I really mean any – kind of website. The book covers information for users at various skill levels, whether creating your first content, customizing the look and feel of your website, using extensions, creating overrides, or using Joomla's CLI.

If anyone can thoroughly guide you through the many options of Joomla, it is Luca. He has been secretary of Joomla's board of directors since 2017 and was in several Joomla teams before that (in case you didn't know, the developers, maintainers, and everyone else working for Joomla are all volunteers). Luca breathes Joomla. He is dedicated, committed, thorough, and meticulous, and he knows virtually everything there is to know. When he told me he was going to write this book, I was thrilled, because I knew it would turn out the way it has: a comprehensive guide for everyone who wants to explore the countless features and possibilities of the world's most powerful CMS.

Enjoy the ride!

Anja de Crom

Team Leader,
Joomla! Community Magazine Team

Contributors

About the author

Luca Marzo is a technology professional with more than 15 years of experience. During his career, he has had the chance to develop websites with Joomla as a freelancer for small to medium-sized companies. He served as an IBMer for 1.5 years. After that, he moved to the web hosting industry. His love for Joomla was born in 2007, a few months after which he started contributing to the Italian Joomla Community. He then progressed to contribute to the global community, where he had the opportunity to serve as the secretary and member of the board of directors for The Joomla Project at a global level for more than 5 years. In The Joomla Project, he has also contributed to the Certification Program, the Community Magazine, and the Extensions Directory.

About the reviewers

Pascal Abatiello is a trainer, editor, and writer. He founded his company in 2012, developing a network of e-learning websites and providing training classes about major CMSes, including Joomla, WordPress, and PrestaShop; SEO techniques; and digital marketing. He's also the co-founder of Host Academy, a leading e-learning portal that has trained thousands of webmasters and website integrators.

Benjamin Trenkle is a Joomla developer and the owner of Wicked Software, a web development company based in Munich, Germany. He is deeply involved in the Joomla! community, serving as a release lead and production department coordinator. In his free time, Benjamin enjoys programming and volunteering. He is passionate about using his skills to make a positive impact on the world. On his home page, www.wicked-software.de, Benjamin showcases some of his work and extensions and provides information on his services and experience.

Table of Contents

3

Advanced Content Management   37

4

Exploring the Flexibility of Modules   59

5

Building Your Site Structure: the Menu System   77

Part 2: Advanced Features

7

11

Command-Line Interface   177

Part 3: Styling and Securing Your Website

12

Styling Your Website – Templates   189

13

Customize Everything with Overrides   209

Part 4: Case Studies

17

Case Study – A Corporate Website in Joomla   279

18

Case Study – Online Academy with Joomla   287

19

Case Study – A B&B Booking System with Joomla   295

Preface

Joomla! 4 Masterclass is a book that explores all the major functionalities of the new version of the software. Joomla is one of the most widely used **Content Management Systems (CMSes)**, powering around 2.7% of the world's websites. Joomla 4.x, released in the third quarter of 2021, is the new major version of the CMS, coming 9 years after the release of Joomla 3.0, and is packed with many new features that empower website integrators, allowing them to build rich websites with ease.

CMSes such as Joomla allow you to develop a website without having coding skills or a command of the PHP, JavaScript, or CSS language. In many cases, you can build composite layouts visually using a drag-and-drop interface. Furthermore, you can extend a CMS's functionalities by adding extensions, such as plugins, so that you can transform your website into an online shop, a reservation system, or an e-learning portal. All the major CMSes on the market benefit from a large ecosystem of developers providing extensions and templates to heavily customize a website and satisfy most of the needs of website developers or owners.

This book will show you how to build a website, using the numerous features included in Joomla, and debunk certain myths related to its perceived complexity.

Use of the Joomla!® name, symbol, logo, and related trademarks is permitted under a limited license granted by Open Source Matters, Inc.

Who this book is for

This book is ideal for all those who want to start using Joomla, irrespective of whether they have used a previous version or not. Joomla newcomers will benefit from the inclusion of screenshots depicting the functionalities and step-by-step guides. Experienced Joomla users will be introduced to the brand-new features of Joomla 4, seeing them in action in the examples and analyzing three real case studies.

This book is suitable for either website developers or CMS integrators, as well as website owners that would like to become independent, managing their websites by themselves. Exercises at the end of each chapter allow the readers to apply and test their knowledge.

What this book covers

Chapter 1, A Powerful and Extensible Core, introduces the Joomla core, presenting the backend interface and its main features, and the opportunities to expand its functionalities using extensions.

Chapter 2, How to Manage Content, explores the content management features, explains how to structure content, and compares Joomla's functionalities with other major CMSes.

Chapter 3, Advanced Content Management, points out some advanced features for handling content, whether scheduled publishing options, custom fields, how to build a custom publishing workflow, or how to produce accessible content.

Chapter 4, Exploring the Flexibility of Modules, explains modules, a basic and flexible element that is used to build both the frontend and backend layouts of the website. Modules can display specific content in a particular position on the website.

Chapter 5, Building Your Site Structure – the Menu System, teaches the reader how to build the navigation system of a website through the menu, build complex navigation structures, handle different menu item lists, manage language associations for multilingual sites, and govern access permissions.

Chapter 6, Managing Users and Their Permissions, demonstrates how to manage user accounts, registration, login, permissions, and much more. Furthermore, it introduces the powerful **Access Control List (ACL)** system.

Chapter 7, SEO at Its Best, details all the integrated features that can improve the **Search Engine Optimization (SEO)** of the website.

Chapter 8, One Site, Multiple Languages, illustrates how to build a multilanguage website in Joomla thanks to the built-in features.

Chapter 9, Planning Operations with Scheduled Tasks, presents the tool for scheduling and automating recurring operations on a website.

Chapter 10, Tailored Communication with Mail Templates, shows the reader how to customize default emails sent by their website.

Chapter 11, Command-Line Interface, describes the CLI offered by Joomla, showing how to execute operations on the website through the terminal.

Chapter 12, Styling Your Website – Templates, provides an overview of the templates and shows how to customize the look and feel of a website using Joomla's options.

Chapter 13, Customizing Everything with Overrides, is all about overrides, a method that allows you to customize how part of a website looks without the need to alter the original template.

Chapter 14, Child Templates, reveals a brand-new functionality of Joomla that allows you to create derived styles and templates, increasing the degree of customization and simplifying maintenance.

Chapter 15, Template Frameworks, goes through the most used template frameworks in Joomla, going through their options and showing how to build a custom style with ease.

Chapter 16, Advanced Features – Access and Security, covers some advanced functionalities dedicated to logging in, multi-factor authentication, and site security hardening.

Chapter 17, Case Study – A Corporate Website in Joomla, makes use of a case study to show how the CMS has been used to build a company's main website, replacing an old JSP frontend with a fast and lightweight website.

Chapter 18, Case Study – An Online Academy with Joomla, implements another case study with a CMS that has been used to build an e-learning portal that sells and provides access to thousands of online lessons for many students.

Chapter 19, Case Study – A B&B Booking System with Joomla, incorporates another practical example of a CMS that has been used to build the website for a tourist rental flat, implementing a full-featured reservation system integrated with online booking portals.

To get the most out of this book

It's recommended to set up a personal installation of Joomla that can be either local (for example, using **XAMPP**) or online (for example, using `launch.joomla.org`). Using an online free instance would be preferable, as you don't have to install and configure local web servers.

Software/hardware covered in the book	Operating system requirements
Joomla 4.x	Windows, macOS, or Linux
SP Page Builder	A modern web browser (Mozilla Firefox, Google Chrome, or Apple Safari)
Solidres	
Helix Ultimate	
T4 Framework	
Gantry	

In the case study presented in Chapter 19, the Pro version of Solidres and some paid plugins were used.

Download the color images

We also provide a PDF file that has color images of the screenshots and diagrams used in this book. You can download it here: `https://packt.link/jaQUU`.

Conventions used

There are a number of text conventions used throughout this book.

`Code in text`: Indicates code words in text, database table names, folder names, filenames, file extensions, pathnames, dummy URLs, user input, and Twitter handles. Here is an example: "Simply create a new file under the `/css` folder of your template called `custom.css`."

A block of code is set as follows:

```
.myfooter {
  font-size: 13px;
  font-weight: 600;
  color: #1c77ba;
}
```

Bold: Indicates a new term, an important word, or words that you see onscreen. For instance, words in menus or dialog boxes appear in **bold**. Here is an example: "From **System Dashboard**, open **Site Templates**."

> **Tips or important notes**
> Appear like this.

Get in touch

Feedback from our readers is always welcome.

General feedback: If you have questions about any aspect of this book, email us at customercare@ packtpub.com and mention the book title in the subject of your message.

Errata: Although we have taken every care to ensure the accuracy of our content, mistakes do happen. If you have found a mistake in this book, we would be grateful if you would report this to us. Please visit www.packtpub.com/support/errata and fill in the form.

Piracy: If you come across any illegal copies of our works in any form on the internet, we would be grateful if you would provide us with the location address or website name. Please contact us at copyright@packt.com with a link to the material.

If you are interested in becoming an author: If there is a topic that you have expertise in and you are interested in either writing or contributing to a book, please visit authors.packtpub.com.

Share Your Thoughts

Once you've read *Joomla! 4 Masterclass*, we'd love to hear your thoughts! Scan the QR code below to go straight to the Amazon review page for this book and share your feedback.

https://packt.link/r/1803238976

Your review is important to us and the tech community and will help us make sure we're delivering excellent quality content.

Download a free PDF copy of this book

Thanks for purchasing this book!

Do you like to read on the go but are unable to carry your print books everywhere?

Is your eBook purchase not compatible with the device of your choice?

Don't worry, now with every Packt book you get a DRM-free PDF version of that book at no cost.

Read anywhere, any place, on any device. Search, copy, and paste code from your favorite technical books directly into your application.

The perks don't stop there, you can get exclusive access to discounts, newsletters, and great free content in your inbox daily

Follow these simple steps to get the benefits:

1. Scan the QR code or visit the link below

https://packt.link/free-ebook/9781803238975

2. Submit your proof of purchase

3. That's it! We'll send your free PDF and other benefits to your email directly

Part 1 – Joomla! Out of the Box

In this part, you will get an overview of the Joomla Core and its functionalities. You will discover the features included in the **Content Management System** (CMS) and how to use them. This part will also cover how to create and manage content through articles and modules. You will then go through some advanced publishing features and see how to create a navigation system for your website. The final part of the section is dedicated to user and permission management functionalities.

This section has the following chapters:

- *Chapter 1, A Powerful and Extensible Core*
- *Chapter 2, How to Manage Content*
- *Chapter 3, Advanced Content Management*
- *Chapter 4, Exploring the Flexibility of Modules*
- *Chapter 5, Building Your Site Structure – the Menu System*
- *Chapter 6, Managing Users and Their Permissions*

1

A Powerful and Extensible Core

One of the major characteristics of Joomla is represented by its core: a modern and robust web application that integrates many features and allows you to plan, build, and manage a complete website without the need to use a high number of extensions.

There have been several discussions over the years within the Joomla development team about decoupling features from the core in favor of a more lightweight core. However, over the years, the application has been constantly enriched by powerful and useful functions.

As of the 4.x version, Joomla includes features to create, organize, handle, and enrich articles and content, which is its primary scope. Plus, it offers a series of additional functions to build multilingual websites, manage users, build publishing workflows, handle media files, and customize the appearance of websites.

Furthermore, the main advantage of Joomla is its extensibility, allowing a website administrator to install additional features through third-party extensions to build complex websites and rich applications.

After reading this chapter, you will have gained the following capabilities:

- An understanding of the Joomla backend application
- To know what a Joomla extension is and the different types of extensions available
- To be familiar with the extensions shipped with the basic Joomla package

Technical requirements

To complete the exercise proposed in this section of the book, you need to have a Joomla instance installed on a **Linux, Apache, MySQL, PHP (LAMP)** stack, either locally or remotely. You can easily install Joomla following the instructions published at `https://docs.joomla.org/J4.x:Installing_Joomla`.

If you don't have an online hosting, you can launch a Joomla instance online for free using the official service at `https://launch.joomla.org`.

> **Note**
>
> LAMP is commonly used to refer to a Linux-based hosting environment, on either local, shared, or dedicated hosting, which offers Apache, PHP, and MySQL services.

Once you have your instance up and running, you can log in to the backend section of the website, accessible from `<yoursiteurl.tld>/administrator`. This represents the Joomla backend application that we'll explore in depth in the next section.

The backend application

Joomla comprises two interconnected applications: a frontend application and a backend one. The frontend is the part of the system that is visible to website visitors. The backend is the part of the system that is used by the webmaster or the administrator to configure, build, and manage the website.

The backend is also the area that hosts most of Joomla's functionality. These features include, but are not limited to the following:

- Log-in/log-out
- Article management
- Category management
- Media management
- Custom fields
- Module management
- Menu management
- Updates management
- Extensions management
- Users management
- Permissions management
- Template management
- Language management
- Application configuration

Joomla also exposes a wide set of APIs that allow extension developers to integrate core features (for example, category management) into their extensions, providing administration users with a consistent experience within the backend application.

Throughout this book, we'll go through the features offered by the Joomla core and explore their options and the possibilities they provide.

The backend experience

One of the novelties introduced in Joomla 4 is a completely redesigned backend user experience, with a collapsible sidebar menu that replaces the previous horizontal top-bar drop-down navigation system provided by Joomla until version 3.10.

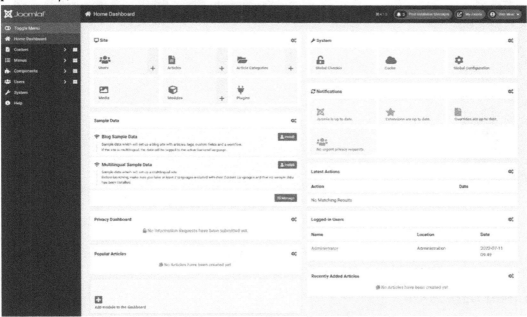

Figure 1.1 – The Joomla 4 dashboard

The new backend design found its origin in UX research conducted by Elisa Foltyn, who published a draft of the administration experience in the Joomla Community Magazine in December 2017 (*A new User Interface for the Joomla Backend, Episode IV*, https://magazine.joomla.org/all-issues/december-2017/episode-iv-a-new-user-interface-for-the-joomla-backend). The draft and preview were discussed extensively among the *community* and core developers, with the final version being slightly different from the original proposal. However, some key concepts are implemented in what we can now appreciate as **Atum**, the backend template.

Now that we know a little about the backend, let's go on to explore the various menus in the dashboard.

Exploring the Joomla dashboards

Beyond the left sidebar menu for administration, Atum features another new concept to Joomla: *dashboards*. Dashboards have been introduced to provide a *summary* page where users can access all the relevant features for a specific area. Some of the dashboards are *pre-defined* and available to all Joomla administrators upon installation, for example, the **Content Dashboard**, **Users Dashboard**, **Components Dashboard**, **Menu Dashboard**, and **System Dashboard**:

Figure 1.2 – Components Dashboard

As shown in the preceding screenshot, dashboards are a collection of links to useful resources and functions. Let us explore these dashboards to see what each one has to offer.

Content Dashboard

In *Figure 1.3*, we can see the **Content Dashboard**, which allows us to access all the most common features to manage content.

Figure 1.3 – Content Dashboard

The dashboard includes the following links:

Item/Link	Description
Content	
Articles	Opens the list of articles
New Article (+)	Creates a new article
Categories	Opens the list of categories
New Category (+)	Creates a new category
Featured Articles	Opens the list of articles that are featured
Popular Articles	Shows the most-read articles
Content Settings	
Custom Fields	Manages the custom fields for articles
Custom Field Groups	Manages the groups of custom fields
Modules & Media	
Media	Opens the Media Manager
Site Modules	Opens the list of modules tied to the frontend
New Site Module (+)	Creates a new module for the frontend
Administrator Modules	Opens the list of modules tied to the backend
New Administrator Module (+)	Creates a new module for the backend
RECENTLY ADDED ARTICLES	Shows the latest articles created on the website
ADD A MODULE TO THE CONTROL PANEL	Allows an administrator to customize the dashboard by adding other modules

Table 1.1 – Content Dashboard

To summarize, the **Content Dashboard** allows an administrator to access almost all aspects of content management for the website, thanks to direct links to the features.

As we can see in *Figure 1.3* and *Table 1.1*, the dashboard can be completely customized. In fact, the administrator can add, move, and remove modules in the **Content Dashboard**, as well as in any other of the pre-defined dashboards. This is particularly important as it allows the administrator to build a personal backend experience, with custom modules and dashboards that are tailored to their specific needs.

Also, as we'll understand further in this book, every block (module) includes *Permissions* management features, allowing the site administrator to create personal dashboards also based on the permission level, differentiating the backend experience for the different access levels and permissions.

Next, we're going to explore the the **Home Dashboard**.

Home Dashboard

The Home Dashboard is a special dashboard that is shown right after logging in to the backend of the website:

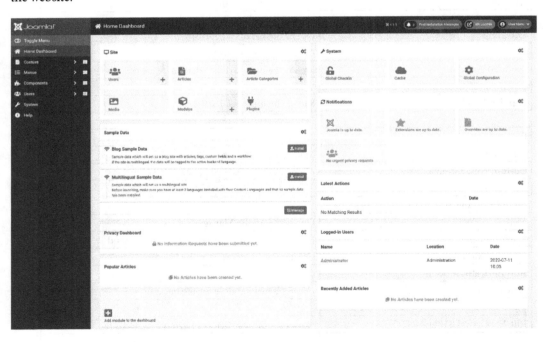

Figure 1.4 – The Home Dashboard serving as the control panel

It allows the administrator to quickly access the most used and useful features, as well as to instantly check the status of the website. Let us explore a few of these in detail, starting with the **Site** module.

The Site module

From the **Site** module under **Home Dashboard**, the administrator can access the following options:

- **Users**
- **Articles**
- **Article Categories**
- **Media**
- **Modules**
- **Plugins**

Figure 1.5 – The Site module

Another key module in this dashboard is the **Latest Actions** module.

The Latest Actions module

The **Latest Actions** module shows the five most recent actions executed by users and administrators on the website. The module takes data from the **User Action Log** feature included in **User Management**, which we will see later in the book.

The System module

Toward the right side of the screen, we can find the **System** module.

Figure 1.6 – The System module

As you can see in the preceding figure, this module displays three buttons:

- **Global Checkin**: This option allows you to check whether some items are locked in the database (for example, articles and contacts)
- **Cache**: This option allows you to check the status of the system cache and purge it
- **Global Configuration**: This option allows you to access the Global Configuration screen

Next comes the **Notifications** module.

The Notifications module

The **Notifications** module shows four status icons/buttons, as seen in the following screenshot:

Figure 1.7 – The Notifications module

Let us look at what each of these does:

- **Joomla! Update Status**: This area checks and provides notifications on the availability of an update for the CMS
- **Available Updates**: This section checks and notifies the user of the availability of updates for any of the installed extensions
- **Override(s) to check**: This section notifies the administrator about the need to verify whether an update of the CMS files may have caused the overrides to be obsolete
- **Privacy Requests**: This section shows whether there are any privacy information or deletion requests that are classified as urgent

In *Figure 1.7*, the status is up to date, but the notifications change based on the status.

> **Note**
> The threshold to classify a request as urgent is completely customizable. We will discuss the core privacy features in *Chapter 6* of the book.

Next, let's look at the **Privacy Dashboard**.

Privacy Dashboard

The **Privacy Dashboard** module shows the list of the most recent privacy information or deletion requests. Just like the notification icon presented in *Figure 1.7*, this module is also directly connected to the Privacy Tool Suite of features that were introduced in Joomla in version 3.9. We will explore the privacy features in depth in *Chapter 6*.

Logged-in Users

The **Logged-in Users** section displays the list of users that are currently logged in to the system, either in the frontend or backend applications. The application to which they are logged in is displayed next to the name of the user. For users logged in to the website frontend, the administrator can also log them out.

The Recently Added Articles module

The **Recently Added Articles** module shows the list of the latest articles created on the website, together with their author and date of creation.

In addition to this, there is the **Popular Articles** module, which shows the most-read articles on the site.

Toward the bottom of the dashboard, there is a button that allows you to add a module to it so that you can customize the appearance of the dashboard. Moreover, each of these modules can also be customized/edited and rearranged in another position or unpublished.

With this module, we have completed the exploration of the **Home Dashboard**. We will now explore another useful dashboard, the **System Dashboard**.

System Dashboard

Another special dashboard is the **System Dashboard**, which collects all the principal options to set up and configure the Joomla installation:

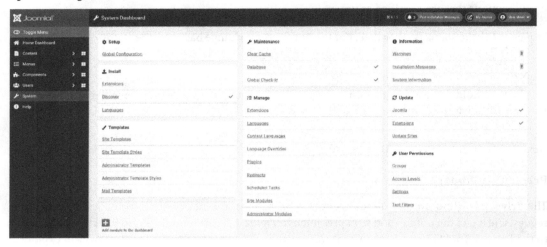

Figure 1.8 – System Dashboard

This dashboard is made up of modules that cannot be edited or unpublished since it is the only path to access some specific features of the application.

Let's explore the commands and options provided by the **System Dashboard**:

Item/Link	Description
Setup	
Global Configuration	Opens the Global Configuration page
Install	
Extensions	Opens the page from which you can install extensions
Discover	Shows the presence of any extensions loaded via FTP that are ready to be installed
Languages	Installs new languages for the website
Templates	
Site Templates	Opens the list of installed templates
Site Template Styles	Opens the list of installed template styles
Administrator Templates	Opens the list of installed administrator templates
Administrator Template Styles	Opens the list of installed administrator template styles
Mail Templates	Lists and manages the email templates for the website
Maintenance	
Clear Cache	Flushes the cache of the website
Database	Checks whether the database structure is aligned and OK
Global Check-in	Checks whether there are locked items in the database
Manage	
Extensions	Opens the list of installed extensions
Languages	Opens the list of installed languages
Content Languages	Opens the list of installed content languages
Language Overrides	Opens the list of active overrides for languages
Plugins	Opens the list of installed plugins
Redirects	Manages redirects and broken links
Scheduled Tasks	Manages scheduled and recurring operations
Site Modules	Opens the list of modules for the frontend
Administrator Modules	Opens the list of modules for the backend
Information	
Warnings	Displays the number of warnings regarding the instance of Joomla
Installation Messages	Displays the number of installation post-notifications to be read
System Information	Opens the system information page
Update	
Joomla	Displays the availability of an update for Joomla
Extensions	Displays the number of updates available for the installed extensions
Update Sites	Opens the list of updated sites used to check the availability of new versions
User Permissions	
Groups	Opens the list of user groups
Access Levels	Opens the list of access levels
Settings	Opens the permissions management page
Text Filters	Opens the text filters setup page

Table 1.2 – System Dashboard

Once again, it is possible to add additional modules to this dashboard to customize its appearance.

We'll now move on to another important dashboard, the **Component Dashboard**.

Component Dashboard

The Component Dashboard represents the access point to the installed components, which we'll explore later in the chapter. This dynamic dashboard will grow automatically as we install other components on our websites.

The dashboard is made up of the same links to component parts that can be found under the **Components** menu in the sidebar.

Every installed component has a specific menu that allows the administrator to access a specific page or function.

For example, the **Contacts** component that is included by default in any Joomla installation has four links both in the **Components Dashboard** and in the **Components** menu. These links allow you to do the following:

- Open the list of created contacts
- Open the list of categories of contacts
- Open the list of custom fields for contacts
- Open the list of groups of custom fields for contacts

There is no standard number of menu items for each component, as the needed number is specific to the needs of the component.

Extensions

As mentioned at the beginning of this chapter, Joomla is a flexible CMS that allows you to extend its functionality with the help of additional software that can be installed on top of its core. Extensibility is a common feature for a CMS and has been key to the success of Joomla. In fact, this aspect allowed the growth of an extensions developer ecosystem, which has resulted in thousands of extensions being published over the years.

So, what is an extension? As the name suggests, an extension extends the CMS, providing additional functionality.

Possible examples are that you need to install a specific extension to add e-commerce features to your Joomla installation, or you need to install a photo gallery extension to build galleries easily on your website.

Extension types

In contrast to the other CMSs, Joomla makes use of several types of extensions. In fact, in Joomla you can have the following extension types:

- Components
- Modules
- Plugins
- Libraries
- Packages
- Templates

There are several differences between the types of extensions, and we will explore each one in brief here (you can refer to the *Further reading* section at the end of this chapter to learn more about these extensions).

Components

Components are mini applications. If you consider Joomla to be your website **operating system (OS)**, you can consider a component as an application that you install on your OS. Components are installed to add features to the website and have two parts—an administration part, accessible via the backend of Joomla, and a site part, accessible through the website frontend.

Several components are provided in the core installation of Joomla, including **Contacts**, **Tags**, **News Feeds**, and **Banners**, which we will explore in a separate section.

You will need a component to add the following features:

- Backup
- E-commerce
- Newsletter

When you install an extension that adds specific functionality, it generally includes a component and other parts such as modules, plugins, and libraries.

Modules

Modules are used to display information or render data from components. They are used to build the page layout, showing specific features, such as the login module and the latest articles modules. Modules are assigned to menu items so that you can show a module on specific pages of the website. It is also possible to create custom HTML modules to show information or custom code.

Modules are used extensively in the backend and the frontend of the website.

Plugins

Plugins are the smallest type of Joomla extensions and provide features associated with trigger events. That means that when an event (for example, a page load) occurs, the function provided by the plugin is triggered.

There are multiple categories of plugins, based on the event type with which they are associated, for example, users, system, content, and authentication.

Also, any extensions can add custom events that trigger the action of specific plugins.

Libraries

Libraries are additional packages of code that provide a group of functionalities. Also, Joomla includes a series of external libraries to provide some features, for example, PDF export features, jQuery, PHPMailer, and a rapid application development framework.

Packages

Packages are a particular type of extension that allows administrators to install multiple extensions at once. For example, if an extension comprises a component, some modules (frontend and backend, for instance), and some plugins, it is common for the developer to provide just a single package. This way, it is easier to install the extension with all the needed *pieces* at the same time instead of executing multiple installations.

Templates

Templates are a type of extension that dictates how a website looks. There are two different types of templates: frontend templates and backend templates.

Frontend templates are used on the publicly accessible side of a website. The default frontend template for Joomla 4 is *Cassiopeia*.

Backend templates are used to render the administration interface. Atum is the default backend template for Joomla 4, and it is the one visible in the screenshots included in this chapter.

Extensions management

The backend application of Joomla includes several functions to manage extensions, allowing the administrator to conduct the following operations:

- Install a new extension
- Update an extension
- Delete an extension
- See the list of installed extensions

All extensions, whether downloaded for free or paid, are provided in the `.zip` file format and can be installed through the dedicated function in the Joomla backend.

The extensions management features are accessible through the **System Dashboard**.

The Joomla! Extensions Directory

From the backend of the application, you can access the **Install from Web** feature, which allows you to install any of the thousands of extensions published on the Joomla! Extensions Directory. This is a web portal in which third-party developers publish their extensions, either free or paid.

Extensions will add to your website additional features and capabilities, on top of those included by default. In the next section, we will explore the components included in the standard Joomla setup.

Exploring the included components

By default, Joomla includes a bunch of components, as well as other extensions, providing some basic features. Let's explore the components shipped with the default package.

The Banners component

Banners is a component that allows an administrator to manage advertising banners on their website. Banners are a piece of content that might include media and/or text that contains advertising material. For each banner, the component allows you to set up the maximum number of impressions and the type of advertising strategy (for example, periodic or unlimited). Each banner should be linked to a client. The number of times a banner is displayed on the website (impressions) and the number of clicks on the banners are tracked by the component.

Banners might be placed in modules on the website frontend, such as common advertising that we are used to seeing on many websites nowadays.

The Contacts component

Contacts is one of the most used components in Joomla. It allows you to create contacts and provide a contact form for each of the contacts created. It is used to handle an *address book* of the different contacts of a company, allowing users to write to the desired person through a contact form published on the website frontend. Contacts can be organized into categories and can be enriched with additional custom fields.

The News Feeds component

News Feeds is a component that allows an administrator to integrate content from other websites. It gets as input an RSS feed and can import the content from a third-party website. Such external content might be displayed in a frontend module. For example, a local news website could use the **News Feeds** component to provide additional national news to their readers, importing RSS feeds of a national news provider.

The Smart Search engine

Smart Search is the internal search engine of Joomla. Smart Search indexes automatically, if enabled, the contents of the website and provides pertinent search results upon request to website users through a search engine module.

It is a comprehensive solution to index the content and provides users with an **OpenSearch**-compatible search engine. Administrators can extend the types of indexable content through additional plugins, allowing the component to index products, users, and much more.

The Tags component

Tags is a *supporting* component that allows administrators to introduce an additional level of categorization to their content. Tags are used to mark related content, surpassing the limit of a category for each item. Also, the same tag can be applied to content items across content types.

Tags are like *labels* that can be applied to content items. The component is used only to create, list, and manage tags.

Summary

In this chapter, we have discovered the overall experience offered by the backend of Joomla, which tools it provides, and how it is structured. We have also learned what dashboards are available in the backend and how they can be customized to fit the needs of any website administrator.

After reading this chapter, you have learned how to navigate the backend of Joomla, understand the difference between the types of extensions available, and know the basics of the components shipped in a default Joomla installation. In the next chapter, we will go in-depth into the content management features.

Further reading

- Component from Joomla! Documentation, `https://docs.joomla.org/Component`
- Module from Joomla! Documentation, `https://docs.joomla.org/Module`
- Plugin from Joomla! Documentation, `https://docs.joomla.org/Plugin`
- Library from Joomla! Documentation, `https://docs.joomla.org/Library`
- Package from Joomla! Documentation, `https://docs.joomla.org/Package`
- Template from Joomla! Documentation, `https://docs.joomla.org/Template`
- Joomla! Extensions Directory: `https://extensions.joomla.org`

2

How to Manage Content

In the previous chapter, we had a look at the backend application of Joomla, introduced the dashboard, and checked the components included in the standard setup of the CMS.

We'll now look at the central functionalities of the application; the features dedicated to content management. We'll see how to structure and manage content within Joomla, comparing the content handling features to other major CMSes.

We'll also have a look at **Categories**, **Featured Articles**, blog functionalities, and the **Media Manager**.

After reading this chapter, you will be able to do the following:

- Understand how to create a new article in Joomla
- Understand how to define a structure and hierarchy for your content through categories
- Explore publishing options
- Explore article options
- Be familiar with the Media Manager, which is integrated into Joomla, and its functionalities
- Understand the difference between Joomla and WordPress in content management

Exploring articles in Joomla

Articles are the basic units of content in Joomla. An article is a piece of content that might include text, HTML code, images, or media that links to other content. Think about a news website: every news story is an article in Joomla, or if you think about a blog, every blog post is an article in Joomla.

Articles have a title, content, and should be assigned to a category. If you do not define any custom categories, there is always a default category called **Uncategorized**.

In the upcoming sections, we will see how to create an article and the features offered by the integrated editor.

Creating a new article

Articles can be inserted into a website either through the backend or the frontend of Joomla.

Both provide an editor that simplifies the content creation process, supplying a **What You See Is What You Get** (**WYSIWYG**) visual experience. This allows website authors and administrators to create HTML content without having to directly type HTML code.

1. To create a new article, click on the + symbol next to the **Articles** button on the backend dashboard of Joomla, as highlighted in *Figure 2.1*.

Figure 2.1 – New article button

> **Note**
>
> There are multiple ways to create new articles. You can also create a new article by clicking the + symbol near **Articles** from the **Content Dashboard** menu item or the **Content** menu item in the left sidebar menu.

2. Once clicked, the default article editing interface will appear. Let's see what it looks like.

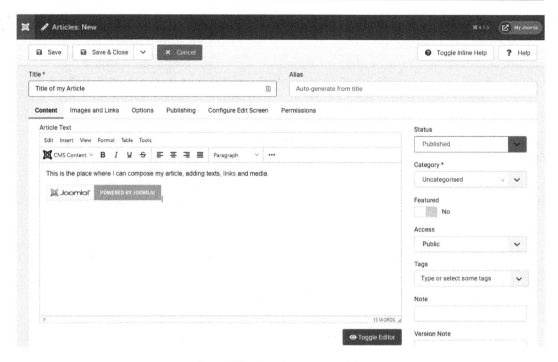

Figure 2.2 – Creating a new article

At the top of the screen, we have the toolbar that hosts the action buttons. These buttons will allow you to save your article, cancel and go back to the previous screen, open the inline help, or check the support pages.

The first field is **Title**, which allows you to specify the title of the article. This can be any short sentence that describes the content of your article.

The second field is **Alias**. The content of this field is used to build the URL of the article page, once published. This field should be filled with an SEO-oriented slug that should not include white spaces or special characters (for example, if your article is named *Title of my article*, **Alias** should be something such as `title-of-my-article`).

After these fields there are some tabs, the first and most important one is the **Content** tab.

Content

The **Content** tab, as the name suggests, is dedicated to the content of the article. The central part of this screen shows a text editor box in which you can insert the content of your article. The editor grants an MS Word-like experience, with a simplified user interface and classic text-editing controls and buttons.

The editor offers more controls and functionalities that can be enabled by clicking on the ... button.

Figure 2.3 – Full editor toolbar

Here, you have all the commonly used features to insert and style rich text: bold, italics, underlined, font size, font style, paragraph style, tables, and much more.

It's also possible to disable the WYSISYG editor and directly type the HTML code in to the article editing window. To disable the editor, just click on the **Toggle Editor** button placed under the editing window.

As you can see in *Figure 2.2*, the right sidebar includes the following fields:

- **Status**: Allows you to define whether an article should be **Published**, **Unpublished**, **Archived**, or **Trashed**.

- **Category**: Allows you to choose the category the article should be tied to. Through this field, you can also create a new category on the fly. We will learn more about categories later in this chapter.

- **Featured**: Allows you to choose whether an article is featured or not. We'll see what this means later in this chapter.

- **Access**: Allows you to select which user group should be granted access to the article.

- **Tags**: Allows you to add tags to the article. There can be one or more tags. Through this field, you can also create new tags on the fly.

- **Note**: Allows you to create an internal note regarding the article. This can be useful for administrative purposes and is not visible on the published website.

- **Version Note**: Allows you to add an internal note related to the specific version of the article. In fact, Joomla includes a versioning system that keeps track of the changes to articles, saving a version of it at each saving action.

One of these fields, **Featured**, has some significance on how and where the article appears. Let's look into this in detail.

Featured Articles

As seen in *Figure 2.2*, one of the options that could be actioned for the article is the **Featured** status. This option allows you to highlight the article and include it in a specific list of articles that are featured.

There is a specific menu item that is called **Featured Articles**, which shows all the articles that are featured and is generally used to build the home page of a website.

Joomla also allows you to define a period for which the article should be featured. This is useful when you want to highlight a specific article for a limited time. This, and other settings, can be configured in the **Publishing** tab of the article creation/editing view, which we will explore in the next section.

Let's move on to the second tab of the editing screen, **Images and Links**.

Images and Links

On this screen, you can enrich your article by adding images and links to it. There are two types of images that can be added to an article: **Intro Image** and **Full Article image**.

Intro Image is the image that is shown with the introduction of the article (the part before **Read More**). It is generally visible when you have a blog layout or a category layout.

The **Full Article** image is shown when you open the article page, that is, on the page where the full content of the article is visible.

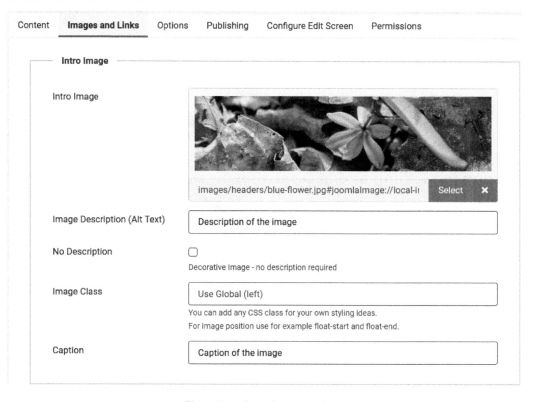

Figure 2.4 – Intro Image options

For each of the images, you can specify several options as you can see in *Figure 2.4*. This includes **Image Description**, which is the alternative text in the HTML markup, a **Caption** box to add a caption that is visible below the image, and **Image Class**, which is the CSS class that should be used to display the image on a public website.

Images can be selected from the image folders of the website or easily uploaded from your computer.

On the same screen, you have also the opportunity to add links to your article. They should be used to add some references to online resources and, depending on your frontend templates, they are displayed on the public website as links to the article. For each of the links, you can specify the target URL, the anchor text, and the browser target window.

Once the article is ready to be saved, you can click on one of the following buttons in the toolbar (as seen earlier, in *Figure 2.2*):

- **Save**: Save the article and continue to work on it. Useful while working on long articles or materials that take a long time to edit.

- **Save & Close**: Save the article and go back to the **Articles** list.

- **Save To Menu**: Save the article and open the new menu item screen to create a menu item that points to the article.

- **Save as Copy**: Create a copy of the article.

With this, we've seen how to create and save our articles. Let's now explore all the options to publish and optimize an article.

Exploring Publishing and SEO settings

The **Publishing** tab is divided into two main parts. The left one is related to the **Publishing** settings, and the right one is dedicated to **Metadata** and SEO options.

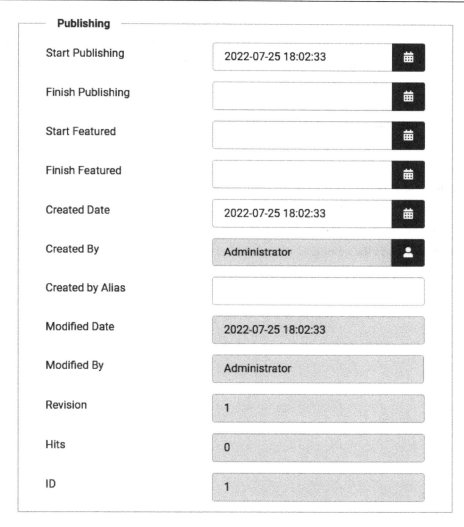

Figure 2.5 – The Publishing settings

Let's analyze the options available on the **Publishing** screen (*Figure 2.5*):

- **Start Publishing**: Allows you to set the date/time that the article should be published. It's automatically set to the current date/time. You can set a date and time in the future, allowing you to schedule the automatic publication of an article.

- **Finish Publishing**: Allows you to set the date/time that the article should be suspended from publication. Generally, this field is empty when the article should not be unpublished automatically.

- **Start Featured**: Allows you to set the date/time that the article should be set as featured. This field is optional and is related to the feature presented in the earlier paragraph.

- **Finish Featured**: Allows you to set the date/time that the article's featured status should end. This field is optional and should be left empty if you don't want to remove the featured status.

- **Created Date**: This field is automatically set with the date and time that the article is created in the system. It can be edited through the calendar button next to the field.

- **Created By**: Shows the name of the user who authored the article. The author of the article can be changed at your convenience, by selecting one of the other users of the system.

- **Created by Alias**: Allows you to set a custom name for the author, even if the author does not have an account on the website.

- **Modified Date**: Displays the date and time that the article has last been changed. This field is not changeable and is filled automatically.

- **Modified By**: Shows the user who last changed the article.

- **Revision**: Displays the number of the current revision of the article.

- **Hits**: Shows the number of hits received by the article. A hit is recorded each time the article is viewed in the frontend of the website.

- **ID**: Displays the unique ID of the article within the system.

The right side of the screen, as mentioned earlier, shows options oriented to the SEO of the website, as seen in *Figure 2.6*.

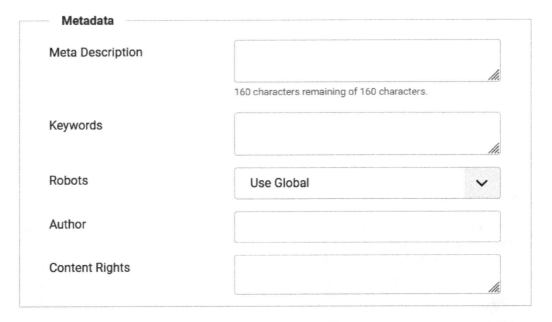

Figure 2.6 – Article SEO options

These settings will allow you to set some important options that affect the SEO of the article:

- **Meta Description**: Allows you to specify a meta description for the article. The field is limited to 160 characters and will produce the respective HTML metatag in the markup of the page.

- **Keywords**: Allows you to specify the keywords of the article. Keywords should be separated by commas. It's recommended that you put a limited number of keywords for each article.

- **Robots**: Allows you to define the rule for the `robots.txt` file for the specific page. You can choose from the most common options or leave the default **Use Global** value that is set in the **Global Configuration** of the website.

- **Author**: Allows you to set the meta tag *Author* for the article.

- **Content Rights**: Allows you to specify the content rights and rules for the article, for example, indicating the license for the article.

Thanks to all the settings seen in this paragraph, you can enrich the HTML markup of your article, optimize the article for search engines, and automate the publication of your content. In the following section, we'll explore the **Options** tab.

Article Options

The next tab on the article editing screen is the **Options** tab, which supplies many settings to customize the appearance and layout of an article.

Options are shown in separate groups: **Layout**, **Category**, **Author**, **Date**, and **Options**. Let's explore each of them.

The Layout group

The settings in this group allow you to customize the layout of the article and offer a few options to select from, as shown in *Figure 2.7*.

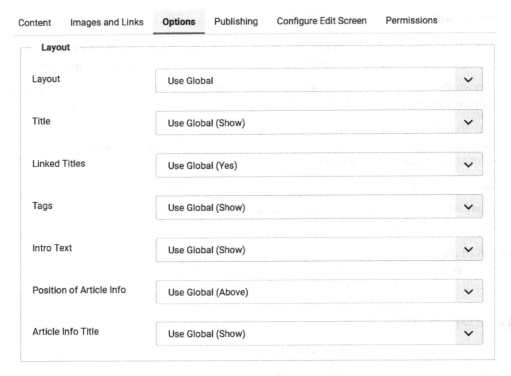

Figure 2.7 – Article options – Layout

These options enable you to choose a specific layout for the article. This is useful if you have **overrides** (which will be covered in *Chapter 13*) for your template and to decide whether or not to show the *title* of the article, the title with a link, the *tags* associated with the article, and the *introduction text*. You can also choose whether or not to show the box with the article details (including author, publishing date, category, and so on) and in which position.

> **Note**
> **Intro Text** is the content of the article that is placed before **Read More. Read More** is an interruption of the content of the article that can be placed in the article to separate the introductory part of the article from the rest of the article. It's generally used on news websites and in blog layouts to show the summary of the article in a multiple-article view.

Next, let's take a look at the **Category** group.

The Category group

The settings in this group allow administrators to choose whether or not to show information about the category next to the article.

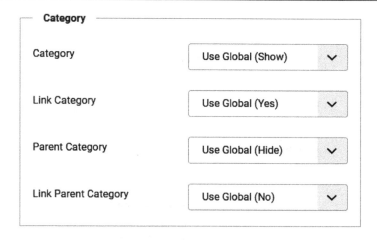

Figure 2.8 – Article options – Category

If you enable the **Link Category** option, there will be a link to the Category view directly in the article details box, allowing your website visitors to navigate to the list of articles in the same category.

The Author group

There are only a couple of options to choose from in this group, as you can see in the following figure:

Figure 2.9 – Article options – Author

The **Author** group holds controls that allow the administrator to choose whether to show the author's name next to the article and whether to link the name of the author to a contact page.

The Date group

The controls included in the **Date** group allow the administrator to choose whether to show the dates of the article or not.

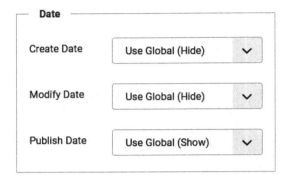

Figure 2.10 - Article options – Date

These dates are the *Creation date*, *Modification date*, and *Publishing date*. They are shown in the article details box and the appearance is controlled by the template in use.

The Options group

The last group of options, as shown in *Figure 2.11*, allows the administrator to show some extra details of the article.

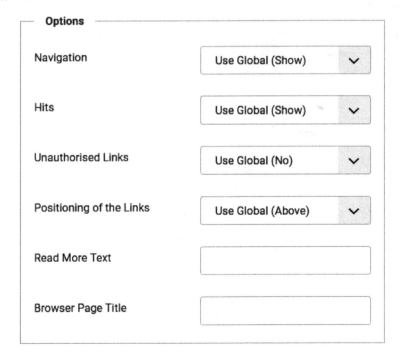

Figure 2.11 – Article options – Options

These include **Navigation**, which shows the previous and next buttons used to navigate between articles of the same category, the hits received by the article, and **Unauthorised Links**. You can also customize **Read More Text** and **Browser Page Title**, shown in the browser tab.

As you might have noticed, for many of the options available, the field is populated with the **Use Global** value. That is because you can set these settings globally for your articles directly in the configuration of the **Articles** component. This way, you do not have to set the configuration specifically for each article.

You can access the configuration of the **Articles** component by clicking on the **Options** button in the toolbar when the list of articles is opened.

With this, we have a full understanding of the article creation options and settings, and we can successfully publish our articles. We will not cover the **Permissions** tab as we will explore the **Access Control List** (**ACL**) and permissions in *Chapter 6*. The settings in the **Configure Edit Screen** tab allow you to change the appearance of the page in which you edit the article.

When creating articles, there is a frequent need to add supporting images and media content (videos, animations, and more). This can be easily done from the **Media** section in the article editing screen, which allows you to upload your media files. In addition, sometimes you need to check the media files that you uploaded to your site and perform certain basic operations on them. To do so, Joomla offers the Media Manager, which we will explore in the next section.

Exploring the Media Manager

The Media Manager is one of the features rebuilt for Joomla 4 and includes many functionalities to load multimedia files and edit them directly online. This has simplified the publishing workflow for website administrators and editors.

The Media Manager is accessible from the **Media** button on **Home Dashboard** or from the **Media** menu item under the **Content** menu in the sidebar.

By default, the component shows a preview of images loaded in the main `images` folder (generally it's the folder named `images` placed under `public_html`), as shown in *Figure 2.12*.

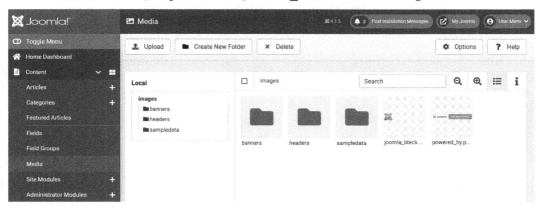

Figure 2.12 – The Media Manager

From this page, you can also navigate through the subfolders holding media files (images, videos, and animations), create new subfolders, and upload media files.

The Media Manager also allows you to perform several operations on the uploaded files. When you select media, you can see the available commands.

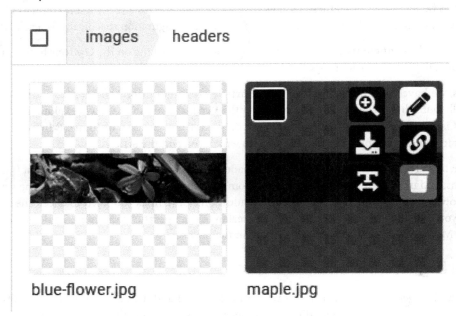

Figure 2.13 – Media Manager commands

In *Figure 2.13*, we can see a number of icons that help perform specific actions. Let us see what each one of them does:

- **Magnifier icon**: Show the preview of the image in real size
- **Download icon**: Download the file onto your device
- **Text icon**: Rename the file loaded on the website
- **Pencil icon**: Edit the media file
- **Link icon**: Copy the link to the media file
- **Trash icon**: Delete the media file

In the next section, we will explore the tools to edit media files online.

Media editing features

The new Media Manager includes some tools to perform basic editing operations directly online, without having to download the file and use graphics software such as **Photoshop** or **GIMP**. Let us take a look at the various features offered by Media Manager.

Crop

The first of the features included allows you to crop an image, set up the quality of the resulting image as a percentage, and define certain parameters to crop the image:

- **X-Axis**
- **Y-Axis**
- **Width**
- **Height**
- Aspect ratio

This feature is useful when you want to crop an image or keep just a part of it, helping you avoid loading huge images and increasing the weight of your web page.

Resize

The second editing feature included in the Media Manager allows you to resize an image, scaling it to the desired size. Again, you can configure some parameters to perform the action:

- **Quality** (in percentage)
- **Width** (in pixel)
- **Height** (in pixel)

The resize feature is very useful to ensure images have the proper size for your website.

Rotate

The last tool included in the Media Manager allows you to rotate images. You can set the quality of the resulting image and the angle of rotation. The tool provides some default angles: 0°, 90°, 180°, and 270°.

With these basic tools, you can prepare and optimize your images directly on your websites, without the need for any external software.

Let's now understand how to organize articles through categories.

Getting to know categories

It's important to know more about categories. Categories can be considered as the folders in which articles are classified and stored.

Each category can have an unlimited number of nested categories, allowing website administrators to create a structure that best fits their needs and accommodates complex website nesting levels.

Each article, as mentioned earlier in this chapter, must be assigned to a category. By default, Joomla supplies an **Uncategorised** category to hold articles. Website administrators can rename it or create any desired category.

It's recommended to plan the structure of the website, prior to adding content, so that you can create all the needed categories and nest them, as it's more convenient for the site structure. Categories are also used to build SEO-oriented navigation paths within the website, thanks to the category aliases included in the URLs of the generated pages.

Categories can be also used to handle different sections of the website, with access to resources differentiated by user groups, thanks to the permission management features included in Joomla. We will discuss more about permissions in *Chapter 6* of this book.

Let us consider a sample scenario where you are building a website to hold your family recipes. A simple category structure could be as follows:

- Main Courses
  - Beef
  - Pork
  - Seafood
  - Vegetables
- Appetizers
- Salads
- Desserts
- Vegetarian

A structure like the one mentioned in the scenario would allow you to categorize your content in a meaningful way and let your users find the recipes easily.

Categories are a common pattern in Joomla. In fact, other components – either built-in or third-party – integrate the category management system.

With this, we're done looking at the basics of content management in Joomla. Let's quickly explore the differences between Joomla and WordPress.

Page, post, or article? That is the dilemma!

Now that we have a clear understanding of how to create and edit an article on our Joomla website, let's spend some time clarifying some key concepts related to the content management features, and do a comparison with WordPress.

At the beginning of this chapter, we mentioned that articles in Joomla are the basic unit of content management. An article could be some news, a blog post, a recipe, a static page, or an announcement. The role of specific content within the website structure is not important while creating it.

This is the first key difference that WordPress users would notice while using Joomla. In WordPress, you should define the role of specific content prior to creating it, choosing, for example, whether you would like to create a blog post (using the **Post** feature) or whether you would like to create a static page (using the **Page** feature).

In Joomla, a unit of content can be created as an article, independent of its role within the website. Furthermore, the role of specific content might be changed at any time, simply because in Joomla you will use the menu items to decide how and where to show specific content.

An article might at the same time be a static page of the website – thanks to a Single **Article** menu item pointing to it – and part of a list of articles or a blog section – thanks to a **Category view** menu item pointing to the category that includes such an article. We'll understand more about Joomla menus and their configuration in *Chapter 5* of this book.

With this parallel between Joomla and WordPress content management features, we have completed the basics of articles. Let's move on to exercises to start trying Joomla in action.

Exercises

It's time to apply the knowledge acquired in the first chapters of the book and start using the Joomla backend.

To complete the exercises proposed in this chapter, you will need to have a Joomla 4.x installation either on your local machine or on a remote server.

Exercise 1 – categories

Open the backend of your Joomla installation, simply typing `<yourwebsite.tld>/administrator` – where `yourwebsite.tld` should be replaced with the URL of your installation – and type the administrator password chosen during the installation of Joomla.

Once logged in to the backend of Joomla, go to **Article Categories** and create a new category called `MyCategory`. You can set a personal description for the category and leave all the other options as their default values. `MyCategory` should be a top-level category. Save and go back to the **Article Categories** view.

Now create a new category named `SubCategory1` and set it as a subcategory of `MyCategory`. Specify a personal description for the subcategory and save it. Then move back to the **Home Dashboard** screen of your backend.

Exercise 2 – articles

From the **Home Dashboard** screen, click on the button to create a new article (*Figure 2.1*). Add content at your convenience or simply two lines of text. Use the text-formatting features to highlight some text with bold and italic styles. Name the article `My Article` and let the system automatically apply the alias for the title. Put the article in the `MyCategory` category that you created in the previous exercise. Save and close the article. Congratulations, you created the first article on your website! You can also preview the article, after saving it, by clicking on the **Preview** button.

Summary

In this chapter, we explored the basic content management features of Joomla and understood how to create an article and configure the settings to customize the appearance of the article on a website, as well as how to use the Media Manager and handle images loaded on the website.

In the next chapter, we'll go deeper into the content management features, introducing **Custom Fields**, **Workflows**, and built-in accessibility functionalities.

3

Advanced Content Management

In this chapter, we will explore some of the advanced content management features offered by the Joomla core. We will look at custom fields, workflows, and accessibility functionalities.

After reading this chapter, you will be able to do the following:

- Enrich your content with custom fields
- Understand the advanced options to manage your website content
- Build your customized publishing workflow
- Produce accessible content for your website

Let's start with custom fields, a feature that was introduced in Joomla 3.7, several years ago.

Enrich your articles with custom fields

For years, since the first release of Joomla, there have been many extensions in the market to enrich or replace the standard article management system, with some extensions called **Content Construction Kit (CCK)**. These CCK extensions allowed administrators to set up additional fields for the articles or content items. So, for several years, many Joomla users adopted such CCKs to manage their content instead of using the standard Article component. The most used CCK extensions were K2, DPFields, Seblod, and FlexiContent. Let's start with understanding what custom fields are.

What is a custom field?

A custom field allows adding additional capabilities to the content. For example, let's consider a website of recipes, where each recipe is an article. If you want to add some standard information that is useful to complete the article, you can create some custom fields for the articles, such as the following:

- Cooking time (in minutes)
- Preparation time (in minutes)
- Difficulty (on a scale of 5)
- Cost (on a scale of 5)

As you might have guessed, these custom fields will enrich the article content, supplying some standard information that is useful for readers.

Let's analyze another example: a directory of teachers on a university website. We will use articles to create a page for each teacher, and for each of the articles, we will use custom fields such as the following:

- Teacher Address (Text)
- Class (Code of lessons subject)
- Phone Number (Number)
- Email address (Email)

These are just some examples of custom fields that might be used to expand the content of your website. There are many diverse types of custom fields that might be used in a website; by default, Joomla can manage the following types of custom fields:

- **Calendar**: This adds a calendar selector to pick a date/time
- **Checkboxes**: This adds a group of checkboxes that can be used to select multiple options
- **Color**: This adds a color picker
- **Editor**: This adds a text editor
- **Integer**: This holds an integer number
- **List**: This adds a list of options that can be selected
- **List of Images**: This adds a list of images
- **Media**: This adds a media file
- **Radio**: This adds a radio button control with alternative options
- **SQL**: This holds an SQL query, generally to supply values for a query
- **Subform**: This adds a repeatable field

- **Text**: This adds a textbox
- **Text Area**: This adds a multiline text editing area
- **URL**: This holds a valid URL
- **User**: This holds a list of user IDs
- **Usergroups**: This holds a list of user group IDs

Recalling the examples presented earlier, we can map the custom fields to the respective type. Let's talk about the recipes:

Field	Type
Cooking Time	Integer
Preparation Time	Integer
Difficulty	Radio (with 5 options)
Cost	Radio (with 5 options)

Table 3.1 – Custom field mapping

It's also possible to install more types of custom fields, such as maps, video galleries, download buttons, video embedding, and more. Furthermore, new types of custom fields can be developed and installed in Joomla.

Custom fields could be added to **Articles** or **Categories**. It's possible to choose which item type to add a specific custom field while creating it. Now, let's see how these custom fields are managed.

Custom field groups

Custom fields are managed through groups. This allows an administrator to enable or disable multiple fields at once, as well as to tie a group of fields to a specific category of articles.

If you create a group of custom fields, you will see a tab with the same name as the group in the editing window of the article, either during the creation of a new article or while updating an existing article.

If a field is not assigned to a group, it will appear in a generic **Fields** tab.

Let's explore the feature in real life by creating a group and adding multiple fields to it.

Adding custom fields to articles

The first thing to do is to create a group of custom fields that is linked to articles. Perform the following steps:

1. In the backend, navigate to the **Fields Groups** option from the **Content Dashboard**.

2. Ensure that the drop-down menu at the top of the page shows **Articles** and then click on the **New** button.

3. Give your field group a title and a brief description in the respective fields. Check whether the **Status** field is set to **Published** and that **Access** is set to **Public**.

    Once the group has been created, we can move on to create the individual custom fields for the articles.

4. To do this, click on the **Fields** menu item in the left-hand sidebar. Then, ensure that the filter on top is set to **Articles**.

5. To create a field, click on the **New** button to see the field creation screen, which is shown in *Figure 3.1*:

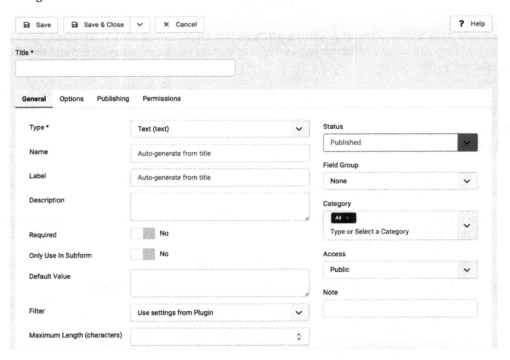

Figure 3.1 – Creating a new custom field: General

In the **Title** field, you can insert the title you want to give to the field.

Let's explore the options of the **General** tab:

- **Type**: The type of the custom field, such as **Text, Calendar, List, Media**, and more.

- **Name**: Specify a name for the custom field. If empty, it's automatically generated from the **Title** field. Note that the name of the field should be unique and must not include any special characters.

- **Label**: This is the text that is visible on the website while editing or showing the field. It might be different from the field title or name.

- **Description**: This is the internal description/note for the field.

- **Required**: This allows you to choose whether the field should be mandatory or not.

- **Only Use in Subform**: This allows you to choose whether the field should be used only in combination with the subform type, as a repeatable field.

- **Default Value**: This allows you to provide a default value for the field.

- **Filter**: This allows you to choose whether to limit the types of characters that can be typed (in the text field).

- **Maximum Length (characters)**: This allows you to set the maximum number of characters that can be typed into the field.

- **Status**: This allows you to set the status of the field to **Published, Unpublished, Archived**, or **Trashed**.

- **Field Group**: This allows you to choose the group of fields to which the field should belong.

- **Category**: This allows you to choose one or more categories (or **All**) of articles to which the custom field should be enabled.

The options shown in *Figure 3.1* are related to the **Text** type of the field. Options can vary based on the type of field selected.

Moving on to the **Options** tab, we can configure some additional aspects of our field, as shown in *Figure 3.2*:

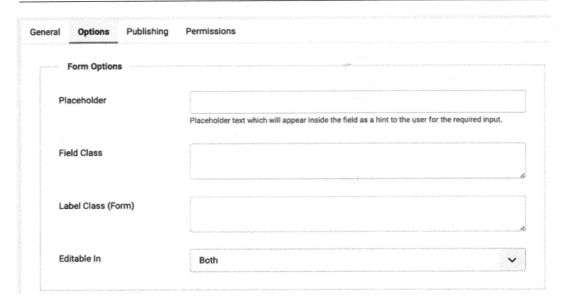

Figure 3.2 – Creating a new custom field: Options > Form Options

In the first group of options, we can configure the appearance of the fields for website operators who input data:

- **Placeholder**: This is the text that is shown within the field as a placeholder
- **Field Class**: This is the CSS class that is used to display the field in the editing screen
- **Label Class (Form)**: This is the CSS class that is used to display the label of the field in the editing screen
- **Editable In**: This allows you to choose where the field can be edited, either in the frontend or the backend or from both sides (the default is **Both**)

The second set of options allows you to edit the appearance of the field on the website while showing an article with its additional fields having content:

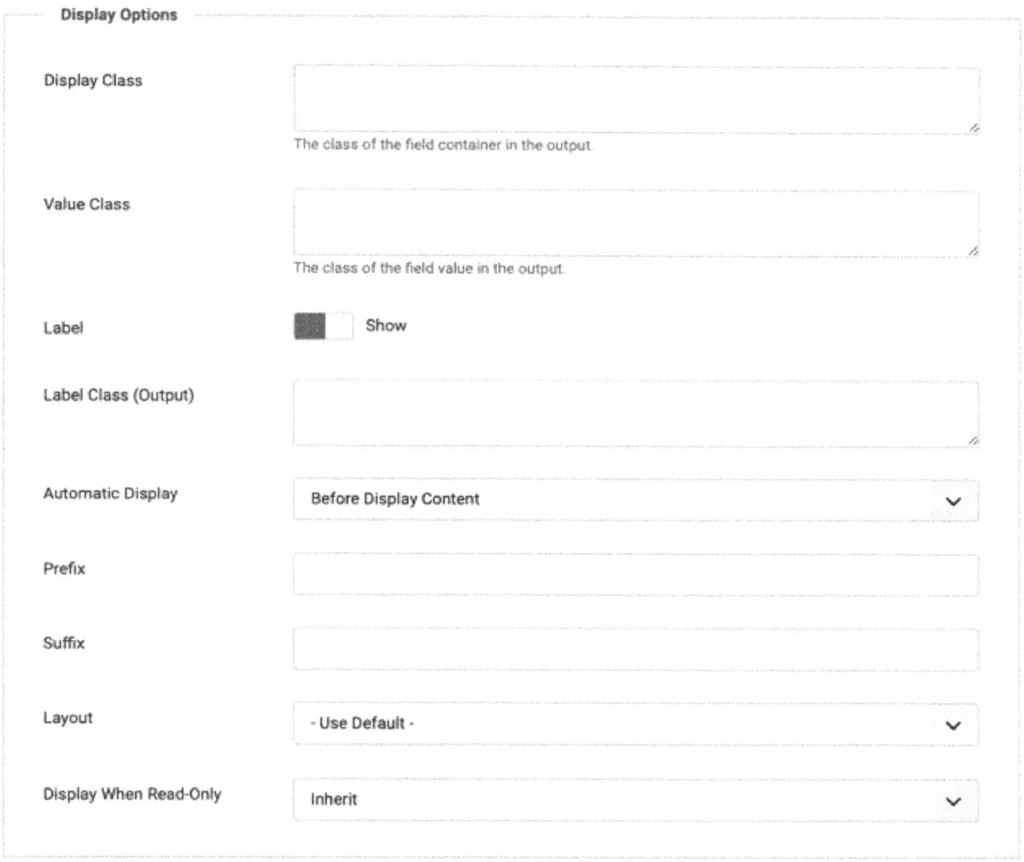

Figure 3.3 – Creating a new custom field: Options > Display Options

The options for editing the appearance of the field on the public website, as shown in *Figure 3.3*, are listed as follows:

- **Display Class**: This is the CSS class to display the field on the frontend of the website.
- **Value Class**: This is the CSS class to display the value of the field on the website.
- **Label**: This allows you to choose whether to show the field label on the website.
- **Label Class (Output)**: This is the CSS class to display the label of the field on the website.
- **Automatic Display**: This allows you to choose whether to display the field on the website automatically. If the field is visible, you can choose whether it should be displayed after the title, and before or after the content of the article.
- **Prefix**: This is the CSS prefix to be added to the field.

- **Suffix**: This is the CSS suffix to be added to the field.

- **Layout**: This allows you to choose a field layout provided by the template in use.

- **Display when Read-Only**: This allows you to choose whether the field should be displayed on the website when it's set to read-only.

The other tabs allow you to set the **Author** and **Creation Date** fields, as well as define permissions for the field. We'll explore permissions in depth in *Chapter 6* of this book.

There are no limits to the number and types of custom fields you can add to your content; this allows you to completely customize your content by enriching it with additional and relevant data.

So, custom fields have been added to the articles, now let's see them in action when editing an article.

Adding content to custom fields

When writing an article, based on the configuration of the custom fields, we can see a new tab with the same name as the field group that we created earlier, in which all the relevant custom fields are displayed, as shown in *Figure 3.4*. This allows website authors or administrators to input their content into the custom fields:

Figure 3.4 – Populating custom fields for an article

As you can see, the custom field we created is displayed within its group and with its description. In the example, the field is called **MyField Name** and is a text field.

Once published, the article will display custom fields on the frontend, as per the configuration of each field, as shown in *Figure 3.5*:

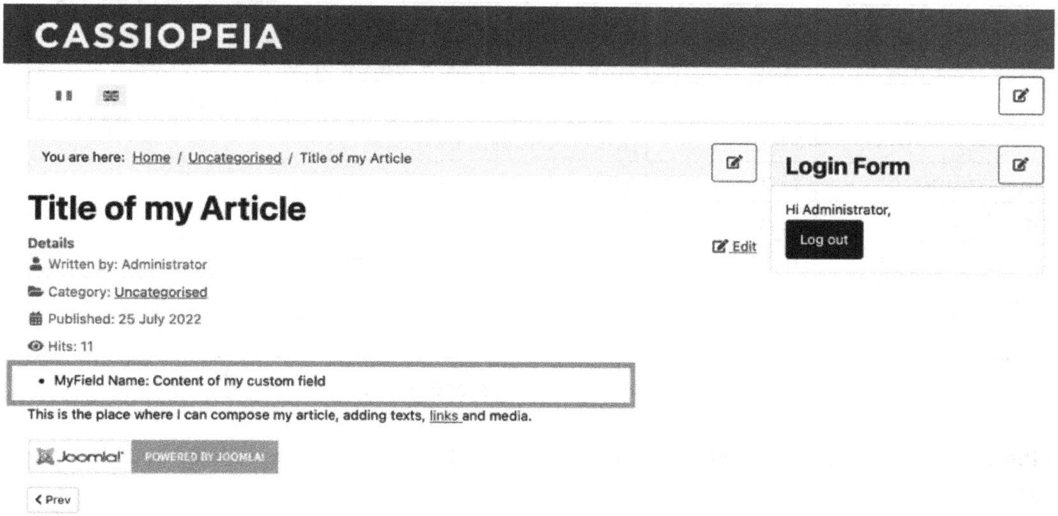

Figure 3.5 – Article with a custom field on the website frontend

In the next section, we will explore a real-case scenario that involves the use of custom fields to enrich your website content.

Case study – building a directory with custom fields

Custom fields might be used for every type of content, from a news website to a recipe collection website, as well as to build an online directory of contacts or businesses. In this case study, we will consider the following scenario: build a directory of professors for a university website. It's very common for universities to provide an address book for their professors, along with a page for each of them that contains a picture, contact data, studio address, and other useful information.

Planning the structure

To build the directory, we will need a *category* for the articles that we will call *Professors*, a *group* of fields called *Professors*, and several custom fields:

Field Name	Type	Description
Role	Text	Role of the professor, for example, Adjunct Professor
Department	List	The department to which the professor belongs
Classes	Checkboxes	The classes held by the professor
Phone Number	Text	The phone number of the professor
Office Address	Text	The office address of the professor
Email	Text	The email address of the professor
Website	URL	The URL of the personal page/website of the professor
Picture	Media	The headshot of the professor

Table 3.2 – The custom fields for Professors

All the custom fields listed in *Table 3.2* should be tied to the *Professors* category and belong to the *Professors* field group.

Each article should have the name of the professor as **Title** and their biography as content, along with the custom fields listed in *Table 3.2*, and the directory will show a standardized and detailed page for each professor at the university.

Custom fields offer unlimited possibilities because you can include a **Map** field to show an interactive map providing directions to reach the office of the professor, or you can add a contact form field to provide a form to get in touch with the professor, directly from their page in the directory. Furthermore, you can have a gallery field to show multiple pictures of the professor, a video field to include a video from YouTube, and more.

With this case study, we conclude this section about custom fields. In the upcoming sections, we will explore other advanced content management features that are included in the CMS. Since version 4.0, Joomla allows you to create completely customized publishing workflows, granting administrators the opportunity to build specific flows, taking into account approvals, notifications, and stages. Let's explore this next.

Custom publishing workflow

Joomla 4.0 introduced an interesting feature that makes the CMS fit the needs of complex publishing scenarios such as those of online magazines, news websites, and corporate websites where there are several people involved during the publishing process with different roles, authorities, and permissions. This feature is called **Workflow** and is meant to add flexibility to the publishing process, allowing administrators to override the standard cycle in favor of a more complex and multi-level publishing flow that might include different stages and approvals. In this section, we will explore this new feature and how to build a custom workflow for our website.

Exploring workflows

By default, the new **Workflows** feature is disabled in Joomla. So, to use it, it's necessary to activate it. You can enable **Workflow** from the **Options** section of the **Articles** component by checking this option from the **Integration** tab.

Once enabled, you will see a new menu item called **Workflows** under the **Content** menu in the sidebar.

Clicking on the dedicated menu item, you will see the list of available workflows, as shown in *Figure 3.6*:

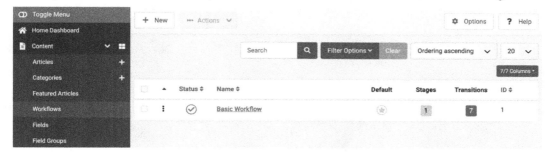

Figure 3.6 – Workflows

From this page, it's possible to create a new workflow or act on an existing one, edit it, or perform actions on it.

In *Figure 3.6*, we can also spot some new terms:

- **Stages**: A stage is each phase of the publishing workflow
- **Transitions**: Transitions represent the move from one stage to the following one

In the preceding screenshot, we can also see that there is a column named **Default** that is used to highlight which workflow has been set as the default for the entire website.

In summary, a workflow is composed of a list of stages and transitions between those stages. The key element is represented by transitions, which we'll explore in the next paragraph:

Transitions

Multiple actions can be defined for the transition between one stage and the next. Let's explore the configuration of a transition. Access the **Transitions** page by just clicking on the number of transitions in the current workflow, and then click on **New** on the **Transitions** page:

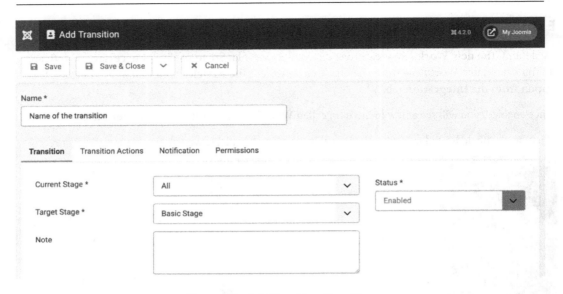

Figure 3.7 – Add Transition: Transition

As you can see in the preceding screenshot, the first field allows us to specify the name of the transition.

We can then set the **Current Stage** field, meaning the stage from which the transition begins. This will allow us to create a sequential flow, setting the proper starting stage for a specific transition every time. The **Target Stage** field represents the stage resulting from the completion of the transition. The **Note** field is for internal notes, and it is only visible to administrators or backend users who have access to this section. The **Status** field is used to make the transition active (*Published*) or inactive (*Unpublished*), like we generally do with other items in Joomla.

In the second tab, called **Transition Actions**, we can configure the operations that are executed when the transition is activated:

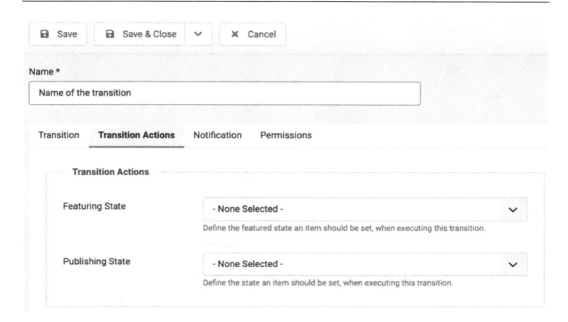

Figure 3.8 – Add Transition: Transition Actions

As shown in *Figure 3.8*, in this tab, you can set the following options:

- **Featuring State**: This enables you to choose whether the article should be marked as **Featured** or not

- **Publishing State**: This enables you to choose the state of the article, for instance, **Published, Unpublished, Archived, or Trashed**

Moving to the third tab, **Notification**, here, we can set automated email notifications to be sent when executing the transition. This is especially useful in workflows that require the approval of specific people/roles prior to publishing an article, allowing reviewers to be notified when there is new content pending their actions.

Figure 3.9 – Add Transition: Notification

As shown in *Figure 3.9*, in this tab, you can enable/disable the notification-sending action, customize the notification text with the **Additional Message Text** field, and choose which usergroups or specific users should receive the notification. If no user group or specific users are selected, the notification will not be sent.

The last tab in the edit screen is **Permissions** and allows you to choose which usergroups can perform certain actions on the transitions (for example, edit, execute, and more). We will explore the Joomla permissions system in depth in *Chapter 6* of this book.

In the following section, we will learn more about the default workflow in Joomla, that is, **Basic Workflow**.

Basic Workflow

Basic Workflow is enabled and used as the system default, as shown in *Figure 3.6*. It has a single stage and seven transitions. The stage is called *Basic Stage* and is set as the default. The seven transitions that are included manage the different status options of an article, as you can see in the following screenshot:

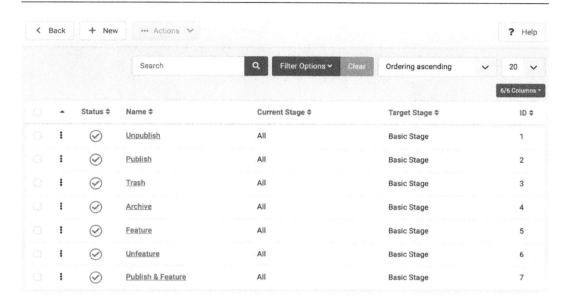

Figure 3.10 – Basic Workflow: Transitions

You can see that the transitions are named as the article status, and each transition can be linked to a **Current Stage** field and a **Target Stage** field. In this case, each transition can be enabled at every stage and only have the **Basic Stage** option as target stage, which we saw as being the only stage set in this workflow.

The following list details the different *transitions* of **Basic Workflow**:

- **Unpublish**
- **Publish**
- **Trash**
- **Archive**
- **Feature**
- **Unfeature**
- **Publish & Feature**

As each of these transitions can be started at any stage and the workflow only has a single stage, this workflow is not meant to be sequential.

Once the workflows are enabled, by going to the list of **Articles**, we can see for each article the **Stage** currently set, as shown in *Figure 3.11*:

	⇕	Stage ⇕	Featured ⇕	Status ⇕	Title ⇕	Access ⇕	Author ⇕	Date Created ⇕	Hits ⇕	ID ▼
☐		Basic Stage		✓	Title of my Article Alias: title-of-my-article Category: Uncategorised	Guest	Administrator	2022-07-25	0	1

Figure 3.11 – Articles view when Workflow is enabled

In the previous two sections, we saw that it's possible to build a completely custom publishing workflow to meet the needs of complex websites.

A website might have multiple workflows since it's possible to set a specific workflow for every single category of the website.

Next, we will see an example of Workflow that can be used in an online magazine.

Case study – an online magazine with Joomla

An interesting scenario to explore when it comes to editorial features such as workflows is the one represented by an online magazine. Generally, an online magazine includes different roles such as the author, reviewers, editors, and more, and each of them has a specific responsibility in the publishing process.

The author is generally the person who inputs the article within the system; a reviewer acts in the second phase and checks the article that has been uploaded by the author, correcting mistakes and typos, and ensuring that the article and all the other related fields are correct (for example, the category, custom fields, and more). During these steps, the article is still unpublished and in draft mode. At the end of the flow, we have the editor who is responsible for approving the article, ensuring that it adheres to the editorial line of the magazine, that it has no typos, that is tied to the appropriate category, and that it has all the additional fields filled properly.

Once the editor has conducted the final review of the article, generally, the article gets approved and published or scheduled for automated publishing. This represents a simplified magazine publishing scenario that can be managed through a custom workflow in Joomla. Of course, magazines might have additional roles such as a creative director who uploads media files, an SEO specialist who might review the article and its metadata to ensure proper placement on search engines, and other roles according to the editorial structure.

> **Note**
> In this example, we will not use permissions since they will be explored in *Chapter 6* of the book, so all users will have the same permissions and belong to the same user group. In *Chapter 6*, we'll come back to this example to improve it using different usergroups and proper access levels.

This example is focused on Workflow creation and configuration. Let's also imagine that the website has three backend users: **Author**, **Reviewer**, and **Editor**.

Our workflow will have the following **stages**:

1. Draft

2. Reviewed Draft

3. Approved

And it will have the following **transitions**:

1. Submit article

2. Review article

3. Approve article

Now that we have a workflow plan in place, let's put the scenario into operation within our Joomla website.

Workflow implementation

Now, let's implement the workflow on the website:

1. From the **Home Dashboard** screen, click on **Content**, and then on **Workflows**. You should see the screen that we saw in *Figure 3.6*. Finally, click on **New**.

2. Let's call this workflow Editorial and click on **Save & Close**. This will create a workflow with one stage and zero transitions.

3. The next step is to create the stages. To do this, click on the number **1** and we will see the default stage called **Basic Stage**. Let's rename it to Draft and click on **Save**. This stage will be kept as the default, as it's the stage that all the new articles should receive when submitted.

4. Clicking on **New** allows us to create the additional stages that we've planned: Reviewed Draft and Approved.

    Now our workflow has three stages and zero transitions. It's time to create the transitions:

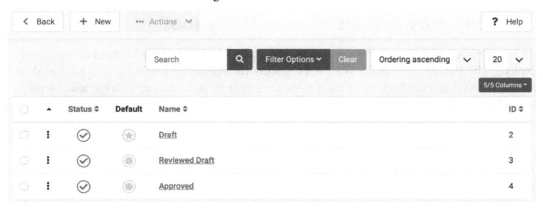

Figure 3.12 – Custom workflow: Stages

5. Click on the **Back** button in the toolbar to move to the **Workflows** screen and click on **0** in the **Transitions** column to start creating transitions for our editorial workflow.

6. Click on the **New** button and create the first transition: `Submit Article`.

7. To make our workflow sequential, we will implement the configuration as shown in *Table 3.3*:

Transition	Current Stage	Target Stage	Article State	Notification Recipient
Submit Article	All	Draft	Unpublished	Reviewer
Review Article	Draft	Reviewed Draft	Unpublished	Editor
Approve Article	Reviewed Draft	Approved	Published	Author

Table 3.3 – Workflow transitions

In none of the transitions did we alter the **Feature** state of the article.

When an author submits the article, the stage will be set to **Draft**, and the reviewer will receive a notification.

When the reviewer checks and corrects the article, the stage will be set to **Reviewed Draft**, and the editor will get a notification while the article is still unpublished.

Once the editor checks and approves the article, it will reach the final stage, **Approved**, and the author will get a notification, informing them that the article has finally been checked and published.

We have created a basic workflow for our online magazine. Throughout the book, we'll expand this workflow by adding permissions and access levels and assigning roles to users.

With this interactive case study, which we recommend you implement in your test website, we have completed our examination of workflow management and the main content management features. In the last section of this chapter, we will explore the tools that Joomla provides to ensure the production of accessible content.

Accessibility by default – the JooA11y tool

Joomla 4 ensures accessibility out of the box; in fact, its default backend and frontend templates are compliant with the AA Level of the **W3C Accessibility Guidelines** (**WCAG**) 2.1. This ensures that both the frontend and the backend of the website are usable by anyone, even with the use of screen readers and similar assisting technologies.

Beyond the technology and the layouts, the most important part that should be made accessible is the content that is produced and loaded by website administrators and other people, depending on the type and size of the website. This is also the hardest part because considering accessibility rules and guidelines is not that easy.

To help with this, Joomla includes a very useful tool, called **JooA11y**, which supports website operators in producing accessible content.

The JooA11y tool is integrated with the article-editing experience of Joomla and executes a series of controls provided by WCAG 2.1 – Level A and AA. It checks formats, images, links, tables, forms, headings, contrast, and more, highlighting errors and warnings, and evaluating the readability of the content.

To access the JooA11y tool, you need to open the article you want to check and click on the **Accessibility Check** button in the toolbar, as shown in *Figure 3.13*:

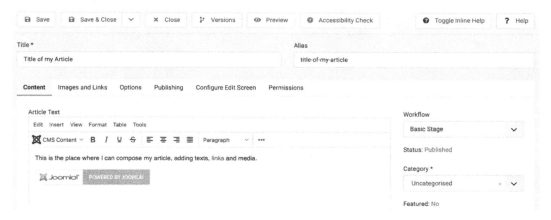

Figure 3.13 – Article editing screen with the Accessibility Check button

By clicking on the **Accessibility Check** button, the public preview of the article will show in a pop-up window, with the accessibility test results on the screen, as shown in *Figure 3.14*:

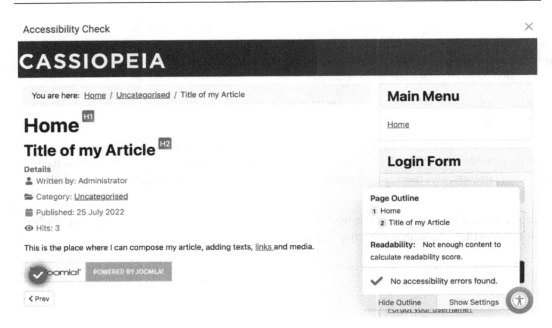

Figure 3.14 – Accessibility Check

The article preview will highlight markup and accessibility errors and warnings, while the tool popup is shown in the bottom-right corner of the screen with the results of the checks and the page outline. This tool is a useful aid to improve the readability and accessibility of your website content.

With the JooA11y tool, we have concluded our discussion of content management functionalities.

Exercises

It's time to apply the knowledge acquired in this chapter and start creating our own custom fields.

Exercise 1 – Create a custom field

In your example Joomla installation, create a custom field group called MyFieldGroup, tied to **Articles**. Then, create a new custom field for **Articles** within MyFieldGroup. The custom field should be called MyCustomText and should be a text field that is always visible after the content of the article.

Create an additional custom field that belongs to the same field group; the field should be a **Text Area** field. Call it MyTextArea, leaving all the options at their default values. Finally, create another custom field, in MyFieldGroup, called Picture, selecting the **Media** field type.

Then, open the article created during the exercises of the previous chapters, check the new tab called **MyFieldGroup**, and populate your additional fields with your desired values. Once complete, click on **Save** and then **Preview** to check the appearance of your article enriched with custom fields.

Summary

In this chapter, we explored the advanced content management features of Joomla, understood what custom fields are, and learned how to create them and organize custom fields in groups. We went through the scheduled publishing options to automate the publication and the featuring status of articles. We have explored the **Workflow** features and built a custom publishing workflow for an online magazine website. At the end of the chapter, we discovered the built-in tools to improve the readability and accessibility of the website content.

In the next chapter, we will discover another key concept of Joomla: **Modules**. We will see what they are, for which purpose they are used, and how to build a custom backend dashboard thanks to **Modules**.

Further reading

- The JooAlly Tool documentation: `https://joomla-projects.github.io/joomla-a11y-checker/`

4

Exploring the Flexibility of Modules

In the previous chapters, we explored the main content management features offered by Joomla, with a specific focus on articles. In this chapter, we will get to explore an additional method to manage content and customize our website: modules.

After reading this chapter, you will be able to do the following:

- Understand what modules are in Joomla
- Understand what module positions are
- Understand the different types of modules available
- Understand how to use modules to customize your website layout
- Build your custom backend dashboard with modules

Let's start with some basic concepts about modules.

What is a module?

As the official Joomla documentation says, a **module** is a basic extension for Joomla that allows you to display content, generally as an output of a component or another extension. A module is generally displayed in a **position** of the template, either the frontend or backend, and is used to show additional content, for example, in sidebars or after the main content position. Modules are extensively used in Joomla, for example, to show a menu, display the login feature, show the footer of the website, display the latest published articles, and so on.

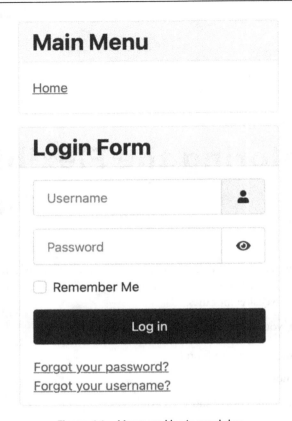

Figure 4.1 – Menu and login modules

In *Figure 4.1*, we can observe two of the most used modules in Joomla: a module that shows the main menu of the website, and the login form module. These modules are shown in the frontend of the website and are connected to a component from which they take their respective functionalities. For example, the main menu takes the menu management component to provide the list of menu items of a specific menu, and the login form takes the user component to provide the login/logout features.

As I mentioned before, modules are also extensively used in the backend of the website. In fact, the whole dashboard is made up of modules.

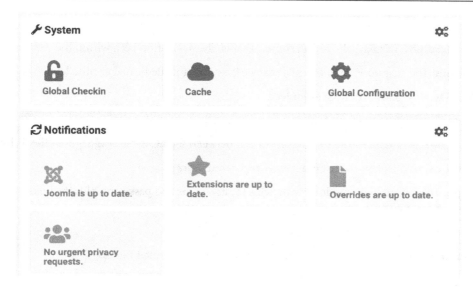

Figure 4.2 – System and notifications modules

In *Figure 4.2*, taken from **Home Dashboard,** we can observe two different modules, **System** and **Notifications**. The **System** module provides some options to access system features, while the **Notifications** module displays the status of the CMS instance including updates of core, extensions, overrides, and the status of privacy requests.

There are many different modules that are shipped by default with Joomla. Let's explore the main types in the next section.

Exploring the types of modules

Joomla includes several types of modules, many of which are connected to the components included by default in Joomla. In the following list, we will review the modules of a standard Joomla installation. You can install many additional modules from the Joomla Extensions Directory or other sources. Please also note that many third-party components include additional modules that display content from them:

- **Articles - Archived**: Displays a list of months with archived articles
- **Articles - Categories**: Displays a list of categories
- **Articles - Category**: Displays a list of articles present in one or more categories
- **Articles - Latest**: Displays a list of the most recent published articles
- **Articles - Most Read**: Displays the list of the most visited articles
- **Articles - Newsflash**: Displays a fixed number of articles from a selected category
- **Articles - Related**: Displays the articles related to the one visited, based on keywords

- **Banners**: Shows the active banners from the **Banners** component
- **Breadcrumbs**: Displays the breadcrumbs, that is, the navigation path within the website
- **Custom**: The custom HTML module that we'll explore in a dedicated section later
- **Feed Display**: Shows an RSS/Atom feed
- **Footer**: Displays the default Joomla copyright and licensing information
- **Language Switcher**: Shows the flags to switch between the available languages of the website
- **Latest Users**: Displays the list of recently registered users
- **Login**: The default login modules with fields for username and password, plus the links to reset password and registration features
- **Menu**: Displays a menu on the public website
- **Random Image**: Shows a random image taken from the selected folder
- **Smart Search**: Displays the Smart Search functionality
- **Statistics**: Shows information and statistics about your Joomla installation
- **Syndication Feeds**: Creates a syndicated feed for the website content
- **Tags - Popular**: Displays a list of most used tags in a list or cloud layout
- **Tags - Similar**: Displays links to other items related by tags to the current one
- **Who's Online**: Shows the number of visitors and logged-in users on the website
- **Wrapper**: Displays a URL within an **iFrame**

The modules in the preceding list are frontend modules that are included in every installation of Joomla. Many additional modules might be available in your installation, given that they are commonly distributed and installed with other extensions, and a great number of them are also available in the **Joomla Extensions Directory**. For example, if you install an e-commerce extension such as **HikaShop** or **VirtueMart**, you will have additional modules available to show the shopping cart, the best-seller products, the latest arrivals, and much more.

Going back to the list of available modules, it's evident that many modules are linked to **components**. For example, seven modules are connected to the **Article** component (com_content), the **Banners** module is connected to the **Banners** component (com_banners), the two **Tags** modules are linked to the **Tags** component (com_tags), and so on. The list also included the custom module, which is a particular kind of module that we'll explore next.

The custom module

The custom module is a specific type of module that allows you to put custom HTML code in it. You can easily input HTML code in a custom module using the WYSIWYG visual editor, similar to the article editing experience.

A custom module can be used to show rich text, images, and media on your website. This type of module is also used to put HTML or JavaScript code that does not have a visible output on the website, for example, a tracking code.

Custom modules are also used in many websites as boxes to show extra information or to handle the footer details (for example, showing the name of the website, some contact information, and so on), and are a very dynamic layout item since you can place them in a specific position, or show them only in selected pages. Let's discover how in the next section.

Module positions and assignments

Modules are considered the most flexible content unit in Joomla, even more than articles, because modules can be placed in specific positions and be assigned to selected pages.

Each module should be assigned to a position. A position is a place in the layout grid in which a module is displayed. Every template has several module positions in which modules can be placed. Depending on the template structure, a position might host one or more modules; we will explore templates and their positions in depth in *Chapter 12*.

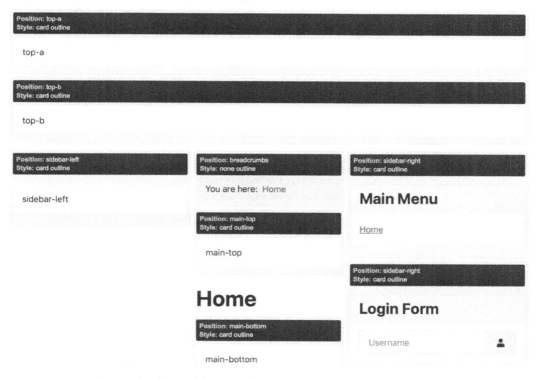

Figure 4.3 – Some of the module positions of the Cassiopeia template

In the preceding figure, you can observe some of the module positions available in the default frontend template of Joomla 4: Cassiopeia. As you can see, each of the positions has a specific name, such as `top-a`, `top-b`, `sidebar-left`, `sidebar-right`, `breadcrumbs`, `main-top`, and `main-bottom`.

In *Figure 4.3*, you can also observe that there are two modules published in the same position: in fact, the **Main Menu** and **Login Form** modules are published both in the position called `sidebar-right`. In this case, modules are shown one after the other vertically. In other cases, they might be displayed inline depending on the template and module configuration and styling.

The position's name and number depend on the template in use.

Modules can be assigned also to a special position called `::None::`. This means that the module is not displayed in any of the available positions. But modules can be placed literally everywhere. In fact, you can place a module in any article by using the dedicated button in the editor.

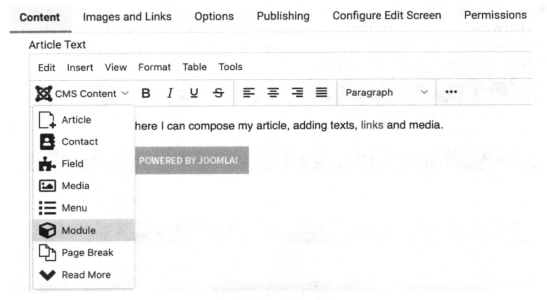

Figure 4.4 – Adding a module

Clicking on **CMS Content | Module**, as shown in *Figure 4.4*, you can choose which module should be displayed within the article.

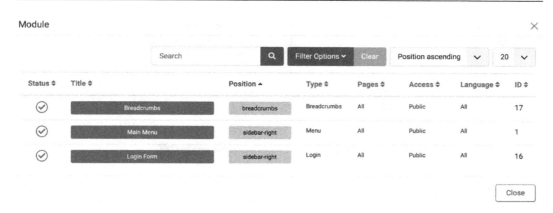

Figure 4.5 – Selecting a module

You can add any of the available modules to any of the articles of your website.

Furthermore, you can show a module on all pages, or only on a selected page, thanks to the **Assignment** features available for each of the modules.

Figure 4.6 – Module Assignment

While creating/editing a module, there is a specific tab called **Menu Assignment**, as shown in *Figure 4.6*, in which you can choose whether the module should be displayed:

- **On all pages** (default)
- **On no pages**
- **Only on the selected pages**
- **On all pages except those selected**

These options grant you a high level of flexibility as to when to show or hide a specific module and is connected to the menu system. In fact, you can select the menu items in which the module is to be shown or hidden, as per the options listed earlier.

When you select **Only on the selected pages** or **On all pages except those selected**, you will be prompted to check the menu items to enable/disable the display of the module, as shown in the following figure.

Figure 4.7 – Menu Assignment | Menu Selection

This level of flexibility allows you to show different modules based on the page the user is visiting. In the next section, we will see how to add a module to our website and explore the available options.

Adding a module to your website

Let's see how to add a module to our website. From the backend of the website, we go to **Content Dashboard** and then to **Site Modules**. On this page, we can see all the modules currently installed/configured on the website.

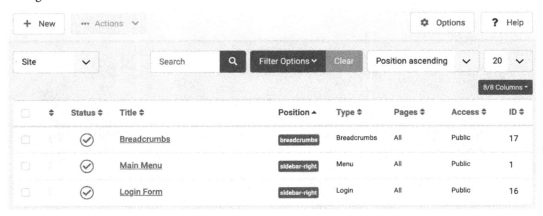

Figure 4.8 – Site modules

To create a new module, just click on the **New** button in the toolbar. We will see the list of available module types, as displayed in the following figure:

Figure 4.9 – Module type selection screen

Let's choose the **Custom** type and create the module by clicking on the plus sign near the desired card. The custom module creation screen will look like this:

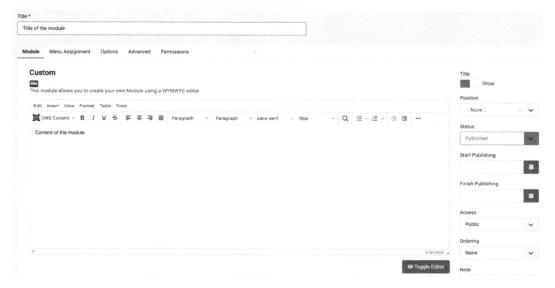

Figure 4.10 – Custom module creation

The first field to fill out is **Title**. The main editing area is meant to host the content of the module that can be inserted through the visual editor.

The other options in the **Module** tab are the following:

- **Title**: Show/hide the title of the module in the frontend
- **Position**: Choose the position in which the module should be published
- **Status**: Choose whether the module should be published/unpublished/ archived/trashed
- **Start Publishing**: Schedule the publishing of the module at a specific date/time
- **Finish Publishing**: Unpublish the module automatically at a specific date/time
- **Access**: Specify the access level for the module
- **Ordering**: Specify the order of the module; useful when there are multiple modules in the same position
- **Note**: Internal notes for the website administrators

The **Menu Assignment** tab includes the controls to decide the pages on which the module should be visible. We went through these controls while describing *Figure 4.7*.

The **Options** tab shows only two controls, as shown in *Figure 4.11*.

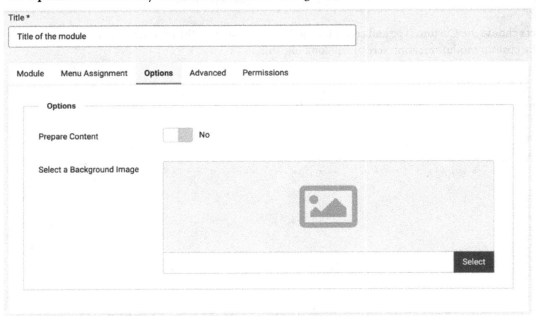

Figure 4.11 – Custom module options

The **Prepare Content** option enables the Joomla content plugins on the contents of the module. This type of plugin generally acts on contents to detect some activation strings to represent galleries, videos, and more.

The other option allows you to select a background image that will be shown as the background of the module.

The **Advanced** tab groups controls to act on the styling of the module, as displayed in *Figure 4.12*.

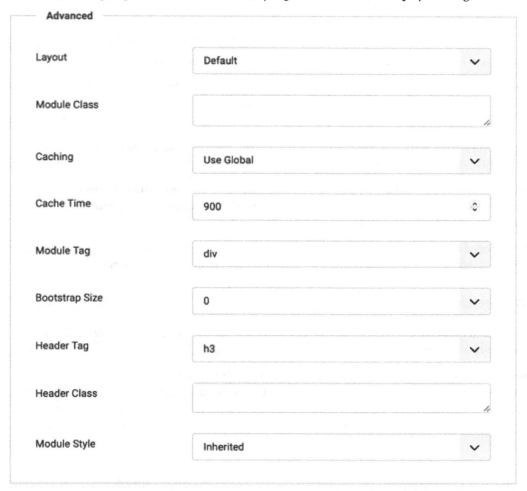

Figure 4.12 – Custom module advanced controls

Let's explore the available options:

- **Layout**: Select a layout for the module if the template provides additional specific layouts.
- **Module Class**: Specify the CSS class to display the module.
- **Caching**: Choose whether to enable cache for the module or not.

- **Cache Time**: Specify the time of the cache.
- **Module Tag**: Choose the HTML markup to be used to represent the module (default is `div`).
- **Bootstrap Size**: Choose how many columns of the 12-columns Bootstrap grid the module should span.
- **Header Tag**: Select the level of header for the module title (default is `h3`).
- **Header Class**: Specify the CSS class to render the title of the module.
- **Module Style**: Choose a style for the module. There are some default styles provided by Joomla and additional styles provided by the template in use.

The latest tab is dedicated, as usual, to permissions, which we will explore in *Chapter 6*. Once we have completed the configuration of the module, we can click on **Save & Close** to save the module we created and configured on our website.

In this section, we explored the settings and controls offered by the custom module, but every module might have additional or different options. Some tabs will be available in every module you install, for example, the **Menu Assignment** and **Advanced** tabs.

As mentioned at the beginning of this chapter, modules are heavily used both in the frontend and the backend of the website. In the upcoming sections, we will explore the backend modules.

Backend modules

The backend dashboard is completely made of modules, which gives us extreme flexibility and the opportunity to customize the layout of the administration side.

Home Dashboard in Joomla 4 includes many modules: **Site**, **System**, **Sample Data**, **Notifications**, **Latest Actions**, **Privacy Dashboard**, **Logged-in Users**, **Popular Articles**, and **Recently Added Articles**. Furthermore, there are other modules to display data such as the version number, the admin menu, a link to the frontend, a logged-user menu, and the notification of post-installation messages.

To check the administrator modules available on the website, you just need to open the **Administrator Module** link from **Content Dashboard**. You will then see the list of available modules as shown in *Figure 4.13*.

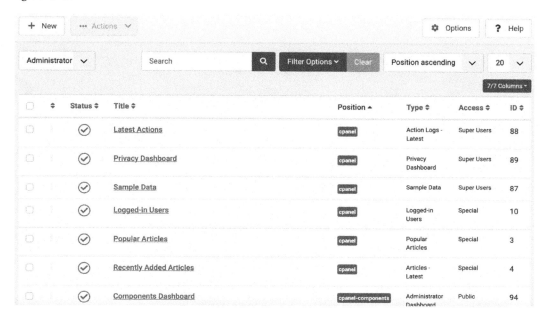

Figure 4.13 – Administrator module

From the list, we can see that the module types for the backend are slightly different, and that in the backend also, modules are published into a position. Available positions differ by template, but it's not that common to use a different backend template.

By clicking on the **New** button, you can create a new backend module, choosing from those available, as displayed in *Figure 4.14*.

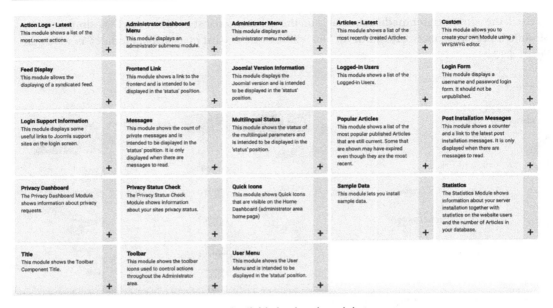

Figure 4.14 – Available backend module types

As for the frontend, the number of available module types might differ based on the extensions installed. Those listed in the preceding figure are shipped by default in Joomla.

Thanks to the available modules, you can set up a completely customized dashboard, placing modules at your convenience to show relevant information.

This feature is very useful, especially when you have multiple administrators for the website and you want to simplify their operations by placing buttons, instructions, and information on a single screen without having them dig through menus and other dashboards.

Also, as you might have noticed, every system dashboard in the Joomla backend has a button that invites you to add another module, as shown in *Figure 4.15*.

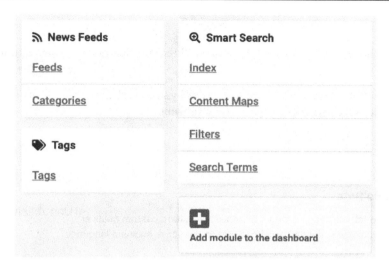

Figure 4.15 – Adding a module to the dashboard

Adding modules to existing dashboards will help you operate your website easier and faster, and your website administration will be tailored to your needs. In the next section, we will learn more about custom backend dashboards with the help of a case study.

Case study – a custom backend dashboard

Throughout this chapter, we discovered that modules increase the flexibility of your website, either on the frontend or backend. We also saw that modules can be used in the backend to customize the administration experience, simplifying paths, and enriching the level of information shown in the dashboards.

With Joomla 4 dashboards, every backend can be different from the others, thanks to the custom modules placed in different positions. In this section, we will analyze, as a case study, a customized backend dashboard.

The scenario

We are building a website for a school, and we will give administrator access (with some limited privileges) to the school's staff to allow them to create articles. We also want to provide some on-screen guidance to them, to remind them where they should go to do the operations. To do so, we need to create custom modules with some text instructions and links to access features. In this case study, we will not operate on access levels and permissions. We will only remove non-useful modules and add additional modules to the dashboard.

Implementation

We will work on the **Home Dashboard**. First, we will remove the modules that are not useful for our users.

Let's remove the **Sample Data** module. We can do this by simply clicking on the gears icon at the top right of the module and clicking on **Unpublish**, as shown in *Figure 4.16*.

Figure 4.16 – Unpublishing a module

We can repeat the procedure for the following modules, if we don't want to have them visible:

- **Latest Actions**
- **Privacy Dashboard**
- **Logged-in Users**
- **Popular Articles**
- **Latest Actions**
- **Recently Added Articles**

We then proceed to create new custom modules in which we can include instructions for the backend users.

To do this, click on **Administrator Modules**, then **New** and **Custom**. We can set the title to `Instructions for Staff` and put as content some text to guide administrators, similarly to what is displayed in *Figure 4.17*.

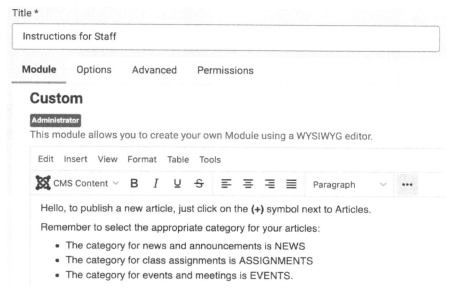

Figure 4.17 – Sample instructions for school staff

This module should be published in the `cpanel` position and will be shown in the dashboard.

With this, we have simplified the administration experience for the school staff. This case study can be heavily improved using access levels in modules and displaying modules only to specific user groups.

Summary

In this chapter, we've explored modules, what they are, how they work, and their usage in the frontend and backend of websites. We saw how to add a module to our website's frontend and to our backend dashboard. We explored the different types of modules and their options and customizations.

In the next chapter, we will explore the **Menu** management system.

Exercises

Let's apply the knowledge acquired in this chapter.

Exercise 1 – creating a custom module

In your Joomla backend, create a new site module, selecting the **Custom Module** type. Give the module the following title: `MyModule`, and configure it to be published on all pages in the `sidebar-left` position. In the content section of the module, type the following text: `This is the text of my first module`. Save and close, then open your website frontend and see how the module looks.

Resources

- Joomla Extensions Directory: `https://extensions.joomla.org`

- *Explore the core! The Joomla 4 Dashboard*: `https://magazine.joomla.org/all-issues/august-2021/explore-the-core-the-joomla-4-dashboard`

- *Joomla 4 for Clients, Part 2: Creating a Streamlined Admin Experience*: `https://magazine.joomla.org/all-issues/february-2022/joomla-4-for-clients-part-2-creating-a-custom-admin-experience`

- *My favourite Joomla 4 feature - customizable dashboard*: `https://magazine.joomla.org/all-issues/september-2021/my-favourite-joomla-4-feature-customizable-dashboard`

Building Your Site Structure: the Menu System

In the previous chapter, we explored Joomla **modules**, the most flexible content unit of the CMS.

We'll now look at one of the most important features of Joomla, the **Menu Manager**.

The menu management features allow you to create menus and menu items to build your personalized navigation system for the website. Menus decide what will be visible on the website, who can see a specific page, what the URL structure of a specific page will be, and much more.

After reading this chapter, you will be able to do the following:

- Understand how the menu system works in Joomla
- Understand how to define a navigation structure for your website
- Handle associations between modules and menu items
- Create a custom menu for your website

So, let's begin!

The menu system

In a website, a menu represents its navigation system, the mechanism that allows users to navigate through the different pages. A menu is a collection of **menu items**; each menu item points to a page, a resource that is displayed when users click on the menu item. Each website might have multiple menus, for example, the main menu shown at the top of the website and an additional menu with some specific items and links displayed in a sidebar. The number of menus and menu items may vary per website since each website has a different structure and complexity.

Also, in Joomla, a menu is a collection of menu items. You can create the number of menus and menu items you need without limits, nest menu items to create submenus, and design a navigation structure that completely fits your needs, as shown in *Figure 5.1*.

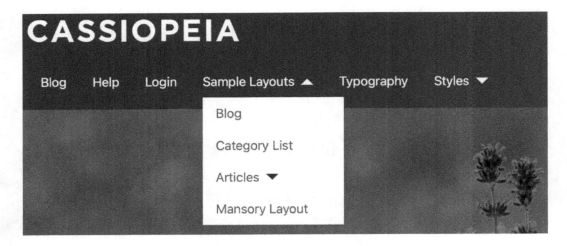

Figure 5.1 – A sample top menu in Joomla

Menu items control many aspects in Joomla – from permissions to the language, and from templates to the URL path, so it's crucial to learn how to structure the menus of your website, to get the most out of it.

Furthermore, the menu items define what type of content should be displayed: a single article, a list of articles, a preview of articles in a category, the main page of a component, a specific component page, and much more, based on the type of menu item selected.

Menus are shown within modules, which control their position, layout, and style within the website.

Let's dig into the Joomla menu-building system, starting from the creation of a new menu for the website's frontend.

Creating a menu

As mentioned in the previous section, a website might have multiple menus, but let's discover how to create a new menu:

1. From **Menu Dashboard** (displayed in *Figure 5.2*), let's click on the **Manage** link shown in the **Menus** module.

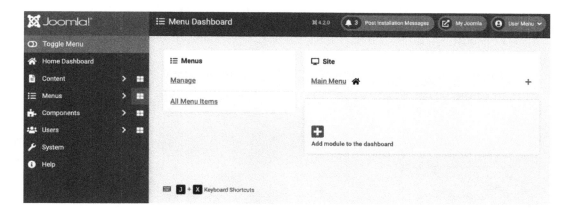

Figure 5.2 – Menu Dashboard

2. The list of available menus will be displayed, as shown in *Figure 5.3*.

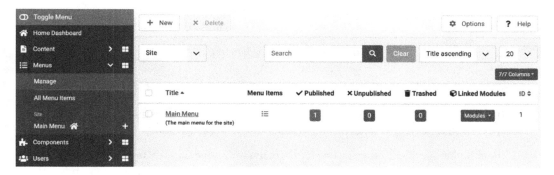

Figure 5.3 – Menus screen

3. Click on the **+ New** button, and let's start creating our menu.

4. The new menu screen has just a few fields, as displayed in *Figure 5.4*.

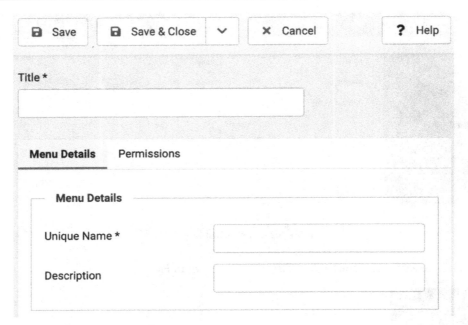

Figure 5.4 – Create a new menu

Let's now explore the fields:

- **Title**: This is the title of the menu. The menu title should be useful to understand which type of menu it is, for example, a horizontal menu, a top menu, or sidebar navigation.

- **Unique Name**: Specifies a unique name for the menu within the site. This field should not contain spaces or special characters. You should only use numbers, letters, hyphens, and underscore symbols. A sample unique name might be `01_sidebar_menu`.

- **Description**: This is an internal description of the menu. This text should help the administrator to remember the scope of the menu while selecting a menu to be shown on the website or when deciding where to put a specific menu item.

The options in the **Permissions** tab allow you to handle permissions and access levels for the menu. We will explore permissions and **ACLs (Access Control Lists)** in *Chapter 6, User Management and ACL*.

To complete the creation of our custom menu, let's just click on **Save & Close** so that we move back to the list of available menus.

After completing these steps, we have created a new menu; now it's time to start creating menu items to be added to the menu we have just created. In the following section, we will explore the available menu item types and how to create a new menu item.

Creating a new menu item

In the previous section, we created a new menu, and it's ready to contain our menu items. As mentioned earlier in this chapter, each menu can host unlimited menu items, even nested in multiple levels. Let's create a menu item and check the available menu item types.

To check the available menu item types in your installation, let's just create a new menu item. To do so, in the list of website menus (**Menus | Manage**), click on the list icon displayed next to the **Sample menu** menu that we created, as displayed in *Figure 5.5*.

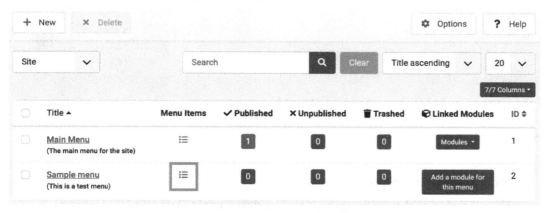

Figure 5.5 – List of available menus and button to open menu items

Clicking on the icon highlighted in red in the previous screenshot allows us to see the list of menu items tied to the **Sample menu** menu. As we can also see from the numbers shown in the columns **Published**, **Unpublished**, and **Trashed**, the menu does not have any menu items.

To create a new menu item, just click on the + **New** button in the toolbar. This action opens the **New Menu Item** screen, as displayed in *Figure 5.6*.

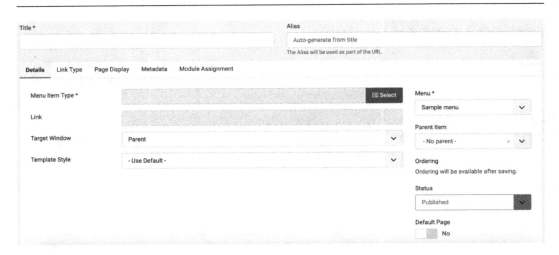

Figure 5.6 – New Menu Item screen

Let's explore the fields and available options to create a menu item:

- **Title**: Specifies a title for the menu item. This is displayed on the menu bar on the public website (for instance, **Home** or **Contacts**).

- **Alias**: Specifies an alias for the menu item. This field is used to build the URL structure.

- **Menu Item Type**: By clicking on **Select**, you can pick the desired type of menu item. We will explore the available menu types in the next section.

- **Link**: This field is automatically populated and shows the deep URL of the page.

- **Target Window**: You can choose whether the link should be opened in a **Parent** window or in a new browser window with or without navigation.

- **Template Style**: Choose the template to be assigned to this menu item. By default, all the menu items will be opened using the template style set as default for the whole website.

- **Menu**: Choose which menus the menu item should belong to. In our example, the menu item will be added to **Sample menu**.

- **Parent Item**: Choose whether the menu item should be a first-level item or nested under another menu item. The drop-down list will show all the menu items in the menu.

- **Ordering**: Choose the position in the list of menu items. This option can be actioned only after the menu item is saved.

- **Status**: Choose whether the menu item should be **Published/Unpublished/Trashed**.

- **Default Page**: Choose whether the menu item should be set as the home page (default page) of the website. This means that if your visitors open mywebsite.com, they will be directed to this page.

- **Start Publishing**: Select the date and time at which the menu item should be published. This is useful if you want to publish a menu item at a specific time, allowing you to schedule the activity. The field is optional, and by default, it's empty.

- **Finish Publishing**: Select the date and time at which the menu item should be unpublished. This is useful to hide a menu item from your website at a specific time. The field is optional, and by default, it's empty.

- **Access**: Specify the access level for this menu item by selecting the **user group** that can see the item and access it. We will explore user groups and ACL in *Chapter 6, User Management and ACL*.

- **Note**: This is an internal note for website administrators.

Note: the importance of menu item aliases

In Joomla, menu item aliases are fundamental in building the URL structure of the website. Through aliases, you can create a custom URL structure to improve the **Search Engine Optimization (SEO)** of your website.

Example: If your website is `mywebsite.com` and you want to have a friendly URL for your contact page, such as `contact-us` string, you should specify as an alias for the menu item of the contact page the `contact-us`. This would result in the following URL for the page: `mywebsite.com/contact-us`. As you can see, it's a friendly URL that is easy to remember and write.

Aliases are important while building the URL structure for the whole website, including blogs and category views.

Please note that the alias should be a string that includes only letters, numbers, dashes, and underscores; special characters are not allowed in this field. Remember that if empty, the alias will be automatically generated based on the content of the **Title** field.

Prior to checking the options offered by Joomla while configuring a menu item, let's explore the different menu types available.

Exploring available menu item types

Available menu item types may vary based on the third-party extensions installed in your Joomla instance. Most components offer one or more menu item types to display their output. Let's explore the menu item types offered in a standard Joomla installation.

After clicking on the + **New** button to create a menu item, we saw in the previous section that you are prompted to input several details and options for the menu item to be created. The most important choice is **Menu Item Type**, which allows you to define what the menu item should have as the target. Click on the **Select** button to see the list of available menu item types in your installation, as shown in *Figure 5.7*.

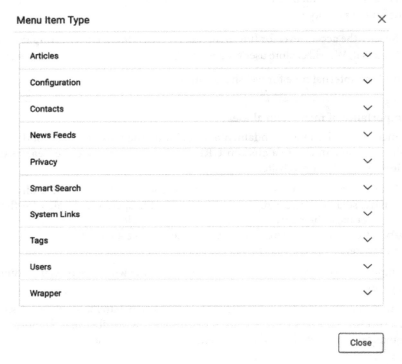

Figure 5.7 – List of the available menu item types

The list shows the installed components and features that offer a specific menu item type. Each of them may offer one or more menu item types.

Let's click on **Articles** to see the menu item types provided by the **Articles** component, as displayed in *Figure 5.8*.

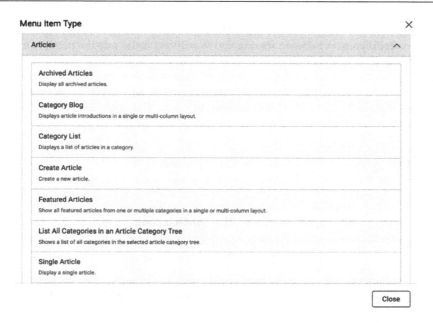

Figure 5.8 – Available menu item types in the Articles component

Let's explore the different types of menu items offered by the **Articles** component:

- **Archived Articles**: Displays all the articles with an **Archived** status.

- **Category Blog**: Displays a list of articles from a category, showing titles and introductory text for each of them. The layout is completely configurable through the menu item options, which allow you to select the number of columns and how articles are displayed.

- **Category List**: Displays a list of articles from a category, showing a minimal table or list with titles and other information. The layout is configurable through the menu item options.

- **Create Article**: Opens the page where users with appropriate permissions can submit a new article to the website.

- **Featured Articles**: Displays featured articles from one or more categories in a customizable layout.

- **List All Categories in an Article Category Tree**: This shows a list of categories nested in the category selected in the menu item. It's useful if you want to build a navigable sitemap or create a section map, given a specific category.

- **Single Article**: Displays a single article. This is one of the most used menu item types since it allows you to create a page. If you only want to show a specific article on a page, this is the right menu item.

> ### Joomla and WordPress: articles, posts, and pages
>
> One of the main differences between Joomla and WordPress is the way the menu is built and managed. This is also reflected in the content. In WordPress, you should decide beforehand whether the content is a blog post (type: *post*) or it is meant to be a static page (type: *page*). In Joomla, you don't have to choose. You simply create an *article*, and thanks to menu items, you can have the article as part of a blog (for example, using the **Category Blog** menu item) or a single page (using the **Single Article** menu item type).

With **Single Article**, we've completed the menu item types offered by the **Articles** component. But as seen in *Figure 5.7*, there are many other components that offer menu item types.

For example, the **Users** component offers menu item types that allow you to create a login/logout page, a user profile page, and a registration form. The **Contacts** component provides menu item types to display a single contact or a category of contacts, to create a new contact, or to show the whole list of contacts.

Third-party components may add specific menu item types. For example, an e-commerce extension will add menu item types to show the shopping cart, the list of orders, the list of products by category, a single product, or the list of invoices.

There are also some menu item types that are provided by the system and are not tied to a specific component.

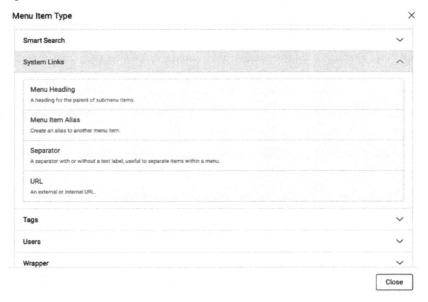

Figure 5.9 – System Links menu item types

Let's explore the menu items type available under the **System Links** group, as displayed in *Figure 5.9*:

- **Menu Heading**: Displays a header in the menu. This is a special type of menu item, not linked to anything, but used when you want to group submenu items.

- **Menu Item Alias**: Creates an alias for another existing menu item. This is useful when you want to have the same menu item in different menus or to link to the same target page using two different anchor texts in menus.

- **Separator**: This is a special item type that creates a placeholder text in a menu without any link.

- **URL**: Allows you to create a link to an external resource, such as a third-party URL.

After the **System Links** menu items, let's explore the unique item type in the **Wrapper** group. **Iframe Wrapper** is a special menu item type that allows you to embed a URL in to a website page, through an iframe.

Having seen the most common menu item types in this section, let's move back to the creation of a menu item process, continuing to analyze the available options.

Menu item options

The options to configure a menu item vary depending on the menu item type. Each menu item type, like those discovered in the previous section, provides a specific set of options in addition to the standard configuration options provided by Joomla itself.

To explore the available options, let's start by selecting a specific menu item type: **Single Article**. Based on this selection, the menu item creation screen changed, immediately showing additional fields, tabs, and buttons, as shown in *Figure 5.10*.

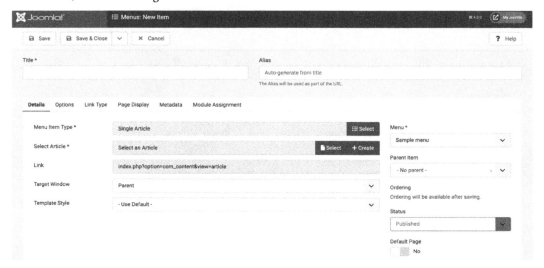

Figure 5.10 – Single Article menu item creation screen

The additional field that appeared is **Select Article**, which shows two buttons:

- **Select**: Allows you to choose an article from existing ones. The article selection screen provides search and filter functionality to find the desired article.

- **Create**: Opens the new article creation screen so that you can write a new article and connect the menu item to it.

The **Options** tab collects a series of options to customize the appearance of the **Single Article** page. For example, you can choose whether or not to display the article **Title**, **Author**, **Category**, the introductory text, **Publishing Date**, and much more.

As mentioned earlier in this section, different menu item types offer different setup options based on the specific item type.

Let's continue to explore the available options, moving to the **Link Type** tab.

Figure 5.11 – Menu item options: Link Type

As shown in *Figure 5.11*, the **Link Type** tab includes options to customize the menu item with some attributes and styles. All these are optional:

- **Link Title Attribute**: Allows you to specify an additional description to the menu item title.

- **Link Class**: Adds a specific CSS class to the link in the menu.

- **Link Icon Class**: Allows you to specify a CSS class for the menu item icon if any.

- **Link Image**: Adds an image to the menu item. Useful when you want to display a small icon near the anchor text in the menu.

- **Image Class**: Allows you to specify a CSS class for the menu item image.

- **Display Menu Item Title: Yes/No**. By default, the title of the menu item is shown. You can disable this option when you want to show only the image or icon instead of the title in the menu.

- **Display in Menu: Yes/No**. By default, the menu item is displayed in the menu. Choose **No** if you want to hide the menu item from the menu.

Let's now move on to the **Page Display** tab, which collects some options related to the page's appearance.

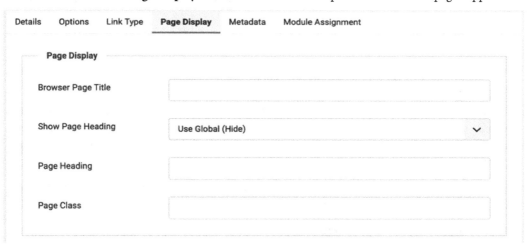

Figure 5.12 – Menu item options: Page Display

As shown in *Figure 5.12*, the options on this page allow you to operate on the appearance of the page linked by the menu item:

- **Browser Page Title**: Defines the title of the page displayed in the browser tab and the `<title>` HTML metatag that impacts your website's SEO.

- **Show Page Heading**: Allows you to decide whether or not to show the page title on the website page. The **Use Global (Hide)** option inherits the setting specified in the component options in **Global Configuration**.

- **Page Heading**: Allows you to specify custom text for the page heading.

- **Page Class**: Allows you to specify a CSS class to be used to render the page.

Let's now move on to the **Module Assignment** tab, displayed in *Figure 5.13*.

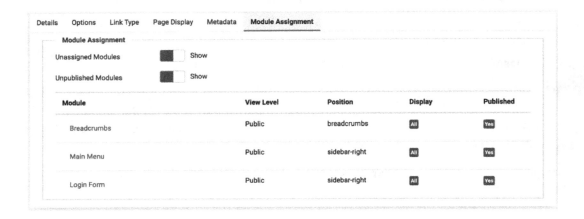

Figure 5.13 – Menu item options: Module Assignment

The **Module Assignment** tab displays the list of modules that are assigned to the specific menu item. It represents a fast method to check which modules are displayed on the page of the website. For each module, you can see the access level, the position, whether it's displayed, and whether or not it's published.

The options above the list of modules allow you to choose whether or not modules unassigned to menu items or unpublished modules should be displayed.

In the next section, we'll explore the **Metadata** tab and other SEO-oriented options.

Menu and SEO configuration

We mentioned earlier in this chapter that menus are important to improve the SEO of your website.

One of the most useful fields is **Alias**, which is used in the formation of the URL structure of the website.

Let's now discover the options offered by the **Metadata** tab, displayed in *Figure 5.14*:

- **Meta Description**: Allows you to specify the description meta tag for the page. You can write up to 160 characters in the field.

- **Robots**: Allows you to specify the rules for the search engine indexing bots (*index, follow / noindex, follow / index, nofollow / noindex, nofollow*).

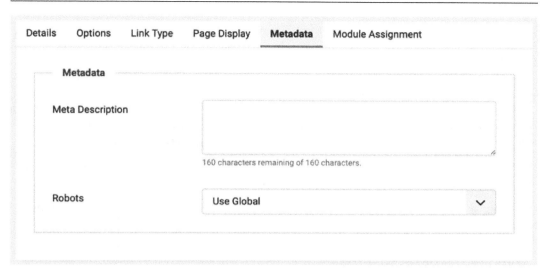

Figure 5.14 – Menu item options: Metadata

We will explore all the features related to SEO in *Chapter 7, SEO at Its Best*.

Let's now discover some of the aspects related to menus on multilingual websites.

Menu and languages

Joomla offers a set of powerful features to manage multilingual websites in a single installation. We will explore multilanguage websites in depth in *Chapter 8, One Website, Multiple Languages*.

We need to know that menus are crucial in the creation and configuration of a multilanguage website. When multilanguage features are enabled, for each menu item, you can choose to which of the languages you want to tie the menu item. A menu item can be tied to a single language or to **All**. When **All** is selected, the menu item is shown in all the languages available.

With this section, we have completed the options to create a menu item. Let's now move on to exercises.

Summary

In this chapter, we have explored the menu management features of Joomla and understood how to create a custom menu for our website, create new menu items, and the different types of menu items available. We have also discovered the settings available for each menu item and their effects on the produced page.

In the next chapter, we'll go deeper into the user management features, introducing **Users**, **Privacy Features**, **Access Levels**, and **User Groups**.

Exercises

It's time to apply the knowledge acquired in this chapter and start building our menus.

Exercise 1 – create a menu and a menu item

In your sample Joomla installation, go to **Menu Manager** and create a new menu called `Sample menu`. You can set a personal description for the menu. Save and go back to the **Menus** view.

Now create a menu item of the **Single Article** type, selecting the article `MyArticle` that we created in *Exercise 2* of *Chapter 2*. The menu item should have `MyArticle` for **Title** and an autogenerated **Alias**.

You can choose the options at your convenience, but ensure that the article's title, category, and author are displayed on the page.

Exercise 2 – a category list

Let's now create a new menu item in `Sample menu`. The new menu item should have as its title `MyList`, as its type **Category List**, and select the `MyCategory` category that we created in *Chapter 2*. The result should be a page on which the list of articles belonging to the `MyCategory` category is displayed.

6

Managing Users and Their Permissions

In the previous chapter, we explored Joomla Menus, and understood how to create menu items, defining the navigation mechanisms for our website.

We'll now dig into users and their permissions management feature.

After reading this chapter, you will understand the following:

- How to create and manage users in your website
- How to manage permissions to access a specific part of your websites
- What access levels are in Joomla and how to create your own custom levels
- How to create and manage user groups
- How to use the features provided by the Privacy Tool Suite

Joomla integrates many functionalities related to users, as you will discover throughout this chapter. Let's start with **Users Dashboard**.

Users Dashboard

The first contact of the website administrator with Joomla's features related to user management is represented by **Users Dashboard**, displayed in *Figure 6.1*.

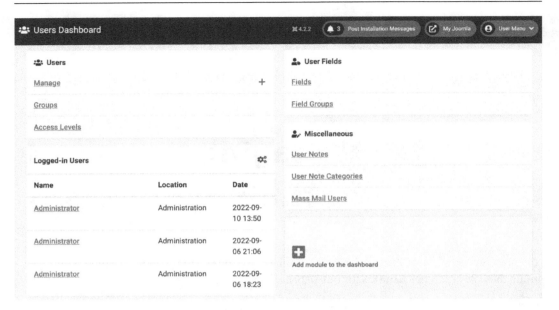

Figure 6.1 – Users Dashboard

Users Dashboard shows three modules with links to user-related functionalities:

- The first module, called **Users**, has links to manage users, groups, and access levels, plus the link to create a new user.

- The second module is called **User Fields** and has links to manage custom fields and field groups. As you can guess, you can create custom fields to enrich your users' profiles with additional data.

- The third module is **Miscellaneous**, and it includes links to the **User Notes**, **User Note Categories**, and **Mass Mail Users** functionalities.

We will explore each of the features linked by the three modules in the following sections of this chapter.

The dashboard also includes the **Logged-in Users** module, which shows a list of the latest accesses to the website, reporting the name of the user, the location (**Site** or **Administration**), and the date and time of the access.

As with all the other Joomla dashboards, **Users Dashboard** can also be completely customized by adding or removing modules.

Let's now present the user account features.

User accounts

Joomla integrates all the needed features to create and manage user accounts out of the box. Accounts allow users to log into the website, perform operations, and access content and pages for which they have the appropriate permissions. Accounts can be created either in the backend of the website by an administrator or in the frontend of the website by the user directly through a self-registration form.

Administrators can choose whether to allow self-registration to the website or not through the options available in the **Users** component's options.

Users on the website may have different permissions and roles. In fact, each user belongs to one or more **User Groups** and, through the group, receives specific *permissions*. We'll explore **User Groups** in depth in a later section.

Let's now see how to create a user account from the website backend.

Creating a new user account

Starting from **Users Dashboard**, displayed in *Figure 6.1*, click on the + sign, next to **Manage** in the **Users** module. The account creation screen is then displayed, as per *Figure 6.2*.

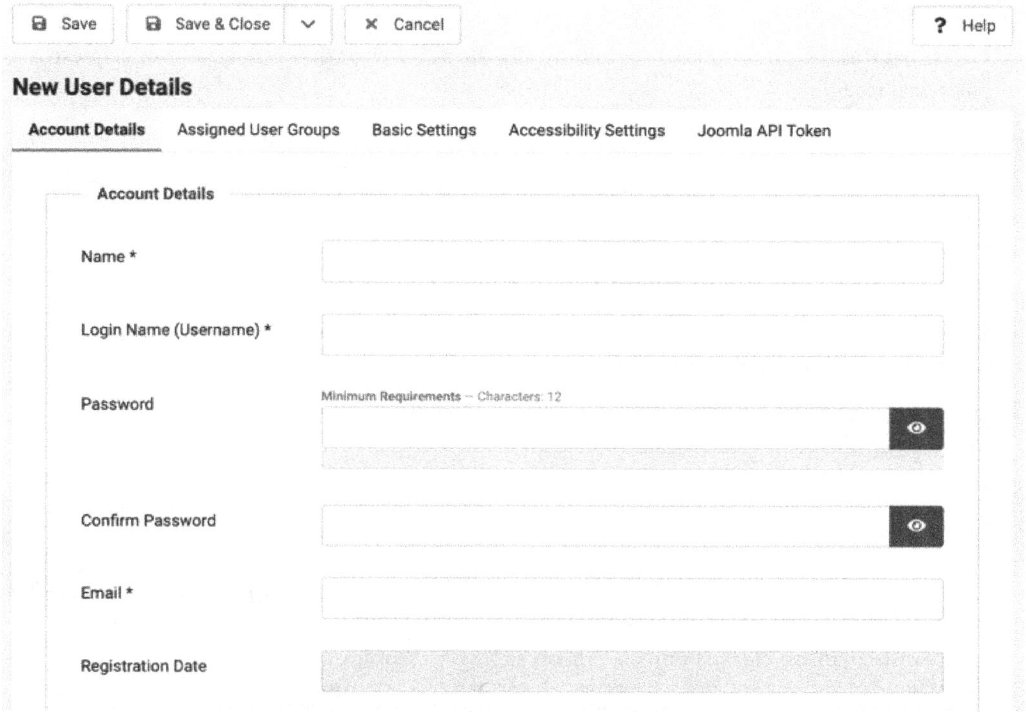

Figure 6.2 – New user screen

Let's analyze the fields proposed in the **Account Details** tab:

- **Name**: This is the name of the user. Generally, this field contains the full name or the legal name of the user.

- **Login Name (Username)**: As per the field name, this field represents the username used to log in to the website.

- **Password**: Specifies the password for the user. This is used when logging in to the website. When empty, the system will generate a random password for the user.

- **Confirm Password**: This is the field where you re-type the password specified in the preceding field to confirm it.

- **Email**: This is the email address of the users. It's used to receive notifications and communications from the website.

- **Registration Date**: This is a read-only field populated automatically with the registration date, once the account is created.

- **Last Visit Date**: A read-only field populated automatically with the last date/time that the user logged in to the website.

- **Last Reset Date**: Reports automatically the date/time that the user requested a password reset.

- **Password Reset Count**: Reports automatically the number of times that the user requested a password reset.

- **Receive System Emails**: Choose whether the user should receive notifications from the system, such as update availability notices or new users' registration messages. The default is **No** and this option should be activated only for administrative users.

- **User Status**: Choose whether the user account should be enabled or not. This option is useful when you want to disable a user account.

- **Require Password Reset**: When set to **Yes**, the user will be prompted by the password change screen at the next login.

- **ID**: An automatically populated field with the unique ID assigned to the user's account, after its creation.

Password requirements

In *Figure 6.2*, there is a visible meter under the **Password** field that indicates the complexity level of the selected password. This evaluation is made against the password requirements specified in the **Options** section of the **Users** component. There, you can specify a series of parameters for your website passwords, including the minimum password length, the minimum quantity of symbols, and the use of lowercase and uppercase characters as well as numbers. Through these options, you can increase the security of the users of your website, forcing them to choose more robust passwords. In **Password Options**, you can also specify the maximum number of password reset attempts and how long in hours must lapse before the count of reset password attempts is restored.

Let's move to the **Assigned User Groups** tab, displayed in *Figure 6.3*.

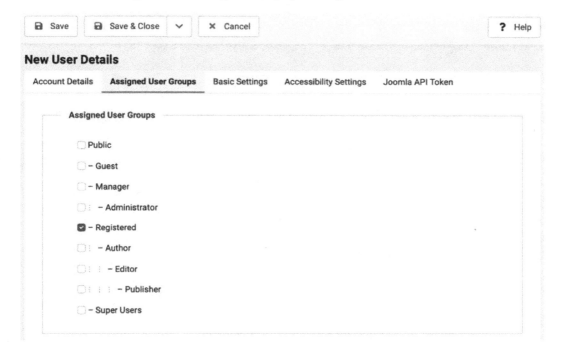

Figure 6.3 – New user: Assigned User Groups

On this screen, you can assign the user account to one or more **User Groups**. By default, all user accounts belong to the **Registered** user group. In *Figure 6.3*, you can see the list of predefined **User Groups**, available in all Joomla installations. You may create, edit, and delete user groups at your convenience. In the next section, we will explore **User Groups** and their importance in assigning permissions on the website.

Let's move on to the **Basic Settings** tab, displayed in *Figure 6.4*.

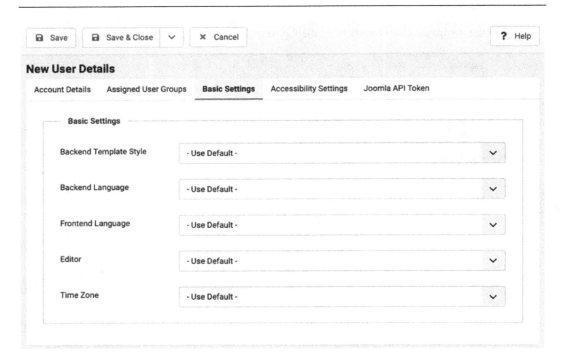

Figure 6.4 – New user: Basic Settings

The controls in this tab allow you to customize the experience of the user, selecting the template style for the backend, the language for either the frontend or backend, the editor to use, and the time zone of the users. Through these options, you can offer an experience tailored to the user, showing the website in a specific language, or allowing the user to input their content using an editor different from the one set as the default for the website. You can also offer the user the ability to apply these options through the profile page on the website frontend.

Let's move on to the **Accessibility Settings** tab, displayed in *Figure 6.5*.

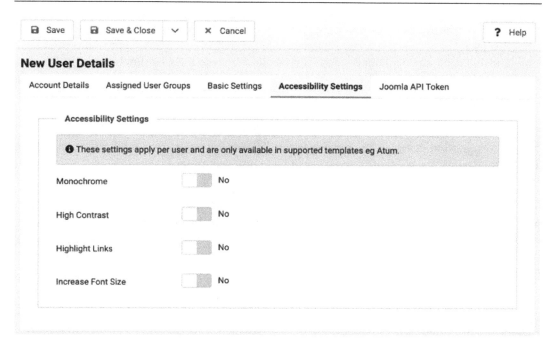

Figure 6.5 – New user: Accessibility Settings

The controls offered by this tab allow you to customize the experience of the user in terms of accessibility, enabling the high contrast or monochromatic version of the website, highlighting links, or increasing the font size, where these options are supported by the backend or frontend template in use. These options are available for each user and can be set by the user through their profile page.

Let's now move on to the last tab, **Joomla API Token**, displayed in *Figure 6.6*.

Account Details   Assigned User Groups   Basic Settings   Accessibility Settings   User Actions Log Options   **Joomla API Token**

Joomla API Token

ⓘ Manage the security tokens used for authenticating to the Joomla API application (remote access to your site). If you are not sure what this does chances are you don't need it and can safely ignore these settings.

Token	c2hhMjU2OjYzMTphY2JkZGNiYTk1ZGQ1NDBjOTk1YmY5ZjRiZjU3MDg2N2E5ZWQzYTJhY2IzNjZmNGQ4MDEwM2RIMmE3MTA1Yzk5 Copy

This is your token. Use it in third party applications requiring remote access to your site through the Joomla API application.

Active	Yes

Set to No to temporarily prevent access to your site with this token.

Reset	No

Set to Yes and save your user profile to create a new token, replacing the old one.

Figure 6.6 – New user: Joomla API Token

This screen shows the unique token that allows you to use the web services offered by the Joomla API, as a specific user. For example, you can authenticate to the website and execute operations through a command line or a script, without the need to type the user credentials, by simply using the token.

On the screen, you can also choose whether the token should be active or not and whether you want to regenerate the token at the next user save.

Once you have completed the mandatory fields in the tabs we explored, just click on **Save & Close** to create the user account. Based on the options selected, the user may receive a notification via email to inform them about the account's creation, with login instructions included.

Based on the user role or the functionalities enabled on your website, the user creation and edit screen may show additional tabs, such as the **User Action Log** tab (only visible to super users) or the **WebAuthn login** and **Multi-factor authentication** tabs, which are displayed only when the respective plugins are enabled.

Editing a user profile

From the list of users, accessible through the **Manage** link on **Users Dashboard**, you can edit the user accounts of the website. To edit an account, just click on the name of the user. You can see all the fields and tabs that we've explored during the creation of a new account.

Being able to create and edit user accounts, we'll now discover **User Groups** and understand their purpose.

User Groups

In Joomla, **User Groups** are used to grant permissions to resources, that is, content, menu items, and extensions, in both the frontend and backend. Each user of the website must be assigned to one or more **User Groups**, as we saw while creating or editing a user account.

Groups are heavily connected to access levels; in fact, each access level should be assigned to one or more groups, granting users of the selected group the permissions defined at that access level. We'll explore access levels in depth in the next section.

Let's now review the User Groups available by default in Joomla, as displayed in *Figure 6.7*.

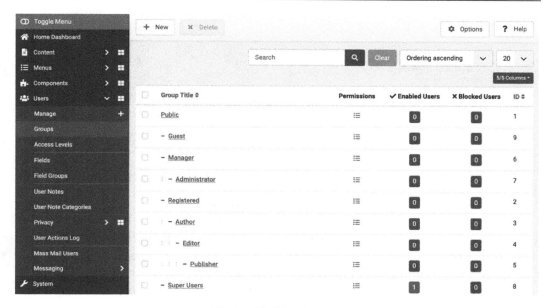

Figure 6.7 – User Groups

To access the **User Groups** page, from the sidebar menu click on **Users** then on **Groups**. You'll then see the list of all the groups created on the website, the number of enabled users in each group, the number of blocked users in each group, and a link to check the permissions that users of each group have on the website.

Groups can also be nested, one under another. In this way, the subgroup inherits permissions from its parent, allowing you to customize only the needed permissions, without re-defining the whole permissions set.

As we can observe in *Figure 6.7*, the root group is called **Public**, and it represents the base for the permissions for the whole website. All the other groups inherit the basic permissions from **Public**.

Creating a user group

You can create and nest user groups at your convenience. To create a user group, click on the **New** button. You will be taken to the screen visible in *Figure 6.8*.

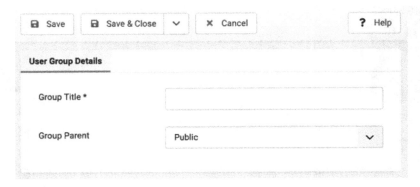

Figure 6.8 – New user group screen

The creation of a new user group is a very simple process that provides only the following two fields:

- **Group Title**: Allows you to specify the name of the user group.
- **Group Parent**: Allows you to select the parent user group for the new group you are creating. By default, all user groups are placed under the **Public** group.

As you can see, groups are basic entities, without many options. We'll now dig into access levels, which allow us to grant permissions to users through user groups.

Access levels

Access levels are very important in Joomla, since they allow us to assign permissions to user groups, and to users. Some access levels are already provided by default in a standard installation, but you can create as many access levels as you need.

Each access level can be assigned to one or more user groups. Let's explore the standard access levels, displayed in *Figure 6.9*.

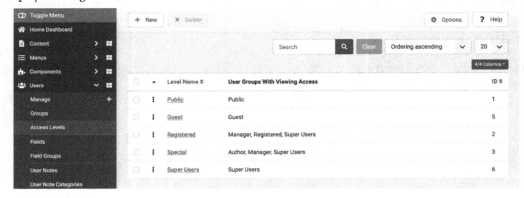

Figure 6.9 – Access Levels

To view the access levels of your website, just click on **Access Levels** in the **Users** sidebar menu. As you can see, Joomla comes with five built-in access levels: **Public**, **Guest**, **Registered**, **Special**, and **Super Users**. For each of the access levels, we can find the list of user groups assigned to them. In the next section, we'll see how to create a new access level.

Creating a new access level

To create a new access level, just click on the **New** button shown in the toolbar. The access level creation screen will look like *Figure 6.10*.

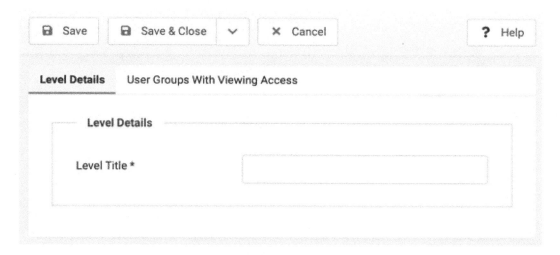

Figure 6.10 – New access level: Level Details

In the first tab, **Level Details**, we can only specify the name of the access level, using the **Level Title** field. The second tab, **User Groups With Viewing Access**, allows you to choose which user groups should receive this access level, as shown in *Figure 6.11*.

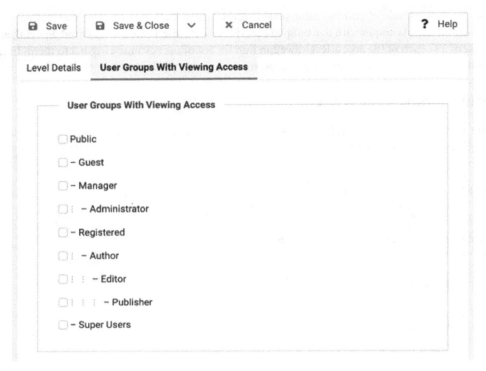

Figure 6.11 – New access level: User Groups With Viewing Access

Creating several access levels will allow us to have a higher granularity in managing permissions on the website. For example, if we are building the website for a school, it would be common to have at least three additional access levels: *Teachers*, *Students*, and *School Personnel*. In this way, we can grant those groups access to the relevant sections of the website or reserved areas, differentiated by role.

In the next section, we'll see how to manage **permissions** using access levels.

Managing permissions and privileges

In this chapter, we've introduced two basic entities that are crucial in the Joomla permission management system: **User Groups** and **Access Levels**. Specifically, through access levels, we can manage permissions and privileges for almost all the entities in the CMS, contents, modules, components, and menu items, either in the backend or the frontend of the website. You can, in fact, create custom permissions sets for each of the sides of the application: limiting features of the backend, allowing only certain parts of the backend to be used, or creating a specific access level for the frontend that allows users with this level to access only a specific set of pages. The Joomla **Access Control List** (**ACL**) is a very powerful feature.

Let's start to understand the permission management functionalities by accessing the **Settings** link from **System Dashboard**.

The page shown will be the **Permissions** tab of **Global Configuration**, as displayed in *Figure 6.12*.

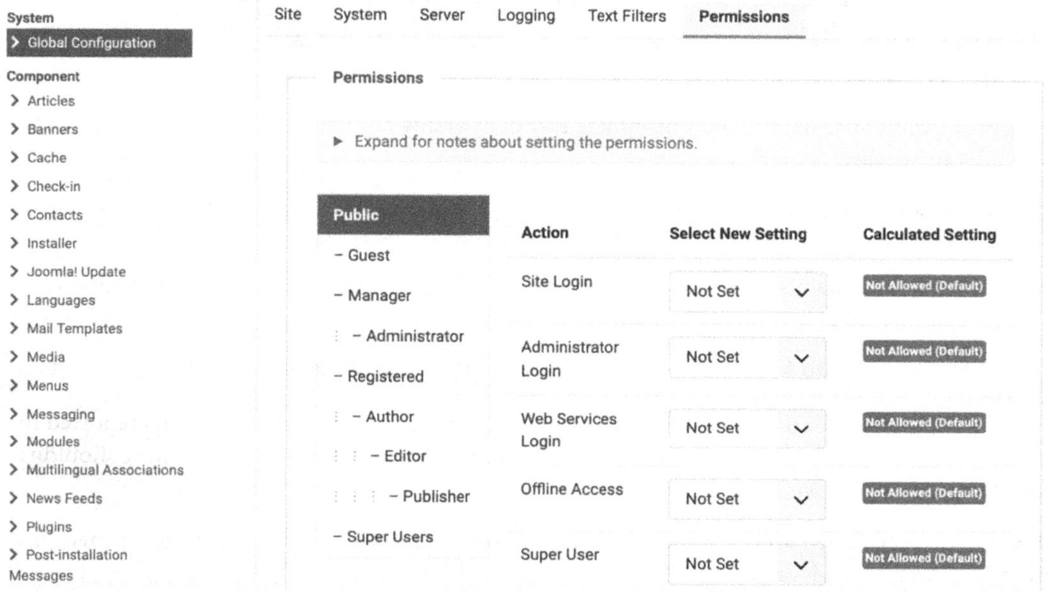

Figure 6.12 – Global Configuration: Permissions

In the tab, we can see the list of **User Groups** on the left and the list of actions on the right side. For each action, you can select a setting through the dropdown. The system will show the result of the permission applied based on the permissions inherited and set there, in the **Calculated Setting** column. For each action you can set one of the three following values: **Not Set**, **Allowed**, or **Denied**. In *Figure 6.12*, we can observe that the permissions shown are intended for the **Public** user group.

Let's now explore the available permission types that can be assigned globally to an access level:

- **Site Login**: Allows the users to access the frontend of the website through their user account.

- **Administrator Login**: Allows the users to access the backend of the website through their user account.

- **Web Services Login**: Allows the users to access the website through their API token.

- **Offline Access**: Allows the users to access the website when it's offline or in maintenance mode.

- **Super User**: Grants the users **Super User** permissions that allow full control over the website.

- **Configure Options Only**: Allows the users to edit the options of any component, except for permissions.

- **Access Administration Interface**: Allows the users to access the backend interface, except for **Global Configuration**.

- **Create**: Allows the users to create any item in any component. For example, they can create new articles, new menus, new menu items, new categories, and new custom fields.

- **Delete**: Allows the users to delete any item in any component. For example, they can delete articles, menus, and menu items.

- **Edit**: Allows the users to edit or update any item in any component. For example, they can edit an article or a menu item.

- **Edit State**: Allows the users to change the state of any item. For example, they can change an article state from *Published* to *Unpublished*, or publish a menu item.

- **Edit Own**: Allows the users to edit only their own items. For example, the author of an article can modify only their article and not those of other authors.

- **Edit Custom Field Value**: Allows the users to edit the value of custom fields, in any extension.

The **Public** access level has the **Not Allowed (Default)** permission on all of the actions reported in the preceding list since it's meant to be the group where website visitors belong and they shouldn't have any specific permissions.

Other access levels have specific permissions; for example, we can see a preview of the permissions for the **Manager** access level in *Figure 6.13*.

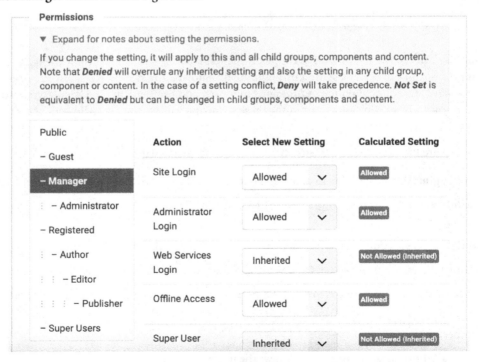

Figure 6.13 – Global Configuration: Permissions | Manager

We can observe that the **Not Set** option – seen in *Figure 6.12* – has been replaced by **Inherited**. This means that permissions are inherited from the parent user groups. That's why it can be useful to nest user groups in a meaningful way.

Beyond **Global Configuration**, permissions can be set on a per-component basis and even on a per-item basis. Let's see how.

Managing permissions of a component

As we mentioned earlier in this section, almost every item in Joomla allows you to define specific permissions for each access level. In this way, you can have full control of privileges on your website.

The permissions management screen for each component can be accessed from **System | User Permissions | Settings**, by selecting the desired component in the list shown on the left side, as we saw earlier in *Figure 6.12*.

Let's explore the permissions manageable for the **Articles** component, displayed in *Figure 6.14*.

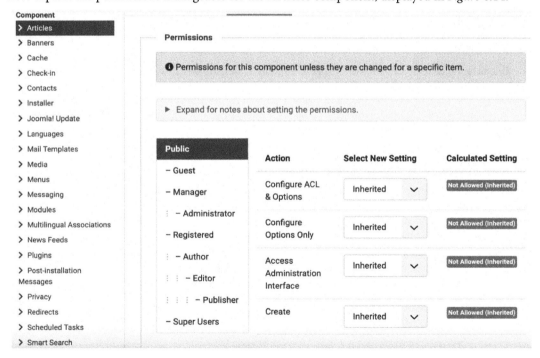

Figure 6.14 – Global Configuration – Articles: Permissions

Actions shown for each component may vary, extending the granularity of the permissions from the standard set of permissions set in **Global Configuration**. Again, the **Calculated Setting** column will ensure you reach the desired permissions result, showing eventual conflicts between global and specific permissions set in the components.

For example, in *Figure 6.14*, we can see that there are some additional permissions for the **Articles** component. Let's check them out:

- **Configure ACL & Options**: Allows the users with a specific access level to access and edit the component options and permissions
- **Configure Options Only**: Allows the users to access and edit only the component options
- **Access Administration Interface**: Allows the users to access the backend interface of the component
- **Create**: Allow the users to create new items (in this case, new articles)
- **Delete**: Allows the users to delete items (articles)
- **Edit**: Allows the users to edit items (articles)
- **Edit State**: Allows the users to change the state of the items (for example **Published**, **Unpublished**, and so on)
- **Edit Own**: Allows the users to edit their own items (the articles they wrote)
- **Edit Custom Field Value**: Allows the users to edit the value of the custom fields linked to articles
- **Manage Workflows**: Allows the users to manage **workflows**
- **Execute Transition:** Allows the users to execute a workflow transition

The number and type of actions may vary based on the component. Some of the actions, such as **Access Administration Interface** and **Configure ACL & Options**, are available for all the components.

Scenario – custom backend permissions

Through the appropriate permissions, you can restrict access to functionalities to specific backend users. For example, for a magazine website, you can create an access level for authors, allowing them to access only the **Articles** component, granting them only **Create** and **Edit Own** permissions, and allowing them to submit new articles or edit their articles. Another backend access level could be useful for editors, allowing them to execute transitions of the workflow, edit items, and change the state of items so that they can review, approve, and publish articles. With an ACL, you can fully apply the principle of minimum privilege.

But permissions can also be managed on a per-item basis. Let's now see how.

Managing permissions for a single item

Almost every item in Joomla allows you to specify the permissions based on the access level. This is specifically useful when you want to restrict permissions of specific articles, categories, or modules.

On an article edit screen, you can see the **Permissions** tab, in which you are allowed to define who can delete, edit, or edit the state for the specific article, as shown in *Figure 6.15*.

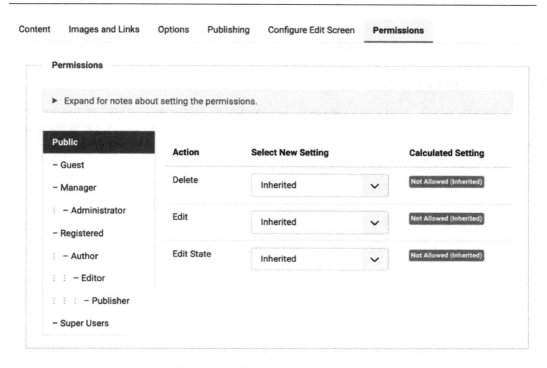

Figure 6.15 – Single article permissions

The same pattern applies to modules; in fact, for each module you can specify who can perform a specific action through the **Permissions** tab, as shown in *Figure 6.16*.

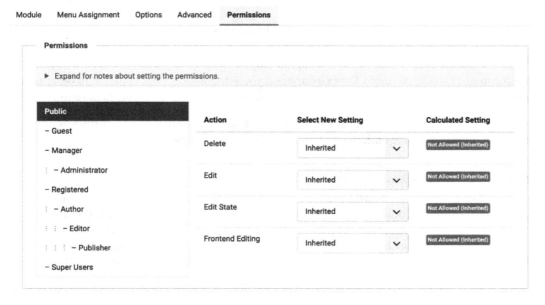

Figure 6.16 – Module permissions

Joomla also allows you to specify who should see specific content, such as an article, a category, a menu item, or even a module. In the next section, we'll see how to restrict access to content to specific users.

Specifying access permission for items

For each item in Joomla, from articles to categories, from modules to menu items, you can specify who should be able to access the item. This is pursued through the **Access** field, visible in the item creation/editing screen, as displayed in *Figure 6.17*.

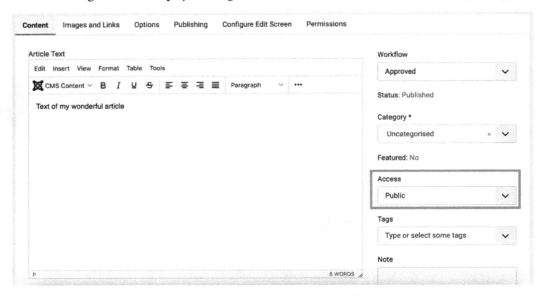

Figure 6.17 – Article edit screen: Access

Through the **Access** field, you can choose from the dropdown the user group who should be able to access the item. If you have nested **User Groups** and you select a group that is parent to other user groups, all the user groups nested under the selected group will be granted access to the item.

This access setting is available on both sides of the application, allowing you to customize access permissions for each item for both the frontend and the backend of the site.

> **Scenario – custom backend dashboard**
>
> You can build a customized dashboard in the backend of the website, hiding some modules and menus and adding other modules to simplify their operations. To do so, just create a user group for those users and assign it to the modules that are meant to be shown to them only. Hide modules that should not be visible to them by selecting a higher user group, such as super users. In this way, you can completely customize the backend experience of your coworkers.

With this section, we completed the part related to permissions and ACLs. We'll now move on to custom fields related to users.

Users – custom fields

In *Chapter 3, Advanced Content Management*, we discovered custom fields, focusing on their usage as enrichment for articles. But Joomla also allows you to add custom fields to users, allowing you to enrich data about your users.

For example, you can use custom fields tied to users to collect data such as a short biography, birth date, province, city, phone number, email, and much more.

Custom Fields are organized in **Custom Field Groups**, which are used to display fields in an ordered way.

Custom Fields will be displayed in the user creation and editing form in the backend, while they are shown on the profile page and registration page on the website frontend.

To create and manage custom fields related to users, from **Users Dashboard** click on **Fields** in the module called **User Fields**. The procedure to create a custom field is identical to the one already presented in *Chapter 3, Advanced Content Management*.

We're now going to explore another feature that is useful for administrators, **User Notes**.

User notes

Joomla allows administrators to add internal notes to users. Notes are organized through **Note Categories**, so you can create different categories to manage your notes, for example, billing, behavior, and so on. You can then create a note, assigning it to the respective category and adding it to the user, noting for example bad behavior on the part of the user, a missing payment, and so on.

Notes are not visible to the users, and they are only displayed to the website administrators.

To create a user note, from the sidebar menu, click on **Users**, then on **User Notes**, and on **New**, as shown in *Figure 6.18*.

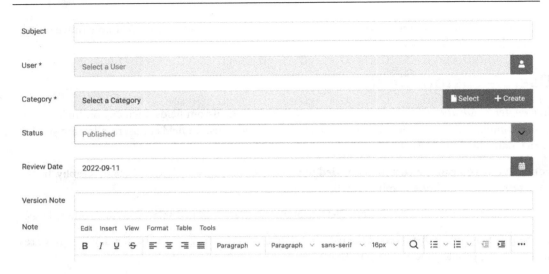

Figure 6.18 – New user note

The user note creation screen includes the following fields:

- **Subject**: Allows you to specify the subject and the title of the note.
- **User**: Allows you to select the user to which you want to add the note.
- **Category**: Allows you to select or create a new category to which you want to add the note.
- **Status**: Allows you to choose whether the note should be published, unpublished, trashed, or archived.
- **Review Date**: Allows you to select the date on which the note has been reviewed. By default, it's the date on which the note has been created.
- **Version Note**: Allows you to specify a name for the version of the note.
- **Note**: Allows you to use the text editor to write the note.

You can add any number of notes you want to any of your users, as well as create all the categories you need to organize your notes. These can be useful while managing your website to remind you of specific things, such as misbehavior, late payments, and much more.

After user notes, we will explore **Mass Mail Users**, which allows administrators to contact website users in an easy way.

Mass mail

Mass Mail Users is a feature that allows administrators to write an email to users of the website easily and quickly. To access the functionality, click on **Users** in the sidebar menu, then on **Mass Mail Users**.

You will be prompted by a screen like the following figure, *Figure 6.19*:

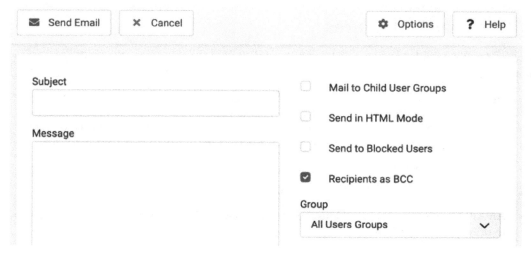

Figure 6.19 – Mass Mail Users

As you can see, using this feature is very easy. You just have to type the subject and the message in the related box and select the desired options:

- **Mail to Child User Groups**: This includes users of subgroups when selecting a parent group.

- **Send in HTML Mode**: This sends the email in HTML.

- **Send to Blocked Users**: This also includes in the recipient list users that are currently blocked.

- **Recipients as BCC**: This puts recipients as a **Blind Carbon Copy** (**BCC**) of the email so that they can't see the list of recipients. This is enabled by default for privacy reasons.

- **Group**: This selects the user group that should receive the message, or if you click the **All Users Groups** option then it will contact all users registered to the website.

Once the message is ready for delivery, click on **Send Email** to send it. Please note that there is no track of sent messages, nor information about the delivery status of your messages.

Note – when you should avoid using Mass Mail Users

As mentioned at the end of the section, **Mass Mail Users** does not track sent email messages, nor the delivery status of the messages. Furthermore, this feature creates a single message with all the selected users as recipients. This might not work in certain hosting environments due to some limits on the number of recipients for a message or the daily email send rate, especially when you have many users selected as the recipient. If you want to send mass communications, schedule the sending process, collect information about the delivery status, and track the openings, then you should use a newsletter component.

Having seen the **Mass Mail Users** feature, it's time to discover the privacy-related functionalities.

Built-in privacy features

Since version 3.9, Joomla includes a series of features dedicated to privacy, simplifying the process to comply with privacy regulations through a set of functionalities called the *Privacy Tools Suite*.

This suite of tools has been designed in line with GDPR requirements and includes the following:

- A feature to collect and manage users' requests for information about their processed data or to delete their data
- A feature to collect and manage consent from users to process their data
- A feature to log user actions that is useful for audits
- An API to connect other extensions to **Privacy Dashboard** and expand those privacy features to third-party extensions

All those features are accessible from **Privacy Dashboard**, which you can open from the sidebar menu by clicking on **Users**, then clicking on the dashboard icon next to the **Privacy** menu item. Let's start exploring **Privacy Dashboard**.

Privacy Dashboard

Privacy Dashboard, as displayed in *Figure 6.20*, shows two main modules and allows you to check at a glance the status of privacy requests and needed actions:

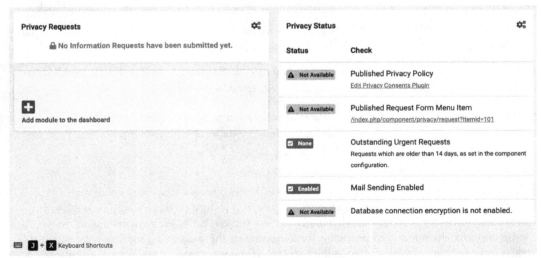

Figure 6.20 – Privacy Dashboard

The first module, **Privacy Requests**, shows the list of outstanding information or deletion requests coming from your website users. We'll see in the next section what a privacy request is and how to submit one.

The second module, **Privacy Status**, shows the status of some checks, including the following:

- **Published Privacy Policy**: This checks whether or not you published a privacy policy and whether you enabled the **Privacy Consent** plugin, which allows collecting consent from the users when they register or log in to your website.

- **Published Request Form Menu Item**: This checks whether or not you published a menu item pointing to **Privacy | Create Request**. This type of menu item publishes a form in which users can submit data information or a deletion request.

- **Outstanding Urgent Requests**: This checks whether you have requests older than 14 days to be processed.

- **Mail Sending Enabled**: This checks whether the website is able to send emails.

- **Database connection encryption**: This checks whether the connection to the database is encrypted or not.

As with all the other dashboards of the backend, you can customize this dashboard with additional modules. Let's see how to set a privacy policy for your website.

Setting a privacy policy

In order to allow the website to collect consent from your users, you need to make them aware of the privacy policy. Joomla can manage two types of privacy policies: an article or a menu item (for example, if you have a specific URL for the policy).

To set your privacy policy, after having created the article or the menu item, open the plugin called **System - Privacy Consent**, which will look like *Figure 6.21*.

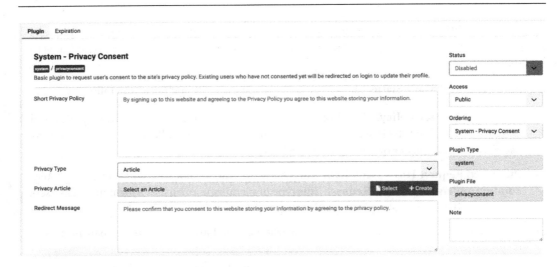

Figure 6.21 – System – Privacy Consent plugin

Let's explore the options offered by the plugin, starting from the **Plugin** tab:

- **Short Privacy Policy**: A short statement about consenting to your privacy policy. The field contains placeholder text that may be used.

- **Privacy Type**: Allows you to choose whether your privacy policy is an article or a menu item.

- **Privacy Article**: Allows you to select the article (or the menu item) that includes your privacy policy.

- **Redirect Message**: A custom message shown to users when prompted to consent to your privacy policy. Also, in this case, you can have placeholder text that may be used in most cases.

Let's now move to the **Expiration** tab, shown in *Figure 6.22*

Figure 6.22 – System – Privacy Consent: Expiration

Through this tab, you can choose to enable the expiration of consent to your privacy policy and set the following options:

- **Enable**: Activates the consent expiration checks.
- **Period check (days)**: Allows you to specify how often the system should check the validity of consent.
- **Expiration**: Allows you to specify the duration of consent provided by the users. The default is 360 days.
- **Remind**: This allows you to specify the number of days to send a reminder about the approaching consent expiration.

After configuring the plugin as desired, it's important to enable it and change **Status** to **Published**, then click on **Save & Close**.

Let's now move to privacy requests.

Privacy requests

A privacy request is a request from a user to either inform them about the data the website holds about them (**information request**) or delete their data from the website (**deletion request**). Those requests are part of the rights to data subjects offered by the GDPR and other privacy regulations.

When processing an information request, the system will produce an XML file containing the data that the website holds about the user (for example, name, email address, and preferences). The contents of the file might not include all the data that the website holds about the user, since not all extensions implement the Privacy API. The data included may differ based on the extensions used on your website.

This type of request is also called an **export request**, as it allows you to comply with the right to data portability provided by privacy regulations.

While processing a deletion request, the system will pseudonymize all the information related to the user. In fact, it's not a complete removal of data, since that could create issues related to the operations of the website (for example, in the case of e-commerce or when deleting data about an author, which might result in having orphan articles).

The first step to collecting privacy requests is to create a menu item on your website pointing to **Privacy | Create Request**. This would result in a page accessible to your users on which they can submit a privacy request, selecting from export and data removal types.

Also, it is important to note that privacy requests cannot be deleted from your website.

When a user submits a privacy request, they will be required to confirm it, validating their email address, through a link included in a confirmation email.

You can also create a privacy request from the backend of the website, but also, in this case, users should confirm it via the confirmation link. This is required to ensure the security of data.

Once a request has been opened, but not yet confirmed, it will show as **Pending** and can be invalidated by an administrator, as you can see in *Figure 6.23*.

Figure 6.23 – An export request pending confirmation

For each request, we can see the email, the status, the type of request, and the date of the request. Also, on the right side of the screen, we have complete tracking of the activity executed on the request.

Each request can have one of the following statuses:

- **Pending**: A request that has been submitted but not yet confirmed
- **Invalid**: A request that has been invalidated by the administrator
- **Confirmed**: A request that has been confirmed by the user, but not yet executed by the administrator
- **Completed**: A request that has 5 been processed by the administrator

By default, only super users are allowed to see and process privacy requests.

Let's now explore the last feature introduced with the Privacy Tools Suite: **User Action Log**.

User Action Log

Even if it's not strictly related to privacy, the **User Action Log** feature has been introduced together with the other privacy functionalities as it's propaedeutic for the work of other mechanisms and tools. In fact, we've seen that a log of actions executed is kept in each privacy request.

As the feature name suggests, **User Action Log** represents a registry of the actions taken by users. In the options of the component, you can choose which type of actions you want to record. By default, the operations executed in the following components are logged: articles, banners, cache, categories, check-in, configuration, contacts, installer, media, menus, messaging, modules, news feeds, plugins, redirects, scheduled tasks, tags, templates, and users.

So, every operation, such as creating an article, editing a menu item, or logging into the website, is logged, with the user involved and the date and time of the operations. These logs are useful for administrators to find out who did an operation and when.

The component allows you to export logs as CSV and execute search/filtering in logs.

User Action Log is accessible from the respective menu item available under the **Users** menu in the sidebar.

With **User Action Log**, we completed our look at the features dedicated to users.

Summary

In this chapter, we explored the functionalities to create and manage users and user groups and grant them appropriate permissions through access levels. We went through the privacy-related features, discovering privacy requests, privacy consent, and the user action log.

In the next chapter, we'll explore the SEO-oriented features offered by the CMS.

Exercises

It's time to apply the knowledge acquired in this chapter to work with users and permissions.

Exercise 1 – user groups and permissions

Create a user group called MyGroup. The group should be nested under the **Registered** user group. Change the menu item called MyArticle (created in the exercise of *Chapter 5, Build Your Site Structure: The Menu System*), to grant access to users in the MyGroup group.

Then create a new user on your website from the backend and add the user to the MyGroup user group.

Exercise 2 – privacy features

Create an article called Privacy Policy and write your policy text. Then, open the **System – Privacy Consent** plugin and set the article created as a privacy policy for the website. Once done, enable the consent expiration with the default values and enable the plugin.

Create a new menu item, selecting the **Privacy | Create Request** type, with the name Privacy Request, setting **Access** as **Registered**, and saving it.

In this way, you created a privacy policy for your website, ensured that your website collects the consent to your policy, and made available a form to receive privacy requests from your users. The menu item will be visible only to registered users.

Part 2: Advanced Features

In this part, you will be introduced to several advanced features of Joomla. You will discover the major functionalities to optimize your website for search engines (SEO). You will also learn how to build a multilanguage website by managing languages and content associations. You will see how to plan and automate recurring operations thanks to Scheduled Tasks and explore the opportunity to completely customize the automated email of your website through Email Templates. Finally, you will discover how to use Joomla through its extensive **command-line interface (CLI)**, a feature for advanced users.

This part has the following chapters:

- *Chapter 7, SEO at Its Best*
- *Chapter 8, One Site, Multiple Languages*
- *Chapter 9, Planning Operations with Scheduled Tasks*
- *Chapter 10, Tailored Communication with Mail Templates*
- *Chapter 11, Command-Line Interface*

7
SEO at Its Best

In the previous chapter, we explored users and how to manage their permissions in the CMS. We'll now look at the SEO features offered by Joomla to ensure your website has a high ranking on search engines.

After reading this chapter, you will be able to do the following:

- Recognize the available on-page SEO options
- Improve the optimization of your website for search engines
- Handle 404 errors

Exploring on-page SEO features

While building a website, it's crucial to keep an eye on **Search Engine Optimization (SEO)** in order to allow your website to reach a high rank on **Search Engine Results Pages (SERPs)**.

The most important thing to optimize is the content of your website, which should be written with users' research intent and their needs in mind. The quality of content is crucial to achieving a good placement in results.

Besides content/articles, there are many options that allow you to optimize your website for search engines. Some options affect the website at a global level, while others are applied to single articles or pages; this refers to on-page SEO.

Let's start to present the major optimization features included in Joomla.

Optimizing an article

As we introduced in *Chapter 2*, article management features allow you to adjust some additional aspects of your content that may improve the optimization of your article for search engines, as we can see in *Figure 7.1*.

Figure 7.1 – SEO options for articles

The first item that can be optimized is **Title**. It's very important as it corresponds to the `title` tag in the page markup and should be structured to be descriptive and concise. The title should not exceed 60-70 characters.

Heavily linked to the title is **Alias**, which is the option that allows you to build your article *URL*. The alias should be structured to be user-friendly and should contain the main keyword.

Another option useful to optimize your article is the **Meta Description** field. You can find this field under the **Publishing** tab while writing or editing an article. As the hint included under the field suggests, the description text should not exceed 160 characters. The field should contain a summary of the article content, including the most important keyword, and it's used to populate the `Meta Description` tag in the page markup. The content of this field is visible on SERPs below the page title.

On this screen, we can also define **Keywords** for the article. Even though, according to many experts, including keywords doesn't really affect the rankings, Joomla allows you to specify the keywords in this field, for each of the articles on your website. As usual, just put a few keywords and phrases and ensure those keywords are contained in the article text to achieve a good **keyword density**. Keywords are also used from the module that shows similar articles to propose relevant articles.

Of course, the most important thing that should be optimized is the text of the article, ensuring that it's relevant, up to date, and well structured.

Using the proper markup (for example, headers, tables, lists, and so on), checking that all internal and external links are valid, adding alternative (and relevant) text for all the images, and ensuring that each article contains at least one **Header 1** (**H1**) header, and contains around 300 words will make your content successful on search engines.

While editing your articles, you can also define which is the title shown in the browser tab/window, as well as the HTML `<title>` tag. To do so, just check the **Browser Page Title** field in the **Options** tab, as displayed in *Figure 7.2*.

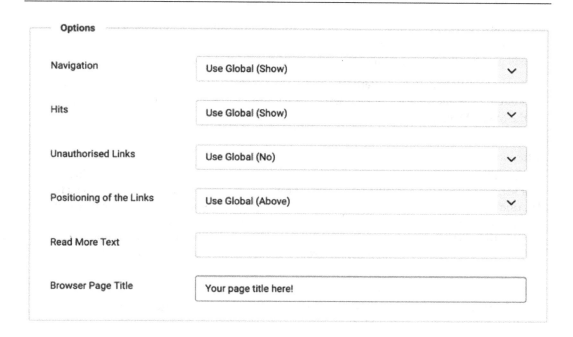

Figure 7.2 – Articles | Browser Page Title

> **Priority of options**
> The SEO options specified in the menu item configuration override the options specified in articles.

Articles may include images, and they play an important role in page optimization. Let's see how.

Optimizing images

If your content includes images, you should optimize them to achieve good results in SERPs. Images can enrich articles, but can also damage their performance, due to their weight or size. Here are some useful tips to optimize images in your content:

- Ensure all images are in a modern format such as **WEBP** or **PNG** and are compressed.

- Make sure that the image file size is not excessive. The smaller the better. A huge file size would decrease your page speed.

- Reduce the number of images included in every article. If you include many images in an article, its load times would increase noticeably When you want to show several images, it's recommended to use thumbnails and load original, bigger images when the user clicks on them.

- Use descriptive filenames. For example, if you are uploading a photograph of Westminster Abbey, a filename such as `westminster-abbey.jpg` is better than `image001.jpg` and will increase the opportunities of the image being seen in the search engine results.

- Ensure that all images have **alternative text**. This will improve the accessibility and SEO of your content. Alternative text can be inserted when inserting the images in the content, through the Media Manager.

> **Alternative text**
>
> When adding an image to your content, as best practice and to ensure the accessibility of your article, you should add alternative text. The alternative text is used by screen readers to describe the image and should include a description of what the image shows. Alternative text is included in the markup of your page and is parsed by search engines, so it can also be used to optimize your content, describe your image, and help search engines to determine what your image is about. Decorative images, as well as images that are part of the template, should not include alternative text.

- Make sure that all images are **lazy loaded**. You can enable **lazy load** for your images while selecting them in the Media Manager.

> **What is lazy load?**
>
> Lazy load is a technology that makes sure that images are loaded only when it is the moment to display them. Let's think of a long page of news in which many articles are displayed and each of them has an introductory image. If such a page has 10 articles, it also loads 10 cover images for these articles. Downloading and rendering 10 images together while loading the page would increase the overall time to display the page to the user.
>
> When lazy load is enabled, only the images that are in the visible part of the screen are loaded, only loading the others at the moment in which the user scrolls the page. Doing so increases page performance, as only the visible images are loaded immediately. This works only when the image's width or height is specified.

Having seen the opportunities to optimize articles and images, we'll now move on to optimization features offered by menus.

SEO options offered by menus

Not all pages display a single article, in fact, many of them are the output of a component. That's why Joomla offers some SEO options directly on the menu items creation screen.

While creating or editing a menu item, besides the **Title** and **Alias** fields, you will see two tabs dedicated to SEO options: **Page Display** and **Metadata**.

Figure 7.3 – Menu item | Page Display

Let's start exploring **Page Display**, shown in *Figure 7.3*:

- **Browser Page Title**: Specify a title for the page to be displayed as the browser tab name. It also affects the HTML markup of the generated page, as it changes the `<title>` tag.

- **Show Page Heading**: Decide whether or not to show the page header on the page. It's rendered as H1 in the markup of the page. If not selected, it won't be displayed.

- **Page Heading**: Specify the text you want to be displayed as the title for the page, before the article title. It's an optional field. If this field is empty, the browser page title is used as a fallback when **Show Page Heading** is set to **Show**.

- **Page Class**: Unrelated to SEO, allows you to specify a `CSS` class to display the page.

After these controls, we'll move to the **Metadata** tab, displayed in *Figure 7.4*.

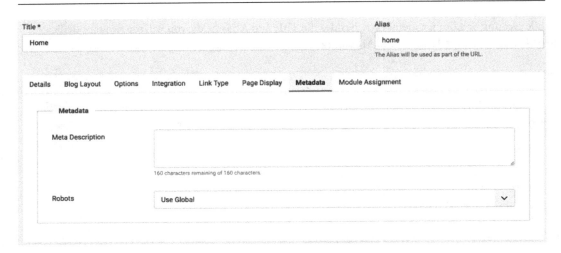

Figure 7.4 – Menu item | Metadata

The **Metadata** tab offers just two options:

- The first one, **Meta Description**, allows you to input the description text for your page. As also seen with articles, the **Meta Description** field can accommodate up to 160 characters of text that can be used to summarize the content of the page.

- The second option is dedicated to command robots, which we'll explore in the next section.

Robots management

A webmaster has the chance to instruct search engines on what they should and should not index on a specific website. These instructions are provided through a simple text file called robots.txt that should be placed in the website root folder.

This file generally contains a set of rules that allow or disallow indexing specific pages or sections of a website. For example, it is advisable to disable indexing of the backend section of the website; or, in certain circumstances, it can be useful to disable indexing of images or a specific type of file (such as PDFs). Or you may want to index a specific section of the website. All these commands can be provided through the robots.txt file.

Joomla comes with a default robots.txt file out of the box that includes the following content:

```
# If the Joomla site is installed within a folder
# eg www.example.com/joomla/ then the robots.txt file
# MUST be moved to the site root
# eg www.example.com/robots.txt
# AND the joomla folder name MUST be prefixed to all of the
```

```
# paths.
# eg the Disallow rule for the /administrator/ folder MUST
# be changed to read
# Disallow: /joomla/administrator/
#
# For more information about the robots.txt standard, see:
# https://www.robotstxt.org/orig.html

User-agent: *
Disallow: /administrator/
Disallow: /api/
Disallow: /bin/
Disallow: /cache/
Disallow: /cli/
Disallow: /components/
Disallow: /includes/
Disallow: /installation/
Disallow: /language/
Disallow: /layouts/
Disallow: /libraries/
Disallow: /logs/
Disallow: /modules/
Disallow: /plugins/
Disallow: /tmp/
```

As you can easily understand from reading the file, Joomla asks the search engines to not index several system folders, such as /administrators, /plugins, and /tmp, for security reasons.

Beyond this set of default rules, the CMS allows you to specify a custom rule for each article and menu item.

In fact, in the **Publishing** tab, while writing or editing an article, we have a field called **Robots** that allows us to define the indexing rules for search engines, as displayed in *Figure 7.5*.

Figure 7.5 – Article | Publishing | Robots

The same option is also available at the menu item level, as displayed in *Figure 7.4*, allowing you to choose the indexing options for each menu item.

For example, you may want to avoid indexing the menu item that points to a reserved area of your website. In this case, you can select **noindex, nofollow** or **noindex, follow**.

In this way, you will have full control over the indexing activities of your website.

In the next section, we'll show you how to build SEO-friendly URLs.

SEO-friendly URLs

Another important task in your website optimization is to make sure it produces URLs that are friendly for users and search engines.

By default, Joomla produces URLs like this: `yourwebsite.tld/index.php/alias-of-the-menu-item`. As you can see, this kind of URL is not friendly as it contains the `/index.php/` string in the path.

Both users and search engines would prefer a URL such as the following: `yourwebsite.tld/about-us`. Immediately, you know that the page provides information about the company and the search engine can read that.

Friendly URLs can be useful to improve the SEO of the website, as they may include the major keywords, creating a direct correspondence between the URL and the page title or main topic.

To enable SEO-friendly URLs, you need to go to the **Global Configuration | Site** tab and operate in the **SEO** group of options, displayed in *Figure 7.6*.

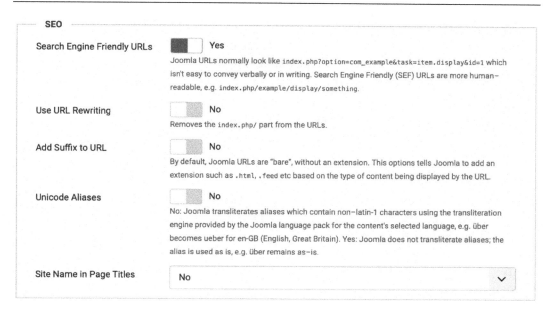

Figure 7.6 – Global Configuration | SEO options

Each option is well documented with the inline help. To make our website produce SEO-friendly URLs, we need to enable the first two options:

- **Search Engine Friendly URLs**
- **Use URL Rewriting**

URL rewriting

The URL rewriting feature requires a valid `.htaccess` file in the root folder of your Joomla installation. By default, Joomla comes with the `.htaccess` file disabled and named `htaccess.txt`. Prior to enabling the **Use URL Rewriting** feature, you need to rename the `htaccess.txt` file in `.htaccess`.

If you are using a different type of server, for example, Nginx, there wouldn't be the `.htaccess` file and you need to work directly on your server configuration as specified at `https://docs.joomla.org/Nginx`. If you are using Windows hosting, then you will have to rename the `web.config.txt` file in `web.config`.

After enabling the URL rewriting options, the URLs of your website will be optimized and easy to remember. Page URLs will be then built upon the content of the **Alias** field in your menu items. Articles' aliases will be used to define the URLs of articles within category views.

The other options in the **SEO** group displayed in *Figure 7.6* allow you to enable page suffixes in URLs, for example, if you want to show `.html` at the end of the URL. Another option allows you to use Unicode aliases, which disable the transliteration feature of Joomla while building the URL structure. The last option of the group allows you to choose whether or not to include the name of the website in the title of the page.

In the next section, we'll explore another useful feature that is useful to improve your website presence in the search engine, managing and fixing 404 errors.

Handling 404 errors

404 errors (page not found) are critical to websites since they can result in lost visits, a bad user experience, and page-ranking loss in search engines. A 404 error happens when a page is not available due to an incorrectly typed URL or because the page has been removed. Besides the unpleasant experience offered to users that couldn't find what they are looking for, as mentioned, multiple 404 errors may result in damage to the SERP ranking, so as webmasters, we need to prevent and avoid a wrong or unavailable URL being indexed by search engines.

Joomla has an integrated tool that supports webmasters dealing with 404 errors. This feature is called **Redirects** and it includes a component and a **system plugin**.

When the **System – Redirect** plugin is enabled, it automatically collects all the 404 errors that occurred on the website and populates the list of errors shown in the **Redirects** component. To use the **Redirects** feature, let's enable the plugin, by clicking on the link shown in the error notice that appears when you open the `Redirects` component for the first time, as displayed in *Figure 7.7*.

Figure 7.7 – Redirects component

To open the **Redirects** component, you need to click on **Redirects** from **System Dashboard** of your website.

If you can't see the warning about **Redirect System Plugin**, from the **System Dashboard**, click on **Plugins**, then filter by **Type**, select **System**, and look for the **System – Redirect** plugin.

Once the plugin is enabled, the system will start collecting 404 errors occurring on the website, allowing you to correct them in the **Redirects** component, pointing the expired URL to a new, valid one.

For each link, you can customize the rule, as displayed in *Figure 7.8*.

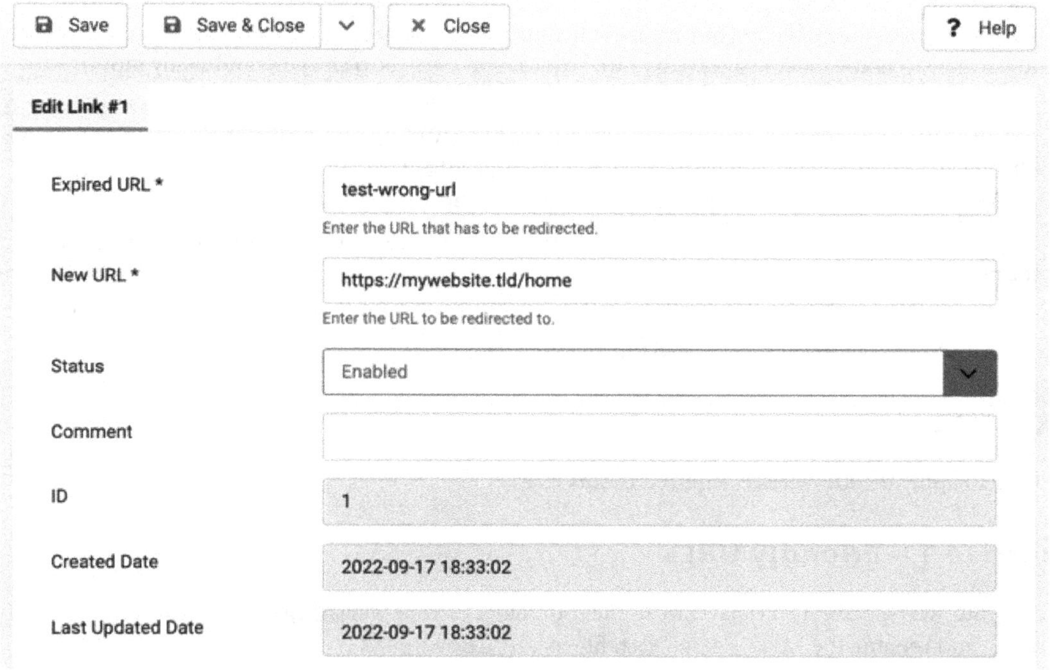

Figure 7.8 – Redirects | Edit Link

Let's explore the fields shown:

- **Expired URL**: Shows the URL that threw a 404 error.

- **New URL**: Enter the new URL to specify where to redirect users. A **301 - Permanent Redirect** rule will be created for the old URL to redirect the user to this new one.

- **Status**: Decide whether the rule should be enabled or not.

- **ID**: Unique identification number of the link.

- **Created Date**: First detection date of the error or date/time when the rule was created.

- **Last Updated Date**: Date and time of the last modification.

The **Redirects** component allows you to create custom rules manually, so you can enter your rules even before a 404 error is triggered by your users. This is particularly useful when you are rebuilding a website and there are massive changes to URL structure.

Note: URL redirects

The **Redirects** feature is very useful and allows you to handle errors, preventing bad user experiences and keeping SERP rankings. This feature records all 404 errors triggered on your website. This may result in a huge table in your database if your website is targeted by cyber-attacks that try to navigate to non-existent pages (e.g., `/wp-admin` or `/wp-login.php` and many more).

So, the recommendation is to enable the plugin to detect 404 errors only after changes in your website URL structure or after migration and disable it after having handled the majority of 404 errors. Alternatively, you could keep the plugin enabled, but you should regularly check the **Redirects** component and purge invalid links that aren't useful to redirect.

Furthermore, it's recommended to use `.htaccess` for redirects, where possible, as it's better for performance.

With the **Redirects** feature, we completed this chapter related to SEO functionalities included in Joomla.

Exercises

It's time to apply the knowledge acquired in this chapter.

Exercise 1 – Friendly URLs

Access your web space via FTP, navigate to the root folder of your website (generally `public_html` or www), and rename the `htaccess.txt` file to `.htaccess`.

Now, access your website's backend and navigate to **Global Configuration** and look for the **SEO** group of options in the **Site** tab. Enable the following options: **Search Engine Friendly URLs** and **Use URL Rewriting**. Now navigate to your website's frontend and check the URLs of the pages.

Exercise 2 – Article SEO

In your Joomla backend, open the article titled `MyArticle` and navigate to the **SEO** options. Type a **Meta Description** in the related field and specify a **Page Browser Title** in the appropriate field in **Options**.

Summary

In this chapter, we explored the features to optimize a Joomla website for search engines. We discovered the on-page optimization functionalities and how to improve the friendliness of website URLs. We got to know the **Redirects** component and how to handle 404 errors, as well as how to manage indexing rules for a website.

In the next chapter, we'll discover how to build and manage a multilingual website with Joomla's core features.

Further reading

- Introduction to `robots.txt`: `https://developers.google.com/search/docs/crawling-indexing/robots/intro?hl=en`
- Create a `robots.txt` file: `https://developers.google.com/search/docs/crawling-indexing/robots/create-robots-txt?hl=en`

8

One Site, Multiple Languages

In the previous chapter, we explored Joomla's SEO options to make your website shine on search engines.

We'll now explore one of the most powerful features included in Joomla: **multilingual management**. In fact, the CMS can handle multiple languages for a website in a single installation.

After reading this chapter, you will be able to do the following:

- Understand how multilanguage management works in Joomla
- Configure a multilingual website
- Handle content in multiple languages

Building a multilingual website

Many businesses need to offer their website in more than one language to reach audiences in different countries, offering them a localized version of the website's content.

There are different ways to build a multilanguage website. One of the fastest (though not the best for quality) is to install a plugin that automatically translates the website content into many other languages through Google Translate or other online translation services. Besides the limits of automated translation, this type of translation service translates content on the fly, although there are limitations to automated translations.

Another approach to providing a multilanguage website, used in Joomla version 1.5, is to create an exact copy of all the website content with extensions such as Joom!Fish, Josetta, and FaLang. The quality offered by this approach is generally better than automated translations if the content is translated by professionals or native speakers of the target language. This method produces duplicates of the website in additional languages so that the website keeps the same structure, appearance, and quantity of content.

Since version 3, Joomla includes complete functionality to handle multilingual websites, providing the opportunity to assign content, menu items, and templates to a specific language. It also supports **Left-to-Right (LTR)** and **Right-to-Left (RTL)** languages, allowing you to handle multiple languages in a single installation of Joomla and create customized experiences and content for each of the languages in which the website is available.

In the next section, we will go through the setup process for a multilingual website.

How to set up a multilingual website

The first thing to do in order to create a multilingual website is to install one or more additional languages to our Joomla instance. To do so, from **System Dashboard**, click on **Languages**. The screen will show the installed languages, as displayed in *Figure 8.1*.

Figure 8.1 – Languages

In our example, we're going to create a website in two languages, English (United Kingdom) and Italian (Italy). The same process also applies to creating websites with more than two languages, independent of the chosen languages.

By default, the website has only one language, in our case, English. This is the language used by Joomla to display its interface. In the case of multiple languages, you can select which one should be used as the default language for either the frontend or backend.

Let's install Italian as an additional language. To do so, click on **Install Languages** in the toolbar and search for the desired language pack among the over 70 available.

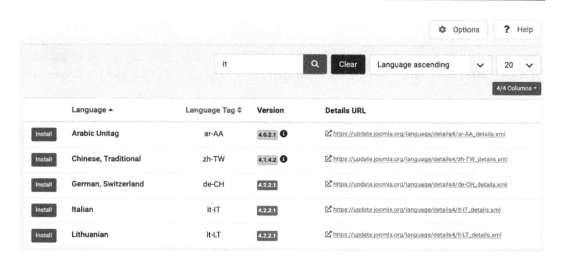

Figure 8.2 – Languages | Install Languages

From the list of available languages shown in *Figure 8.2*, let's click on the **Install** button next to the Italian language.

The language will appear in the list of available languages for the website. During the installation of the language pack, we automatically created Italian as **Content Language**. This means that the website is aware of the possibility of hosting content in Italian in addition to English.

To check which languages are available, from **System Dashboard**, click on **Content Languages**, and you will see a list like the one in *Figure 8.3*.

		Status ⇕	Title ⇕	Native Title ⇕	Language Tag ⇕	URL Language Code ⇕	Image ⇕	Access ⇕	Home ⇕	ID ⇕
☐	⋮	⊗	Italiano (it-IT)	Italiano (it-IT)	it-IT	it	it_it	Public	No	2
☐	⋮	⊘	English (en-GB)	English (United Kingdom)	en-GB	en	en_gb	Public	No	1

Figure 8.3 – Content Languages

As seen in *Figure 8.3*, the Italian language is installed and configured, but not yet active. We need to enable it by clicking on its status icon to make it **Published**.

If the language is not listed, you can click on the **+ New** button and manually create a new content language.

From the same screenshot, we can see also that for each language the system handles a **Title**, **Native Title**, **Language Tag**, **URL Language Code** (used in URLs), and **Image** (flag). All of those parameters are customizable; just click on the language title. Furthermore, the **Content Language** screen allows you to customize **Meta Description** and the site name for the specific language, as displayed in *Figure 8.4*.

Figure 8.4 – Content Languages | Edit Language

Language tags can be reused across languages that share the same base language (e.g., German – Germany, German – Austria).

With the preceding steps, we have ensured that Joomla can manage content in both English and Italian and can display its interface in both languages.

Now, let's make the website multilingual and ensure that Joomla can detect user language preference to show them the relevant version of the website. To do so, we need to enable two plugins:

- Language Filter
- Language Code

Let's explore them.

Plugin: System – Language Filter

The **System – Language Filter** plugin is responsible for the correct language being set in the system. It builds the correct URLs and redirects the user after logging in to the page displayed the correct language. The plugin is disabled by default, so we need to enable it when building a multilanguage website.

From **System Dashboard**, click on **Plugins** and filter by type for **System**, then select **System - Language Filter** from the list. We'll see the plugin configuration screen, as shown in *Figure 8.5*.

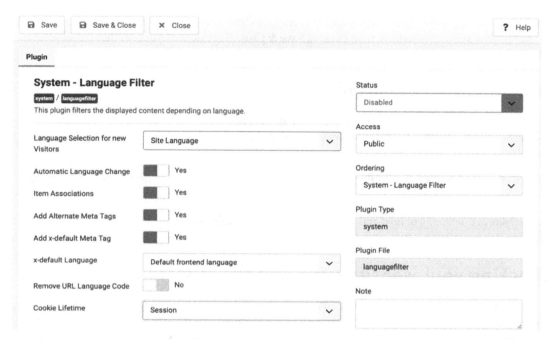

Figure 8.5 – System - Language Filter plugin

Let's explore the options offered by the plugin:

- **Language Selection for new Visitors**: Allows you to choose the language in which to display the website to new visitors, either through the default site language or by detecting the user's language from their browser.

- **Automatic Language Change**: Allows you to automatically change the content language shown to the user when their language changes.

- **Item Associations**: Allows associations between items when switching languages.

- **Add Alternate Meta Tags**: Add alternate meta tags to menu items that have other menu items associated with them in other languages.

- **Add x-default Meta Tag**: Improve SEO by adding the x-default meta tag. This tag is added to pages that are not targeted at any specific languages.

- **x-default Language**: Select the x-default language for your website.

- **Remove URL Language Code**: Decide whether or not to remove the language code from the URL structure. For example, the Italian version of your website will not show `yourwebsite.tld/it/` in its URLs. This is valid only for the site's default language.

- **Cookie Lifetime**: Choose the expiration period of the technical cookie used to detect and remember the preferred language of the user.

The default settings represent the recommended setup for most cases; we just need to enable the plugin by changing its **Status** to **Enabled**, then clicking **Save & Close**. Let's now move on to the second plugin called **System – Language Code**.

Plugin: System – Language Code

This plugin is used to improve the HTML markup of the produced pages, adding the language code, and allows you to replace short tags. It does not require any setup but needs to be enabled from the website's backend.

From **System Dashboard**, click on **Plugins** and filter by type for **System**, then select **System – Language Code** from the list. Change its status to **Enabled**, then click **Save & Close**.

Our website is now ready to host and manage content in multiple languages. We'll now explore a tool that helps us make our multilanguage website fully operational.

Checking your website's multilanguage status

Creating a multilingual website is not that easy. That's why Joomla includes a tool for administrators that allows backend users to check the configuration status for multiple languages. This tool is a backend module called **Multilanguage Status**. When enabled, it shows a **Multilingual Status** icon in the top bar of the backend system, as shown in *Figure 8.6*. If it's not enabled, you just need to publish it from the **Administrator Modules** list.

Figure 8.6 – Multilingual Status icon

By clicking on the **Multilingual Status** icon, we can check the progress of making the website multilingual, as shown in *Figure 8.7*.

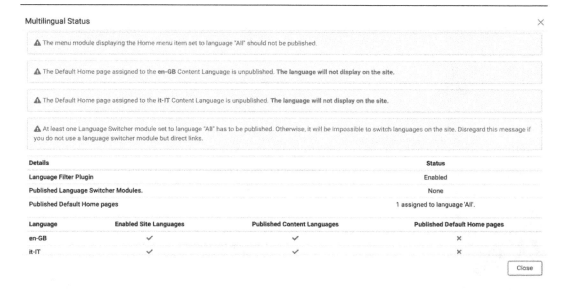

Figure 8.7 – Multilingual Status

As you can see from the screenshot, our website is not yet completely ready. The module suggests the following required actions:

- Remove the module that holds the menu item for the home page for all the languages.
- Publish a home page assigned to the English language.
- Publish a home page assigned to the Italian language.
- Publish a **Language Switcher** module, assigned to all languages. This is optional but highly recommended.

The table at the bottom of the screen shows the status on a per-language basis so that you know what is missing to complete your multilingual website.

Let's proceed with the required steps.

Remove the module that holds the home for all languages

The first step is to hide the module that holds the home menu item for all languages. How can we identify this menu item? We start by looking for the menu that holds the menu item listed as home for all languages. That's made easy, as **Menu Dashboard** holds the menu where the home page is marked by the home symbol, as displayed in *Figure 8.8*.

Figure 8.8 – Menu Dashboard displaying the menu holding the home item

By clicking on the menu name in the list of menu items, we can easily spot the menu item assigned as the home page for all the languages, as shown in *Figure 8.9*.

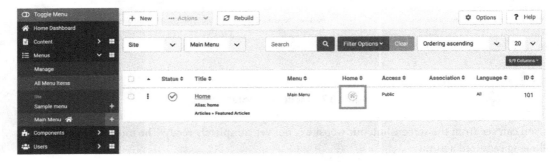

Figure 8.9 – Home menu item

The yellow home symbol shows that the menu item is assigned as the home page for all the languages. Now that we have found out which menu holds the home menu item assigned to all languages, we need to unpublish the module that displays this menu. To do so, let's move to **Content | Site Modules** and filter by type by selecting **Menu**, as displayed in *Figure 8.10*.

Figure 8.10 – Modules | Menu

To unpublish the module, just click on the green check in the **Status** column. We have now completed the first step of those proposed by the **Multilingual Status** module, so let's proceed with the next ones.

Publishing home pages for each language

Each language of a multilingual website should have a home page assigned, to be shown to visitors once the specific language has been selected. That means that we need to create a menu item marked as **Home** but assigned to a specific language. Let's see how.

Let's suppose that we already have the articles for each of the languages, called `Home page italiana` (for Italian) and `English Home Page` (for English). We now need to create a menu item for each of them.

While creating a new menu item, we select **Articles | Single Article**, then choose the article called `Home page italiana`. For this menu item, we also need to select the **Default Page** option and select **Italian (it-IT)** as the language, as displayed in *Figure 8.11*.

Figure 8.11 – Setting a home page for the Italian language

In the menu items list, this item will look like *Figure 8.12*, with the Italian flag, and the respective menu will show the language tag (e.g., **it-IT**) near the menu name in the sidebar.

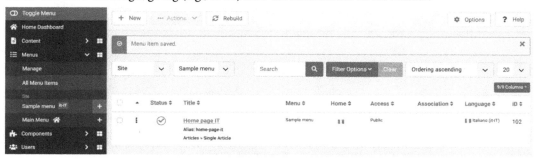

Figure 8.12 – Home page for the Italian language

We have now set the home page for Italian. We need to repeat the same process for the English language.

> **A home page for each menu**
>
> Each menu in Joomla can hold just one menu item marked as the home page. That means if you have a website in two languages, you should have at least two different menus, one for each language.
>
> As a tip, you can create a menu for each language to hold the home menu items assigned to the respective language. Then use a single menu to hold all the other menu items of the website for all the languages. Selecting the language of each menu item, in fact, makes it visible only when the selected language is the active one, hiding it while using other languages.

With the home menu items for both languages, we completed the second step of those listed in the **Multilingual Status** module. To complete the procedure, we need to publish the Language Switcher module.

Publishing the Language Switcher module

The **Language Switcher** module, as the name suggests, is a particular module for the website's frontend that allows visitors to choose their desired language among those available on the website. It can be configured to show language flags or language names and is generally published on the top bar of the website, allowing users to spot it immediately.

In **Content | Site Modules**, click on **New**, then choose **Language Switcher** as the module type. We can then see the module configuration page, as in *Figure 8.13*.

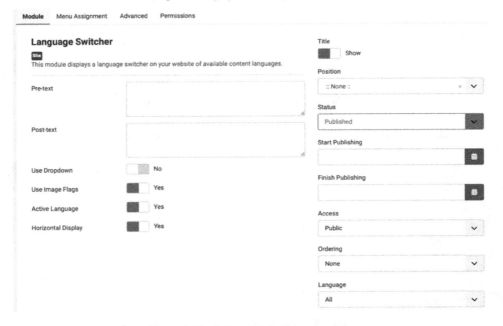

Figure 8.13 – Language Switcher module

Let's explore the module configuration options:

- **Pre-text**: Allows you to specify custom text to be shown prior to the language selection part
- **Post-text**: Allows you to specify custom text to be shown after the language selection part
- **Use Dropdown**: Choose whether the language switcher should be displayed as a drop-down list of languages
- **Use Image Flags**: Choose whether the language switcher should display country flags for each language
- **Active Language**: Decide whether or not to show the current language in the list of available languages
- **Horizontal Display**: Choose whether the list of languages should be displayed as a horizontal list or a vertical one

All the other options are like other modules that we explored earlier in *Chapter 4*. What we need to focus on is the **Language** option, which, for the language switcher, should be set to **All**, to make it visible on the website regardless of the active language.

The **Language Switcher** module can be placed in a position of your choosing, based on the frontend template you are using. When published in the frontend, the module will look like in *Figure 8.14*.

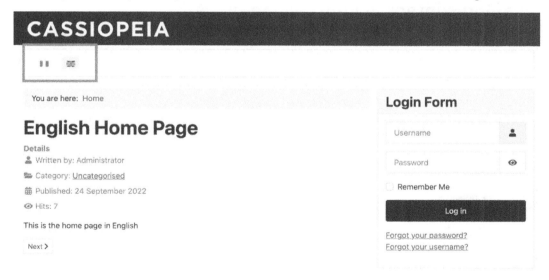

Figure 8.14 – Language Switcher

As you can see, the module will show the flags of the available languages, highlighting the currently active language, and allowing visitors to select their desired language.

With this step, we completed the setup of our website as a multilingual one. In fact, the **Multilingual Status** module doesn't show any additional messages, as seen in *Figure 8.15*.

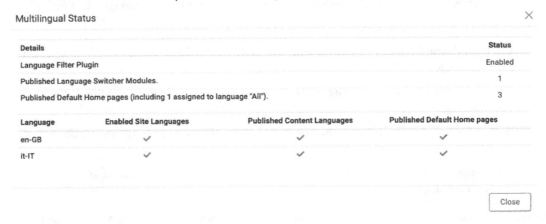

Figure 8.15 – Multilingual Status module when the setup is completed

Let's now see how to organize content for the different languages in which our website is available.

Managing content in multiple languages

After completing the setup of the website, we need to add content to each language. This can be easily done by simply selecting the language to which each content item should be assigned.

While creating or editing an article, in fact, we can see a new field called **Language**, which allows you to choose the language to assign to the article, as displayed in *Figure 8.16*.

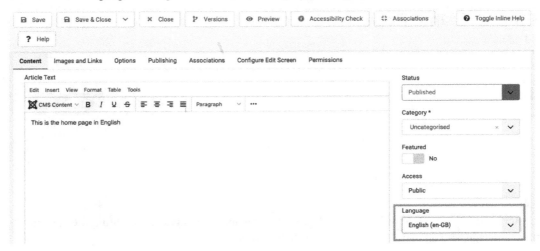

Figure 8.16 – Assigning a language to an article

The dropdown highlighted in *Figure 8.16* will list the languages enabled on the website; in our example, we can find: **English (en-GB)**, **Italian (it-IT)**, and **All**.

When **All** is assigned to content, it is available in all the languages of the website.

> **Language assignment**
>
> It is good practice to assign a language to each piece of content when working on a multilingual website. This allows you to show only the correct content to your visitors and prevents showing content in mixed languages.

In the next section, we will explore **Multilingual Associations**, the way to connect the same content in different languages.

Multilingual Associations

In many cases, the same content should be made available in multiple languages. This will result in having the same article written in multiple languages and assigned to the respective language. For example, you may have the *About Us* page in both English and Italian. It would be convenient, in such cases, to connect the same content in different languages, allowing visitors to switch languages and see the respective version of the same content. This can be done in Joomla through a specific component, called **Multilingual Associations**, which you can find under the **Components** menu of the website backend. The component will show the active associations between pieces of content in different languages. Let's now see how it works.

On our website, we have two articles called **English Home Page** and **Home Page Italiana**, respectively, the first assigned to English and the latter assigned to the Italian language. We want to associate them both. To do so, let's open the **English Home Page** article and click on the **Associations** button shown in the toolbar, as displayed in *Figure 8.17*.

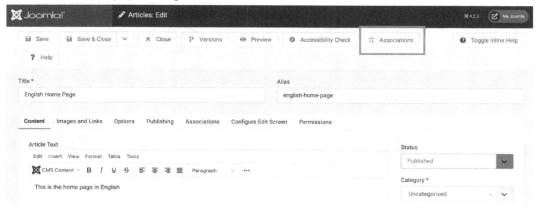

Figure 8.17 – The Associations button visible on the article editing screen

The displayed screen allows us to configure the multilingual association for the article, as shown in *Figure 8.18*.

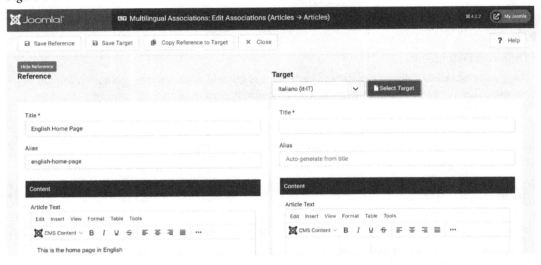

Figure 8.18 – Multilingual Associations | Edit Association

On this screen, we can continue to edit the original article, called **Reference**, and create a new version of the article in another language (the right part of the screen). Such content is called **Target**. If the target content is already available, we can click on the **Select Target** button, which allows us to select the article in the target language (Italian, in our example). In *Figure 8.19*, we can see the same screen after selecting the article called **Home Page Italiana** as the target article.

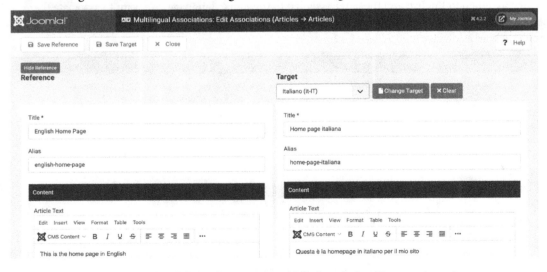

Figure 8.19 – Multilingual Associations | Edit Association | Target selected

Once the setup has been completed, we just need to click on **Save Target**. If the original article has been modified during the setup process, we should save it by clicking on **Save Reference**.

Going back to **Articles**, we can see that the **Association** column is populated with the respective associated language for the articles that we linked, as displayed in *Figure 8.20*.

Figure 8.20 – Articles with associations

Each article may have one or more associations. If a website handles more than two languages, an article may have as many associations as languages published on the website. Articles may also have no associations; this can happen when content is available in just one language within the website, or it's specific to a region and it's not necessary to publish it in multiple languages.

Associations are available not only for articles and their categories but also for contacts and their categories, news feeds and their categories, as well as menu items. Using associations correctly allows your users to easily switch the language and see the respective version of the same page.

The Multilingual Associations component allows you to check all the associations configured in your website, filtering by type of item and language, as displayed in *Figure 8.21*.

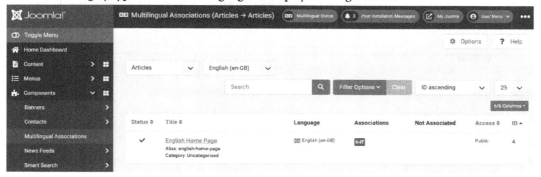

Figure 8.21 – Multilingual Associations | Articles | English (en-GB)

Now we can assign content to a specific language and handle associations of content between languages.

If you open an article with active associations, you will then see a tab called **Associations**, in which you can check and change the target content for each language, as shown in *Figure 8.22*.

Figure 8.22 – Articles | Associations

Let's now explore how to customize the visitor experience based on their language.

A different website for each language

Once a website is set as multilingual, Joomla automatically adds to each item an additional option that allows the administrator to assign the item to a specific language or to all languages. This is valid for articles, modules, menu items, and templates. This option practically allows you to create a different website for each language, given that you can choose the template, the modules, and the menu items that you want to display based on the language.

This is one of the major advantages of the built-in multilanguage management feature of Joomla. Each language can offer a tailored experience to website visitors, showing relevant content for their location/culture, eventually switching from LTR to RTL layouts, and much more. You can easily hide non-relevant parts such as modules or menu items, by simply assigning them to the correct language. This will prevent them from being displayed in other languages.

Exercises

It's time to apply the knowledge acquired in this chapter and use the multilanguage management features.

Exercise 1 – Set up a multilingual website

1. From your backend, install the French and Italian languages, as Language Packs.

2. Check that the respective content languages have been created correctly and enable them. Your website now has three languages: English (en-GB), French (fr-FR), and Italian (it-IT).

3. Enable the **Language Filter** and **Language Code** system plugins.

4. Check the status of your setup through the **Multilingual Status** module and proceed with any missing steps. Remember that you need to create articles that serve as the home page for each language and that each of these articles should be assigned to one language.

5. Create three menus called `English Menu`, `Italian Menu`, and `French Menu`.

6. Create a menu item in each of them, showing the respective article that should serve as the home page. Each of these menu items should be marked as **Default Page** and assigned to a specific language. You now have the three home pages, one for each language.

7. Finally, publish a **Language Switcher** module, hiding its title and making it display flags using a horizontal layout placed in the `topbar` position of the Cassiopeia template.

8. Check your website frontend to ensure that all three language flags are displayed.

Exercise 2 – Multilingual Associations

Let's use the **Multilingual Associations** feature to link the home page articles of the three languages:

1. In **Articles**, open the article you wrote to serve as the home page for English and click on the **Associations** button.

2. Select **French (fr-FR)** as the target language and click on **Select Target** to see the list of available articles.

3. From the list, select the article you wrote to serve as the home page for French.

4. Once done, select **Italian (it-IT)** as the target language and click on **Select Target** to see the list of available articles, then pick the article you wrote as the home page for Italian. In this way, you connected the three articles as associated content.

5. To check the result, open your website and ensure that the English language is enabled from the **Language Switcher** module.

6. Click on the different language flags to verify that the associated article is shown in the respective languages.

Summary

In this chapter, we explored the multilanguage management features of Joomla and understood how to configure a multilingual website, associating content to languages and customizing the experience for each language.

In the next chapter, we'll get to know one of the newest features included in Joomla: Task Scheduler.

Further reading

- Managing multi-regional and multilingual websites: `https://developers.google.com/search/docs/specialty/international/managing-multi-regional-sites`

## 9

Planning Operations with Scheduled Tasks

In the previous chapter, we explored Joomla's multilanguage features, which allow you to manage a website in multiple languages with only one instance of the CMS. Now, we'll look at one of the most recent functionalities added to the CMS: **Scheduled Tasks**.

After reading this chapter, you will be able to do the following:

- Understand how the Scheduled Tasks component works
- Know which type of tasks can be scheduled
- Create customized scheduled tasks

What is a Scheduled Task?

Websites often require repetitive actions to be executed, such as maintenance operations, ongoing optimizations, and processing queues regularly.

To handle these kinds of repetitive actions, over the years, webmasters used `cron`, a job scheduler available on all Linux-based environments and generally made available on all the major shared hosting services. Cron allows you to execute tasks on a planned basis; this includes choosing the command to execute and the frequency with which such a command should be actioned.

Even though cron is generally available among hosting providers, sometimes, it has some limits in terms of frequency or the number of tasks you can set up. Furthermore, it's not easy to set up a cron because you need to know the path of the PHP executable if you want to execute a PHP script, or the path to the `curl` function if you want to call a web page or an API endpoint.

To avoid such limits and simplify the setup process, Joomla 4.1 introduced a feature called **Scheduled Tasks**, which allows you to set up a cron directly through the CMS backend with a couple of easy steps. Let's learn how to create our first scheduled task.

Creating a scheduled task

To set up our first scheduled task, we need to open the **Scheduled Tasks** component, which we can access through the **System Dashboard** area on our website's backend. The component dashboard will look as shown in *Figure 9.1*:

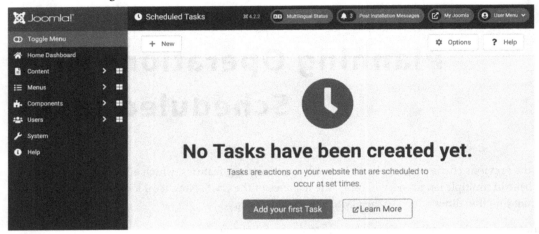

Figure 9.1 – The Scheduled Tasks component screen

Then, we need to click on the **New** button in the toolbar. Since we don't have any other tasks, we could even click on the **Add your first Task** button, which is visible on the welcome screen of the component.

We will be asked to choose the types of tasks we want to create, as shown in *Figure 9.2*:

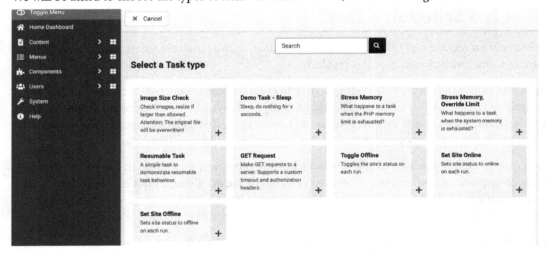

Figure 9.2 – The Select a Task type screen

From this screen, we can select the type of task we want to schedule. There are several types of tasks available by default. Additional types of tasks may be added after installing third-party extensions.

In this example, we will create a task that calls a specific URL at a given interval. To do so, we must select the **GET Request** type of task from the list. The **New Task** creation screen looks as shown in *Figure 9.3*:

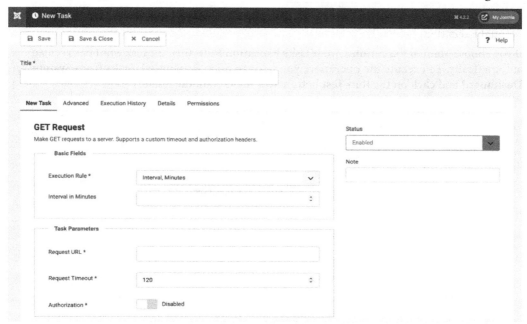

Figure 9.3 – New Task | New Task options

After giving our task a **Title**, we must go through various options, starting from the **New Task** tab:

- **Execution Rule**: Here, you can select the rule with which to execute the task. The available options are **Interval, Minutes**; **Interval, Hours**; **Interval, Days**; **Interval, Months**; **Cron Expression (Advanced)**; and **Manual Execution**.

- **Interval in Minutes**: This field name may vary based on the interval selected. It allows you to specify the length of the interval in minutes.

- **Request URL**: Specifies the URL to be called through a GET request.

- **Request Timeout**: Specifies the timeout for the request, in seconds. The default is **120** seconds.

- **Authorization**: This allows you to set eventual authorization parameters for the request. If enabled, additional options will appear, such as the type of authorization required (**Bearer** or **Joomla Token**) and a field to provide the token.

The classic **Status** field allows you to select whether the task should be enabled, disabled, or trashed.

Each cron type has fields and options

Some of the fields reported are specific to the type of cron you want to set up. For example, if you use the **GET Request** type of cron, you will see the **Request URL**, **Request Timeout**, and **Authorization** fields. Different types of fields may be proposed based on the type of cron selected.

Manual Execution

If you choose **Manual Execution** as your task's **Execution Rule**, then the task won't be executed automatically. To execute the operation, you need to open **Scheduled Tasks** from **System Dashboard** and click on the **Run Test** button near the task, in the task list.

Now, let's move on to the **Advanced** tab's options, as shown in *Figure 9.4*:

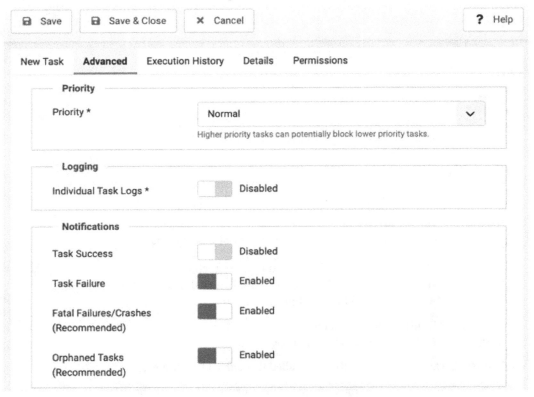

Figure 9.4 – New Task | Advanced options

The **Advanced** tab contains the following options:

- **Priority**: Here, you can select the priority of the task; you can choose between **Low**, **Normal**, and **High**. **Priority** is useful for defining the order and importance of tasks when your server is busy.

- **Individual Task Logs**: Here, you can decide whether to create a log for a single task or not. When enabled, you are asked to define the name for the task file log. Log files are saved under the `/administrator/logs/` folder.

The other options grouped under the **Notifications** title allow you to choose when you want to receive a notification: **Task Success**, **Task Failure**, **Task Failure/Crashes**, or **Orphaned Tasks**.

> **Task notifications**
>
> If you have many tasks or frequent tasks (several times during the day), it is recommended to avoid opting in for **Task Success** notifications. If you enable **Task Success** notifications, you may become overwhelmed by email notifications.

Let's move on to the **Execution History** tab, as displayed in *Figure 9.5*:

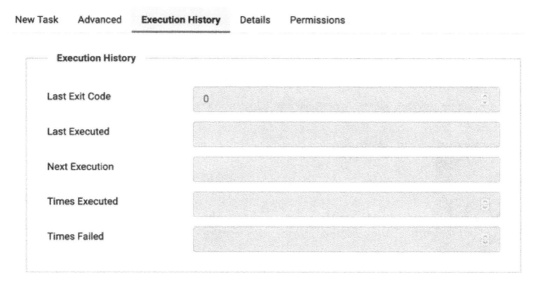

Figure 9.5 – New Task | Execution History

Since we're creating a new task, it's normal for this tab to show empty values in its fields. Once the task is active and regularly executed, you will see meaningful values in the fields, such as **Last Exit Code**, the date and time of the **Last Execution** and **Next Execution** properties, the overall number of times it has been executed, and the number of failures.

The **Details** tab shows some additional information about the task, as displayed in *Figure 9.6*:

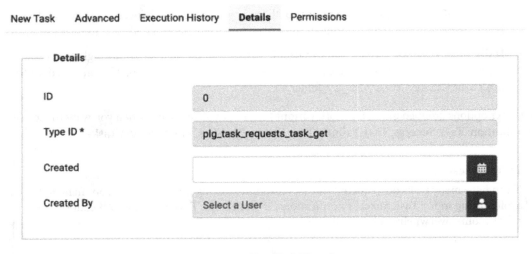

Figure 9.6 – New Task | Details

The details shown include the **ID** property of the task – assigned after saving it – the **Type ID** property, the date and time of creation, and the user who created the task.

The **Permissions** tab completes the new task creation process and shows the common permissions management controls that we explored in *Chapter 6, Managing Users and Their Permissions*.

Once you've set up the task, just click on **Save and Close** to be taken back to the task list screen, as shown in *Figure 9.7*:

Figure 9.7 – Scheduled Tasks | Task list

From here, we can observe some details about each task, including its **Title**, **Task Type**, **Last Run Date**, **Task Priority**, and **ID**. There's also a button in the **Test Task** column that allows us to manually execute the task to test it.

A **GET Request** task may be used to either call an internal URL to trigger a specific action or an external URL. Some common scenarios include triggering how the sending queue in a newsletter extension is processed, triggering an automated backup at a specific time regularly, and launching a regular synchronization between calendars. Generally, for these scenarios, you will be provided with a URL that should be called through a cron.

In the next few sections, we'll explore two examples: setting up a regular maintenance window and automatically optimizing images on a website. Let's start with the maintenance window.

Example – scheduled maintenance window

A common use case in large websites, especially e-commerce ones, is the need to set up a regular maintenance window in which some batch operations are executed, such as to align with the warehouse for the availability of products, synchronize with shipping companies, and similar operations.

To avoid creating inconsistencies with customer orders, it may be useful to define a maintenance window for the website, suspending it from operations for a certain amount of time. Let's suppose that you need to take the website offline for 1 hour, every day from midnight to 1:00 A.M. Doing so is very easy with **Scheduled Tasks** – you just need to set up two tasks:

- One to make the website go offline at a given time
- Another to make the website go back online at a given time

Let's start with the first task.

In the **Scheduled Tasks** component, create a new task by selecting the **Set Site Offline** type. For the **Execution Rule** property, select **Cron Expression (Advanced)**, as shown in *Figure 9.8*:

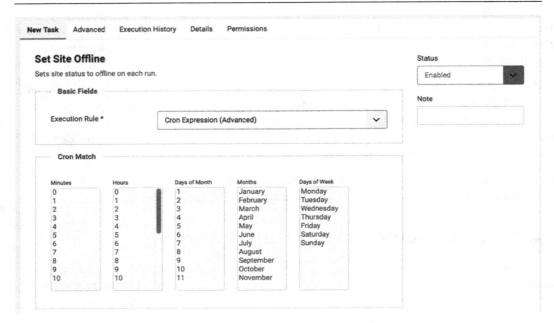

Figure 9.8 – New Task | Cron Expression (Advanced)

In the **Cron Match** section, we can define the time to execute our task. In our case, we can set up the task like so:

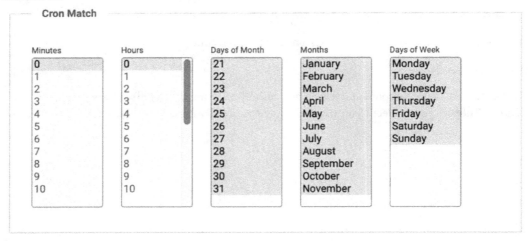

Figure 9.9 – Cron Match selection

The selection depicted in *Figure 9.9* ensures that our task is executed every day of the month, of every month, independent of the day of the week, at hour 0 (midnight) minute 00. As you can see, these controls give you maximum flexibility over the setup of your recurring operations.

Click Save and Close for this task and create a new one by selecting the **Set Site Online** type. The only difference with the previous task is that, in the **Cron Match** section, we will select **1** in the **Hours** field instead of **0**. **Click Save and Close for** this second task.

Now, the website has been configured to go offline at midnight and come back online at 1.00 A.M., every day. Now, let's look at another example that shows us how to optimize the images of a website.

Example – automatically optimizing your images

Images' weight and size are crucial to ensure the performance of a website. When multiple operators publish content on a website, the image sizes and formats might not be optimized or uniform.

A scheduled task can help us optimize the images of our website, ensuring a proper size and weight. Let's create a new task and select **Image Size Check** as the type. The task creation screen looks like that shown in *Figure 9.10*:

Figure 9.10 – New Task | Image Size Check

Let's suppose that we want to execute this task every day at 22.00. In the **Execution Rule** field, select **Interval, Days**. Additional fields will appear, allowing us to select the execution interval in days and the time at which the task should be executed, as shown in *Figure 9.11*:

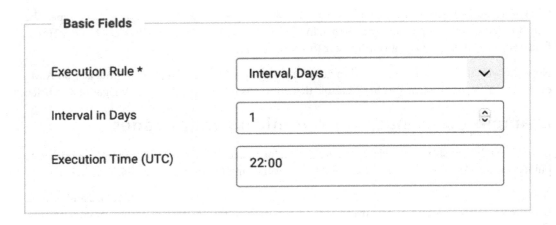

Figure 9.11 – Execution interval in days

Going back to the controls shown in *Figure 9.10*, we can select a **Directory** where the images to check and optimize will be stored, a **Dimension** to check – for example, **Width** – and a **Limit** in pixels. The **Maximum Images** parameter allows you to choose the number of images to process at each cron execution.

Once the task has been configured, click on **Save and Close** to finish creating it. Now, the website will check every day at 22.00 whether the images are wider than 1,080 px and eventually resize them to fit this value.

> **A website with many images**
>
> If you add a consistent number of images to your website every day, it would be opportune to keep the number of images to process at each execution low and increase the execution frequency of the task.

With this example, we have finished exploring the **Scheduled Tasks** feature.

Exercises

Now, it's time to apply the knowledge you've acquired in this chapter and use the **Scheduled Tasks** feature.

Exercise 1 – handling planned maintenance

Create two scheduled tasks to handle planned maintenance weekly. The website should be taken offline every Saturday at 23.00 and should be set back online every Sunday at 1.00 A.M. You can use **Interval, Daily** or **Cron Execution (Advanced)** as the **Execution Rule** property for these tasks.

Exercise 2 – calling an endpoint

Create a scheduled task to call the following URL every Monday at 8.00 A.M. The URL to be called is your website's `index.php`.

Summary

In this chapter, we explored the **Scheduled Tasks** feature and learned how to set up some basic repeatable actions.

In the next chapter, we'll learn how to customize the communications of our website thanks to **Mail Templates**.

Further reading

To learn more about the topics that were covered in this chapter, take a look at the following link:

- Cron: `https://en.wikipedia.org/wiki/Cron`

10

Tailored Communication with Mail Templates

In the previous chapter, we explored the brand-new **Scheduled Tasks** feature, which allows you to configure your website so that it automatically executes actions regularly.

Now, we'll look at **Mail Templates**, a feature that allows you to completely customize the communication style of your website.

After reading this chapter, you will be able to do the following:

- Use notifications as a branding item
- Understand how **Mail Templates** works
- Customize the look and feel of your website's automated notifications

Let's understand why customizing emails matters for a website.

Notifications as a branding item

Every company has a brand style guide that is used among all types of communication: newsletters, press releases, documents, and much more. Websites, especially those with advanced features such as e-commerce sites, generally send a lot of automated emails as a result of user actions (think about user registration, account activation, order confirmation, subscription expiration, and similar notifications).

Even for large corporate sites, some of those communications differ from the usual *corporate style*, especially automated emails for processes such as account creation/activation, where those emails are generally sent as simple text without graphics or style. This is in contrast to newsletters, which are well-styled and prepared with specific graphics.

Furthermore, in some countries, a company may be obliged by the law to include some company details, such as the company's name, VAT ID, registration number, or address in the footer of each communication. So, there could be multiple needs to customize and harmonize all website's emails.

Joomla 4 allows us to implement our corporate style in any communication sent through the website. This can be done through the **Mail Templates** feature, which allows us to customize every automated email style and its appearance, creating a uniform way to communicate with the same look and feel.

Let's see how it works.

The Mail Templates feature

The **Mail Templates** feature can be found in the **System Dashboard** area. Once opened, it looks like what's shown in *Figure 10.1*:

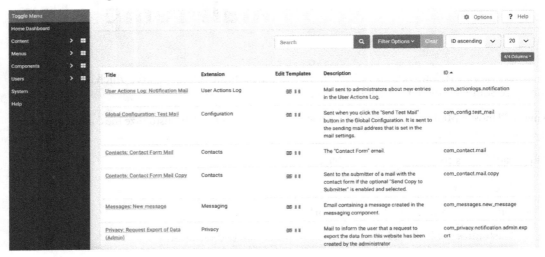

Figure 10.1 – Mail Templates

The main screen of **Mail Templates** shows a list of all the notification messages that are sent by Joomla, each one connected to a specific **Extension** and with a **Description** that specifies when a message is sent.

Search and filtering functionalities allow us to look for a specific email or filter emails by extension. It's useful when you want to customize emails sent by a specific extension (for example, e-commerce, newsletter, contacts, and so on).

For each of the emails, in the **Edit Templates** column, flags of the available languages are visible. Here, we can edit the email in the desired language, granting us a high degree of flexibility.

Now, let's see the feature in action by customizing our first email template.

Customizing an email template

To explore the functionalities of the **Mail Templates** feature, we are going to customize the first template shown in *Figure 10.1*, called **User Action Log: Notification Mail**. Let's click on the English flag in correspondence to the email we want to edit.

The **Edit Template** screen looks like what's shown in *Figure 10.2*:

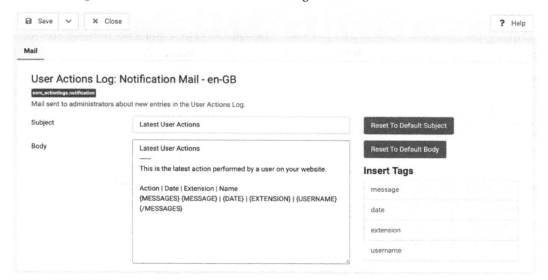

Figure 10.2 – Mail Templates | Edit Template

In the preceding figure, we can observe several details: the email's title and language, the label with an internal name, and a description of the email template. Such a description generally includes the purpose of the communication and the recipient.

Then, we have the **Subject** field, which corresponds to the email subject that the users will receive in their mailbox, and the **Body** text area, in which you can see the actual text of the email and customize it.

On the right-hand side of the screen, two buttons allow you to reset either the **Subject** or **Body** properties of the email to the respective default value, canceling any eventual variation you made.

The **Insert Tags** section lists all the variables – called **Tags** – that you can add to this email. In *Figure 10.2*, we can see that the message, date, extension, and username tags are listed. Tags are automatically converted into their values when the email is generated and sent to the recipients.

Email tags

Do not forget to add tags to your email when they need to show variable values. Tags are used to display the username or the email address of the user, or – as shown in *Figure 10.2* – some messages and data from extensions.

If we look at the **Body** section of the message, as shown in *Figure 10.2*, we can see that the text of the email is shown in plain text format and includes some of the tags we've seen.

Customizing the message is very easy – we just need to type some text in addition to the default content of the message. For example, if we want to add a footer, we can add one, as shown in *Figure 10.3*:

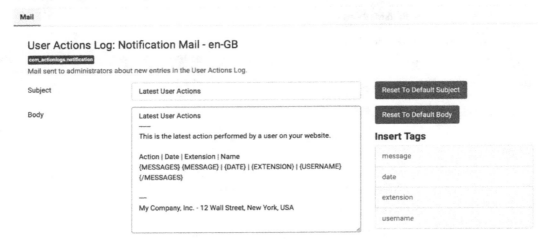

Figure 10.3 – Mail Templates | Edit Template – modified

Once the text has been changed, we can simply click on **Save & Close**.

Plain text versus HTML

You may have noticed that, by default, all system notifications are sent in plain text mode, without any HTML tags and styles. If you want to customize the look and feel of your website's email, you should enable HTML mode so that you can add images, headers, footers, and much more. You can enable HTML from the **Mail Templates** feature's **Options** screen by selecting **HTML** under the **Mail Format** option. Bear in mind that not all email clients support HTML emails, so ensure that you can test your messages to ensure they can also be read when opened in a simple text format.

When HTML mode is enabled, editing mail templates is more user-friendly. For example, if we look at the same mail template, named **User Action Log: Notification Mail - en-GB**, we will see something similar to the following:

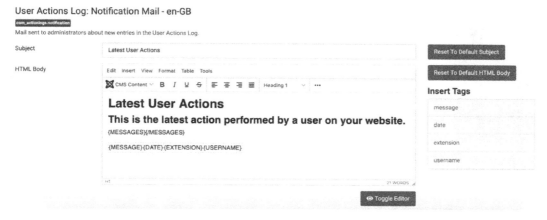

Figure 10.4 – Mail Templates | Edit Template | HTML mode

As shown in *Figure 10.4*, the email's content looks more structured, thanks to the use of headers and the table in which we can find tags.

With the standard content editor integrated into Joomla, it's much easier to input your content and format it, adding images and other items to the message.

Earlier in this chapter, we mentioned that you could edit each email template for each of the languages available on the website. This is useful for a multinational company website, for example, where there could be different corporate addresses or contact details based on the country. With **Mail Templates**, you can have a custom footer that's different for each language so that you can put the regional office for Italy in emails to Italian users, the global office for those who receive emails in English, and so on.

In the next section, we will customize the user registration email by completing a case study.

Case study – customizing the user registration email

In this case study, we are going to customize the email message that the user receives after registering to our website. This scenario is one in which users register by themselves to the website without the need for account approval either by administrators or users.

In the **Mail Templates** feature, filter by **Extensions** and select **Users**, as shown in *Figure 10.5*:

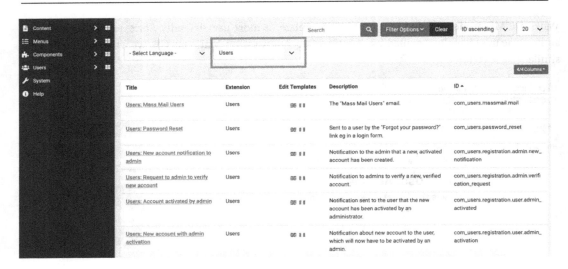

Figure 10.5 – Mail Templates | Extensions – Users

In the list of emails, find the one named **Users: New account without activation**, as highlighted in *Figure 10.6*:

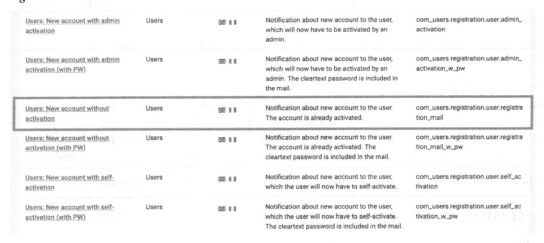

Figure 10.6 – Mail Templates | Detail

To start editing it, click on the English flag. The edit screen will look as follows:

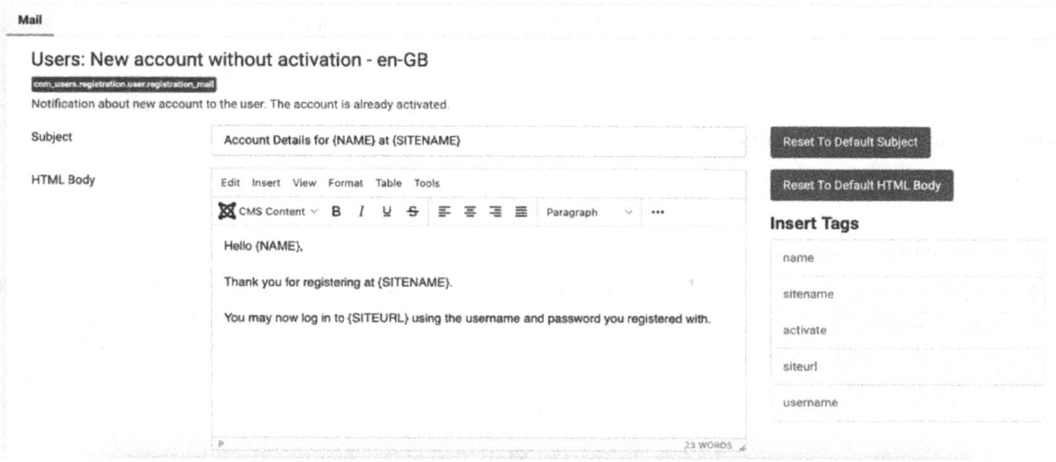

Figure 10.7 – Mail Templates | Edit new account without activation email

Now, we can customize the email template. Let's start by changing the email's **Subject** to something more attractive, such as {NAME}, welcome to {SITENAME}!.

This string would look like Paul, welcome to MyCorp!.

Here, Paul is the name of the user and MyCorp is the name of the website. This subject is more personal and friendly for the user.

Now, we can work on the email's content. First, we will add our logo as the heading of the email; then, we can add a footer for the message. *Figure 10.8* shows what the message will look like after making these additions:

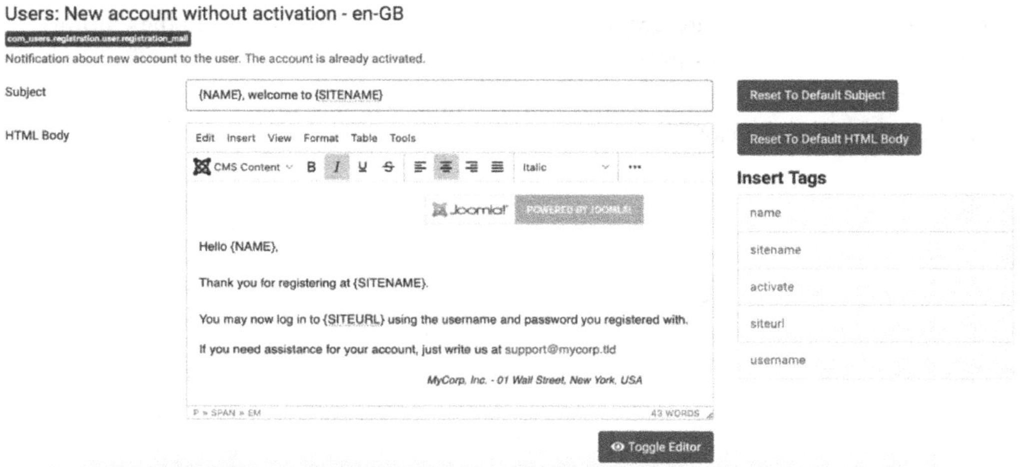

Figure 10.8 – Modified mail template

Here, we have added a logo to the header of the email, then instructions on how to get support. The email was completed with a footer that shows the address of the company.

Once the email is ready, we just click on **Save & Close** to complete the operation. Remember that it's opportune to update emails in other languages so that your users across the world can have a consistent experience.

Standardize your style

To give your users a consistent experience throughout their relationship with your website, it's opportune to adopt a standardized design and layout for your email templates. This will also make your users immediately recognize your emails as legitimate, as they will all have the same look and feel.

With this case study, we have finished exploring the **Mail Templates** feature. Try it by yourself in the proposed exercises.

Exercises

It's time to apply the knowledge you've acquired in this chapter regarding **Mail Templates**.

Exercise 1 – customizing the courtesy Contact Form Mail Copy

You have been asked to customize the email that a user receives after submitting a contact form on your website. The mail template we want to edit is called **Contacts: Contact Form Mail Copy**.

Check the email's format

Before editing the mail template, ensure you enable **HTML** as **Mail Format** in the **Options** area of the **Mail Templates** component.

The email template will look as follows:

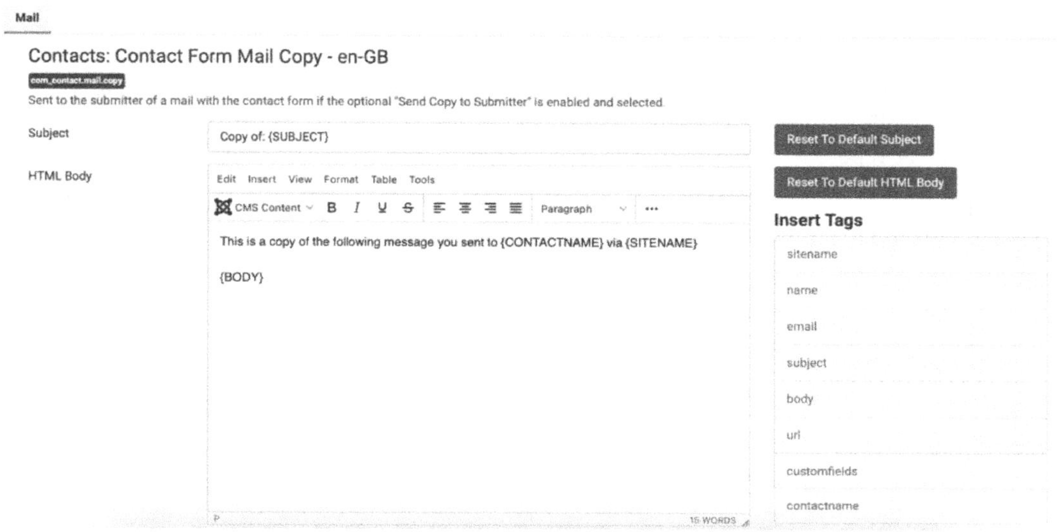

Mail

Contacts: Contact Form Mail Copy - en-GB

`com_contact.mail.copy`

Sent to the submitter of a mail with the contact form if the optional "Send Copy to Submitter" is enabled and selected.

Subject	Copy of: {SUBJECT}	Reset To Default Subject
HTML Body	Edit Insert View Format Table Tools	Reset To Default HTML Body

CMS Content ∨ B *I* U S̶ ☰ ☰ ☰ ☰ Paragraph ∨ ⋯

This is a copy of the following message you sent to {CONTACTNAME} via {SITENAME}

{BODY}

P   15 WORDS

Insert Tags

sitename

name

email

subject

body

url

customfields

contactname

Figure 10.9 – Mail Templates | Edit template – Contact Form Mail Copy

1. Change the **Subject** property to `Thank you for contacting {SITENAME}`.

2. Update the text, adding the following lines before the actual content:

    ```
    Hello {NAME}, thank you for contacting us.
    Your message {SUBJECT} has been received.
    ```

3. At the end of the message, add the following text as a footer, after two blank lines:

    ```
    MyCorp, Inc. - 01, Wall Street - New York, USA
    ```

4. Remember to center the content of the footer using the proper button in the toolbar.

5. Once done, **Save & Close** the mail template.

We customized the email message received by the users who contacted us through the website. Proceed to the next exercise to add a custom logo to your messages.

Exercise 2 – modifying your emails with your logo

Open the template you edited in the previous exercise (**Contacts: Contact Form Mail Copy**) and modify it by adding your logo.

You can either upload a custom image file from your device or pick one of the default images shipped with Joomla. Place the logo at the top of the email template, before the text. Once done, click **Save & Close** for your email template.

Now, your website's users will receive a nicer confirmation email when they contact you.

Summary

In this chapter, we explored the **Mail Templates** feature, understood how to edit the messages and confirmation emails sent by the system, and learned how to give all the website's emails a uniform look and feel. The reported case study and exercises helped us learn how to customize emails.

In the next chapter, we will learn how to use Joomla through its **Command-Line Interface (CLI)** and how to perform basic operations via the CLI.

11

Command-Line Interface

In the previous chapter, we explored the **Mail Templates** feature, where we learned how to customize the look and feel of the communication for our website. Now, we'll look at a hidden gem of the CMS known as the **Command-Line Interface (CLI)**, which allows us to use Joomla through a terminal.

After reading this chapter, you will be able to do the following:

- Understand how to use the Joomla CLI
- Perform basic operations through the CLI

Using Joomla via the CLI

Joomla offers a CLI to perform operations on the website without the need to access it through a web browser. This CLI can be accessed through an SSH session in a terminal opened from your device.

> **Where is the terminal?**
>
> To access Joomla through the CLI, you can use the Terminal app on macOS or Linux. If you are using a Windows machine, you can use the built-in Command Prompt or SSH software such as Solar Putty or Termius. It's common to refer to the terminal as a *shell*.

The CLI is less user-friendly than the web interface, but it's faster and more efficient when you want to perform some maintenance options than via the web as they may require several clicks, especially when you are managing several instances of Joomla in the same web hosting account.

When you activate your hosting account, you should also receive the SSH credentials in the activation email, specifying when SSH access is allowed by the hosting service provider. To access Joomla through its CLI, we need to establish an SSH session. Follow these steps:

1. To do so, open the terminal on your device and type the following command:

```
ssh username@mywebsite.tld
```

2. Then, press *Enter* on your keyboard. The system will request your password. Generally, it's the same as the main FTP password, but this may vary, depending on your hosting service configuration and characteristics.

3. At the first login attempt, the system may request you to add the host to the list of known hosts on your machine. If requested, type `Yes` and press *Enter*:

```
Last login: Sun Oct  2 16:27:08 on ttys000
[lucamarzo@Air-di-Luca ~ % ssh uhpskeg2@joomla.sviluppo.host
[(uhpskeg2@joomla.sviluppo.host) Password:
Last login: Sun Oct  2 00:35:28 2022
[uhpskeg2@web122 ~]$
```

Figure 11.1 – Logged into the server

4. Once logged in, you can start inserting commands, as shown in *Figure 11.1*.

5. To start using the CLI, you need to navigate to the folder in which the feature resides. After logging in, you will be on the home page of the user in the remote server. From here, you need to reach the `public_html` folder and its `cli` subfolder.

6. To see the folder structure, type `ls` and press *Enter*. The `ls` command will display a list of files and folders under the current folder. You should see a folder called `public_html` or a link to it. The `public_html` folder is the root folder of your web space; this is where all the Joomla files will be located.

> **Which is your root folder?**
>
> Based on the remote server configuration, the name of your root folder may vary. Common names include `public_html`, www, and `htdocs`. The root folder may also be a subfolder of other folders; in fact, it's common to have a path such as `/home/<username>/domains/<domainname.tld>/public_html/`. Refer to your hosting service's instructions to find out which is your root folder. If you installed Joomla in a subdomain or a subfolder, when we talk about the root folder, we mean the folder in which your Joomla instance resides.

7. To navigate to the `public_html` folder, just type `cd public_html` and press *Enter*.

8. If you type `ls` again and press *Enter*, you will see the list of files and folders of your Joomla installation, as shown in *Figure 11.2*:

```
[[uhpskeg2@web122 public_html]$ ls
administrator   components          index.html_    LICENSE.txt   robots.txt.dist
api             configuration.php   index.php      media         templates
cache           htaccess.txt        language       modules       tmp
cgi-bin         images              layouts        plugins       web.config.txt
cli             includes            libraries      README.txt
[uhpskeg2@web122 public_html]$
```

Figure 11.2 – Contents of the Joomla root folder

9. To access the Joomla CLI, you need to move to the `cli` folder. To do so, use the `cd cli` command and press *Enter*.

10. You should now be in the right folder. To start the CLI, you need to execute the `php joomla.php` command and press *Enter*. You will see something similar to what's shown in *Figure 11.3*:

```
[[uhpskeg2@web122 cli]$ php joomla.php
Joomla! 4.2.2 (debug: No)

Usage:
  command [options] [arguments]

Options:
      --live-site[=LIVE-SITE]   The URL to your site, e.g. https://www.example.co
m
  -h, --help                    Display the help information
  -q, --quiet                   Flag indicating that all output should be silence
d
  -V, --version                 Displays the application version
      --ansi                    Force ANSI output
      --no-ansi                 Disable ANSI output
  -n, --no-interaction          Flag to disable interacting with the user
  -v|vv|vvv, --verbose          Increase the verbosity of messages: 1 for normal
output, 2 for more verbose output and 3 for debug

Available commands:
  help                          Show the help for a command
  list                          List the application's available commands
 cache
  cache:clean                   Clean cache entries
```

Figure 11.3 – Joomla CLI start screen

Now that you've opened the Joomla CLI, it is now ready to accept your commands. As shown in *Figure 11.3*, the welcome screen shows the available options and commands.

The Joomla CLI allows us to perform a long list of operations, from managing users (creating/removing/updating) to checking for Joomla updates, from managing extensions (installing/removing/updating) to performing a database backup.

Furthermore, through the CLI, you can create custom bash scripts that can be automated with a cron (or via a scheduled task) to perform operations automatically, such as checking for updates, cleaning the cache, and much more.

Now, let's explore the commands that are available in Joomla 4 through its CLI.

Available commands

The Joomla CLI offers a long list of commands. To explore this list, type `php joomla.php list` in your Terminal and press *Enter*.

You will be provided with the list of available commands. This will look as follows:

Command	Description
help	Shows the help/guide of a command
list	Shows the list of available commands
cache:clean	Cleans the cache of the website
config:get	Shows the current value of a configuration or option
config:set	Updates the value of a configuration or option
core:check-updates	Checks if there are available updates for Joomla
core:update	Performs a Joomla update
database:export	Exports the database of the website
database:import	Imports the database
extension:discover	Explores whether there are extensions to be installed
extension:discover:install	Installs the extensions discovered
extension:discover:list	Lists the extensions discovered
extension:install	Installs an extension from a URL/path
extension:list	Lists all installed extensions
extension:remove	Uninstalls an extension
finder:index	Purges and re-builds the index of Smart Search
scheduler:list	Lists all scheduled tasks
scheduler:run	Runs one or more scheduled tasks
scheduler:state	Enables/disables/trashes a scheduled task
session:gc	Performs session garbage collection
session:metadata:gc	Performs session metadata garbage collection
site:down	Puts the website offline
site:up	Puts the website online
update:extensions:check	Checks for updates for extensions
update:joomla:remove-old-files	Removes old files related to updates
user:add	Creates a new user
user:addtogroup	Adds a user to a user group
user:delete	Deletes a user
user:list	Lists all users
user:removefromgroup	Removes a user from a user group
user:reset-password	Changes the password of a user

Table 11.1 – List of CLI commands

The CLI commands listed in *Table 11.1* can be launched from the terminal by preceding them with the php joomla.php command, as shown in the following example:

```
php joomla.php cache:clean
```

After executing this command, the system will prompt us with the result of the operation, as shown in *Figure 11.4*:

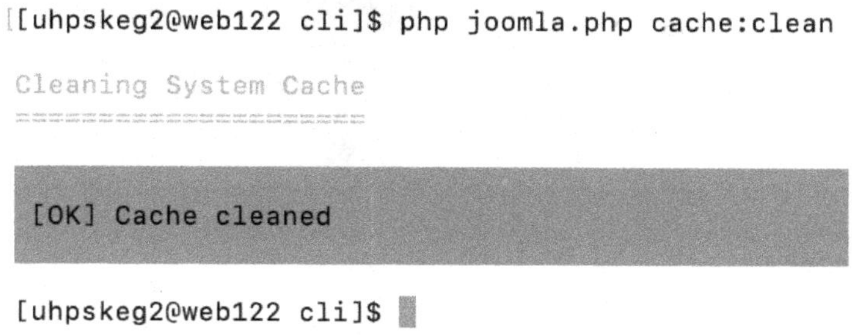

```
[uhpskeg2@web122 cli]$ php joomla.php cache:clean

Cleaning System Cache
========================

[OK] Cache cleaned

[uhpskeg2@web122 cli]$
```

Figure 11.4 – CLI | cache:clean command

In the next few sections, we will explore some real-life scenarios where we will use the CLI to perform operations on users and update our website.

Example – managing users through the CLI

In this example, we will explore the commands that allow us to manage users through the CLI. Follow these steps:

1. Let's create a user using the php joomla.php user:add command:

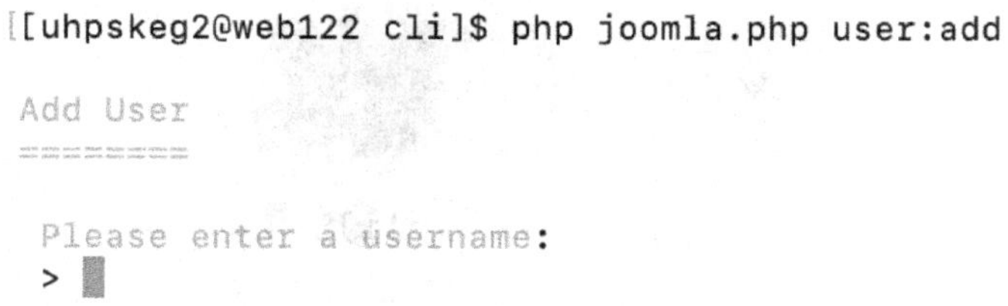

    ```
    [uhpskeg2@web122 cli]$ php joomla.php user:add

    Add User
    =========

    Please enter a username:
    >
    ```

    Figure 11.5 – CLI | Creating a new user

2. As shown in *Figure 11.5*, the system becomes interactive and requests us to input a username. In this case, we will type testuser as the username and press *Enter*.

3. The system will then ask for the full name of the user. Type Test User and press *Enter*.

4. The system will request the user's email address. Insert their email address and press *Enter*.

5. Next, we'll be asked for the password of the user. Type their password and press *Enter*.

6. The system will then request us to choose a User Group, as shown in *Figure 11.6*:

```
Please enter a username:
[ > testuser

Please enter a name (full name of user):
[ > Test User

Please enter an email address:
[ > no-reply@packt.com

Please enter a password:
[ >

Please select a usergroup (separate multiple groups with a comma):
 [0] Public
 [1] Registered
 [2] Author
 [3] Editor
 [4] Publisher
 [5] Manager
 [6] Administrator
 [7] Super Users
 [8] Guest
 >
```

Figure 11.6 – CLI | New user creation

7. In our example, we are creating a registered user account without any additional privileges, so we want to add the user to the **Registered** user group by typing 1 and pressing *Enter*.

The system will then confirm the creation of the user account, as shown in Figure 11.7:

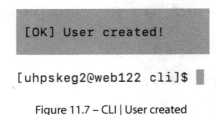

```
[OK] User created!


[uhpskeg2@web122 cli]$
```

Figure 11.7 – CLI | User created

With that, the user has been created. Now, let's look at the list of all user accounts in our installation. To do so, we can use the following command:

```
php joomla.php user:list
```

The system will respond with a list of all users, as shown in *Figure 11.8.*:

```
[[uhpskeg2@web122 cli]$ php joomla.php user:list

List Users
==========


  -----  ----------  ----------------  ----------------------  ---------  -------------
   ID    Username    Name              Email                   Blocked    Groups
  -----  ----------  ----------------  ----------------------  ---------  -------------
   631   admin       Administrator     luca.marzo@.    .com    0          Super Users
   632   testuser    Test User         no-reply@packt.com      0          Registered
  -----  ----------  ----------------  ----------------------  ---------  -------------

[uhpskeg2@web122 cli]$
```

Figure 11.8 – CLI | List of all users

You can also delete a user by using the following command:

`php joomla.php user:delete`

The system will request the username of the user to delete. In our example, we want to delete the user we created previously, so we will type `testuser` and press *Enter*. The system will then ask whether we are sure we wish to remove the user. Confirm this by typing `Yes` and pressing *Enter*. With that, the user will be deleted.

In the next example, we'll check for updates and update our website.

Example – updating your site through the CLI

In this example, we will update our website using various CLI commands.

First, we will check for updates by using the `php joomla.php core:check-updates` command and pressing *Enter*.

The system will notify us of whether a new version can be installed, as shown in *Figure 11.9*:

```
[[uhpskeg2@web122 cli]$ php joomla.php core:check-updates

Joomla! Updates
===============

 ! [NOTE] New Joomla Version 4.2.3 is available.

[uhpskeg2@web122 cli]$
```

Figure 11.9 – CLI | Checking for updates

To perform the update, we can execute the `php joomla.php core:update` command and press *Enter*.

The system will then process the update. This may take several minutes, depending on the size of the update package. Once the update is completed, the system will prompt you with a confirmation message, as shown in *Figure 11.10*:

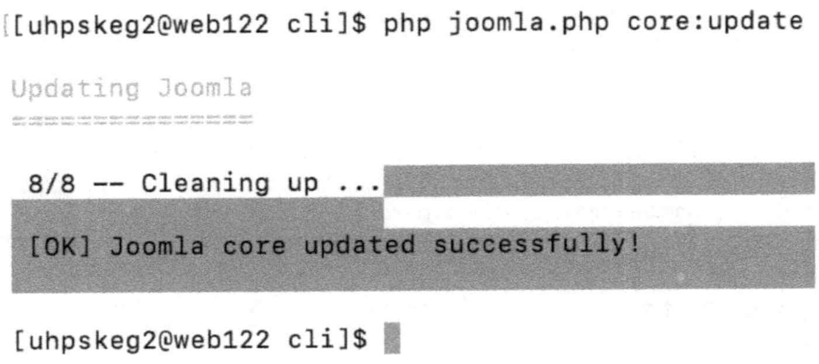

```
[[uhpskeg2@web122 cli]$ php joomla.php core:update

Updating Joomla
==================

8/8 -- Cleaning up ...

[OK] Joomla core updated successfully!

[uhpskeg2@web122 cli]$
```

Figure 11.10 – CLI | Joomla core updated successfully

As you can see, updating Joomla through the CLI is very easy.

With this example, we have finished exploring Joomla 4's CLI.

Exercises

It's time to apply the knowledge you've acquired in this chapter by using the CLI to perform some basic operations.

To complete the exercises proposed in this chapter, you will need to have SSH access to your web hosting. If you are not sure of this, check with your hosting service provider.

Exercise 1 – accessing Joomla's CLI

Access your Joomla installation via SSH and locate the root folder – for example, public_html. Then, navigate to your root folder and then to the cli folder using the cd command. Start the CLI using the php joomla.php command and press *Enter*.

Check the available commands by using php joomla.php list.

Exercise 2 – Scheduled Tasks via the CLI

Using your Joomla CLI, check whether the website has some Scheduled Tasks configured. Use the php joomla.php scheduler:list command and press *Enter*.

Disable the two scheduled tasks we created in the exercises in *Chapter 9, Planning Operations with Scheduled Tasks* (put your website offline, put your website online). To do so, use the php joomla.php scheduler:state command and press *Enter*.

When requested by the system, disable the state of the task. Repeat this for both tasks we created in *Chapter 9*.

Summary

In this chapter, we explored the CLI offered by Joomla 4 and its commands. We went through multiple examples, which included managing users, performing updates, and cleaning the website's cache.

In the next chapter, we will dig into **Templates**, exploring how they work and how we can customize the appearance of our website.

Further reading

To learn more about the topics that were covered in this chapter, take a look at the following resources:

- Joomla 4: A powerful CLI application: `https://magazine.joomla.org/all-issues/june-2022/joomla-4-a-powerful-cli-application`
- Joomla 4 CLI documentation: `https://docs.joomla.org/Category:Joomla_CLI`

Part 3: Styling and Securing Your Website

In this part, you will learn how to customize the look and feel of your website. You will discover what templates and styles are and how to customize the templates, and you will explore style options. You will discover overrides and learn how to use child templates. Furthermore, you will be introduced to template frameworks and will discover the most used frameworks to quickly and easily build layouts for your websites. To complete this part, you will discover some advanced functionalities dedicated to access and security, such as multifactor authentication, webAuthn, and HTTP header management features.

This part has the following chapters:

- *Chapter 12, Styling Your Website – Templates*
- *Chapter 13, Customize Everything with Overrides*
- *Chapter 14, Child Templates*
- *Chapter 15, Template Frameworks*
- *Chapter 16, Advanced Features – Access and Security*

12

Styling Your Website – Templates

In the previous chapter, we explored Joomla's **command-Line interface**, a different way to perform actions on a website without accessing its backend.

We'll now learn how to customize the appearance of our website through templates. Templates define how the website will look – the style, colors, fonts, module positions, and much more.

After reading this chapter, you will be able to do the following:

- Understand what a template is
- Understand the difference between templates and styles
- Understand how to customize a template through the website's backend

What is a template?

A **template** is a special type of Joomla extension that is used to style a website. It is a package that includes all the files needed to provide a different look to the website: images, CSS files, JavaScript files, and PHP files.

A template may incorporate styling libraries, such as Bootstrap, Tailwind, or other technologies, to provide some common graphic patterns. For example, the Joomla 4 frontend template, Cassiopeia, is based on Bootstrap 5.

Incorporating popular libraries, such as Bootstrap, simplifies the process of building a template, as it can use all the components and assets from the library.

In Joomla, a template has full control of the appearance of a website, defining its layouts, colors, font type, and size, the available module positions and style variations, and the opportunity to customize the template through the backend.

Templates can be installed as a regular Joomla extension and are provided as a `.zip` file package. Sometimes, template designers also provide a `Quickstart` package for their templates. You can install a template at any time, and it allows you to change the look of your website without the need to build it again from scratch.

> **What is a Quickstart package?**
>
> A **Quickstart package** is a Joomla installation with a specific template installed and set as the default and comes with some placeholder images. These packages are used to allow users to replicate the look and feel of the demo installation of a specific template, as shown on their designer's website. Quickstart packages can't be installed on live sites, as they include a whole Joomla installation, but they should be used to start a new site.

The following are the two types of templates in Joomla:

- Frontend templates
- Backend templates

Backend templates are very rare, and they customize how the website's backend looks. Frontend templates are the most common type of templates. In this chapter, we'll talk about frontend templates, as they allow us to customize the style of our website.

Joomla offers several features to manage templates. Let's start exploring them.

Template management – templates

Template management functionality is accessible through **System Dashboard** and is collated into a module named **Templates**, as shown in *Figure 12.1*.

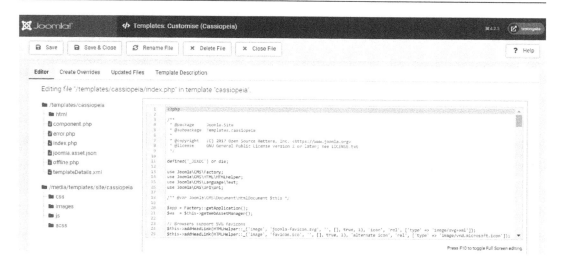

Figure 12.1 – Templates module in System Dashboard

The module displays links to access the various functionalities regarding both frontend and backend templates. Let's start by clicking on **Site Templates** to start going through the available features.

By clicking on **Site Templates**, we can access the list of installed frontend templates, as shown in *Figure 12.2*.

Figure 12.2 – Templates | Site Templates

Each installed template has an entry in the table where we can see its name, a preview/demo image, its version, the release date, information about its author, and whether or not overrides are up to date.

To enter the details and use a template, just click on the name of the template.

We will then see a screen with the list of the template's files and folders, as shown in *Figure 12.3*.

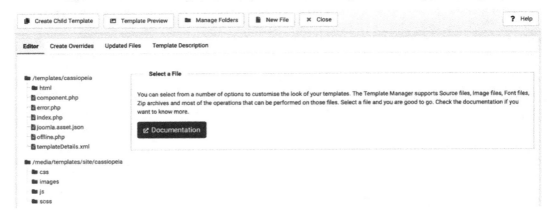

Figure 12.3 – Templates | Site Templates | Cassiopeia Details and Files

By clicking on any of the files from the tree displayed on the left part of the screen, we can see the content of the file and edit it through the integrated editor offered by Joomla. By clicking on the name of the file, it's possible to edit PHP, CSS, JavaScript, HTML, and other types of files online, without the need to download and update them on your computer. In *Figure 12.4*, you can see how to edit a file directly within the template manager.

Figure 12.4 – Templates | Site Templates – online file editing

File and folder structure of a template

It's opportune to dedicate a few moments to understanding how template files and folders are structured. Each installed template has a dedicated folder under the /templates folder of your website; for example, Cassiopeia's folder is /templates/cassiopeia. This folder holds the files needed by the template in order to function properly, such as index.php, error.php, offline.php, and components.php. Those files define how the site is structured in certain cases, for example, when displaying a component, when the website is offline, or when there is an error, as the filenames suggest. The /html folder within the /templates folder holds the **overrides** – the views that the template implements differently from the standard Joomla layout. For example, it includes the PHP files to provide a specific layout for blog pages or category views. We'll get to know overrides in *Chapter 13, Customize Everything with Overrides*. Each template may have its own overrides for standard layouts. In the folder structure, we can also see the folder with the /media/templates/site/cassiopeia path that is outside of the /templates folder. This folder is meant to hold media files such as image, CSS, JavaScript, and SCSS files.

The template manager also allows you to create and manage folders, as well as to create and manage files, thanks to the **Manage Folders** and **New File** buttons in the toolbar. The toolbar also hosts the **Create a Child Template** button, which we'll explore in *Chapter 14, Child Templates*.

These features allow you to customize your template, edit the template files, and add your custom files directly from the backend without the need to download files, edit them offline, and re-upload them via FTP. Be careful of updates, as changes applied to files may be lost. But in most cases, it's not required to operate directly on the source code of your template files, as most templates offer several options to customize them through a configuration panel. This can be done by switching to the **Site Templates Styles** view in the backend of the website. You can access this feature by clicking the **Styles** button in the toolbar, as seen in *Figure 12.5*.

Figure 12.5 – Templates | Site Templates – switch to Styles

In the next section, we'll go through template styles and the options provided.

Template management – styles

Each template installed may have one or more styles. Furthermore, you can create additional template styles for any of the installed templates. Styles allow you to have different configurations for a single template. This feature is useful when you want to differentiate the appearance of your website across different pages or languages by assigning a certain template style to a specific menu item.

A template style should be assigned as **Default** for the website, and it will govern the look and feel of all the website pages that don't have a different template style assigned.

When opening the **Site Templates Styles** view from **System Dashboard**, or by clicking on **Styles** on the **Site Templates** page, we can see the list of available styles, as shown in *Figure 12.6*.

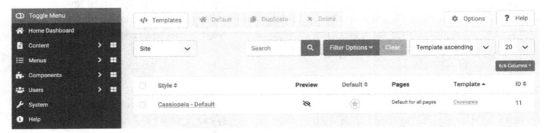

Figure 12.6 – Templates | Site Templates | Styles

In *Figure 12.6*, we can see that there is just one template style installed, called **Cassiopeia – Default**. We can also observe that this style is set to **Default** for all pages. For each style, we can also see which templates they are derived from.

By clicking on the name of the style, we can open the template configuration and customization page. The options available for each template may vary depending on the template itself.

Most templates offer options to change the font and background colors, choose the type of layout, implement a specific footer, link to social networks, and much more.

For each style, you can also specify to which menu item the style should be assigned; this way, you can customize the way the website looks based on the active page. This can be done through the **Menu Assignment** tab on the style management page, as shown in *Figure 12.7*.

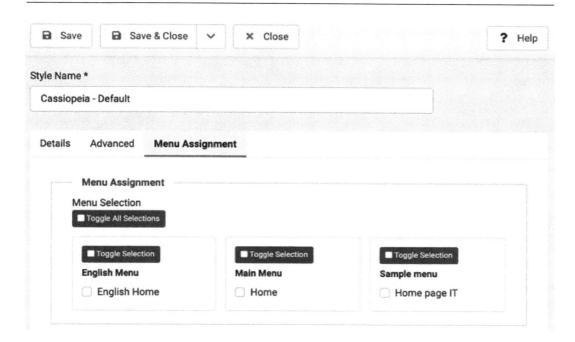

Figure 12.7 – Templates | Template Style | Menu Assignment

The **Menu Assignment** tab shows all the menu items of the website, grouped by menu. From this page, we can select to which menu items the template style should be assigned. Furthermore, template styles can be assigned directly from each menu item configuration in the menu management.

You can duplicate styles as needed and assign them to specific menu items so that every part of the website looks different. In the next section, we will explore the customization option offered by the Joomla default frontend template, Cassiopeia.

Example – a powerful frontend template, Cassiopeia

As an example, we will explore the options offered by Cassiopeia, the default template of Joomla 4. To access them, from **Site Templates Styles**, click on **Cassiopeia – Default**, then click on **Advanced**, and the screen will look like *Figure 12.8.*

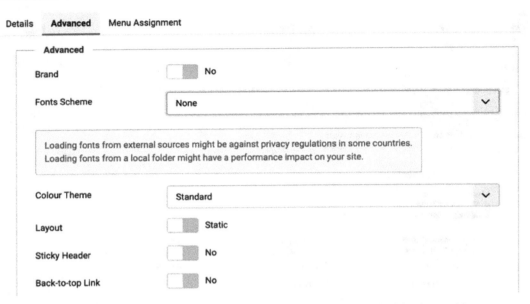

Figure 12.8 – Templates | Site Templates Styles | Cassiopeia – Default | Advanced

The first option is called **Brand**, and it allows us to decide whether to include branding elements on our website. In fact, if allowed, additional fields are displayed, as shown in *Figure 12.9*.

Figure 12.9 – Details of the Brand options of the Cassiopeia template

These additional fields, as displayed in *Figure 12.9*, allow us to select an image as a logo of the website, specify a title to be shown as an alternative to the logo – when the image is not present – and a tagline, a short line of text to be shown after the logo or the title.

Continuing with the options displayed in *Figure 12.8*, the **Fonts Scheme** field allows us to select the font family to be used on the website, selecting from locally installed fonts (included in Joomla) or remote fonts, such as from Google Fonts.

Other options are defined in the following list:

- **Colour Theme**: Allows you to choose between the default or an alternative color palette.
- **Layout:** Choose whether to use a **Static** or **Fluid** layout. The **Fluid** layout is generally fullscreen.
- **Sticky Header**: Allows you to enable or disable the sticky header. This blocks the header part of the template – where the logo and the menu are displayed – while scrolling.
- **Back-to-top Link**: Allows you to choose whether or not to show a link to go back to the top of the page. This is useful when it is a long page.

In *Figure 12.10*, you can see what the original version of the Cassiopeia template looked like.

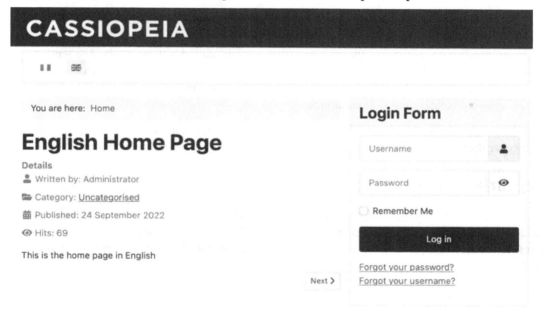

Figure 12.10 – Cassiopeia template, standard configuration

We then uploaded a custom logo, specified a tagline, selected a different remote font, and applied an alternative color scheme. In *Figure 12.11*, you can see the results of the changes to the template.

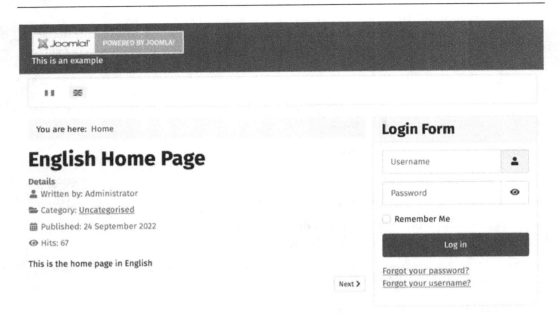

Figure 12.11 – Cassiopeia template, alternative color scheme, custom logo

In this section, we have explored the customization options offered by Cassiopeia. As mentioned earlier, the number and type of options offered may vary depending on the template. In *Chapter 15, Template Frameworks*, we'll see that some templates offer a wide number of customization features, including layout builders and style variations.

We have completed the exploration of the Cassiopeia template options. In the next section, we're going to discover the features dedicated to backend templates and their customization options.

Exploring backend templates

The same features seen in the template manager for frontend templates apply to backend templates, including template file and folder modification functionality and style management options. You can access the backend template management screen by clicking on **Administrator Templates** in **System Dashboard**, as shown in *Figure 12.12*.

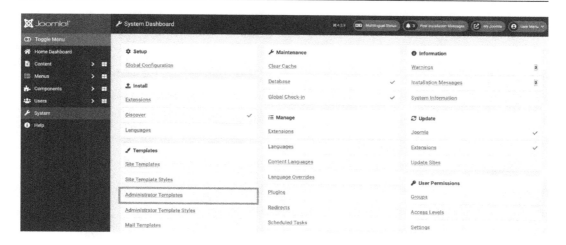

Figure 12.12 – System Dashboard | Administrator Templates

You will then see the list of installed backend templates. By default – and in most installations – you will see only one template, *Atum*, as shown in *Figure 12.13*.

Figure 12.13 – Templates | Administrator Templates

You can open the template's list of files and folders by clicking on the name of the template, as shown in *Figure 12.14*.

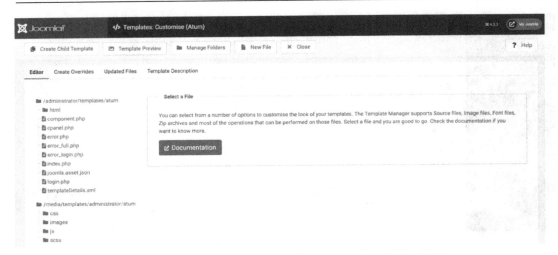

Figure 12.14 – Administrator Templates | Atum Details and Files | Editor

The available features are the same as those offered for frontend templates. In fact, you can edit each of the template's files directly online, you can click on **New File** to create new files and folders within the template structure, go to the **Create Overrides** tab to create an override, or click on **Create Child Template** to create a child template.

Going back to **System Dashboard**, let's now discover the backend template style features by clicking on the **Administrator Template Styles** link.

You can then see the list of backend template styles, as shown in *Figure 12.15*.

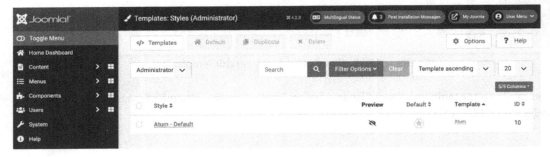

Figure 12.15 – Templates | Administrator Template Styles

In the list of template styles, click on the name of the style – **Atum - Default** – under Style to open the customization options offered by the template, as shown in *Figure 12.16*.

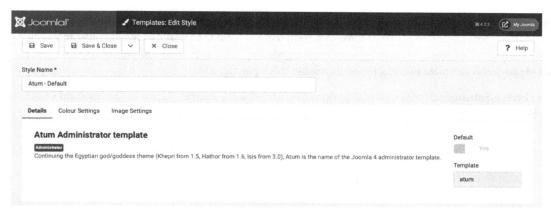

Figure 12.16 – Templates | Administrator Template Styles | Atum - Default

The number and name of the available tabs may vary depending on the template.

On the screen shown in *Figure 12.16*, we can see the name of the style, its description, whether it is set as **Default**, and the name of the template to which the style belongs.

The Atum template offers the following two tabs of options:

- One related to colors

- One related to images

Let's start exploring the options of the **Colour Settings** tab, shown in *Figure 12.17*.

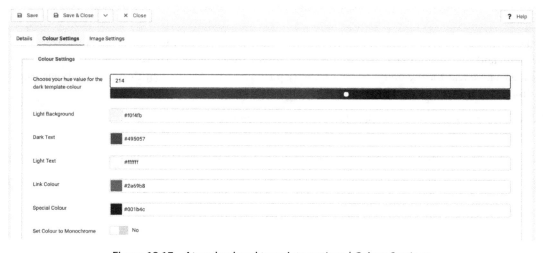

Figure 12.17 – Atum backend template options | Colour Settings

All the options available in the tab allow you to change the color used in the backend template. Default colors have been chosen to ensure **WCAG-AA** compliance so that the website backend is also accessible to users who suffer from different types of color blindness. You can even disable all colors, setting the whole backend template to use a monochromatic color palette.

The **Image Settings** tab offers several options to customize the images shown in the backend of the website. Those options are organized into several groups.

The first group of controls is related to **Login Logo**, as shown in *Figure 12.18*.

Figure 12.18 – Atum backend template | Image Settings | Login Logo settings

You can upload a custom logo/image in **Image,** which is shown on the login page of the website backend, and specify an image description in the **Image Description (Alt Text)** field that is used as the alternative text for the image for accessibility purposes. The **No Description** option allows you to disable the image description.

The second group of options is related to brand logo, as shown in *Figure 12.19*.

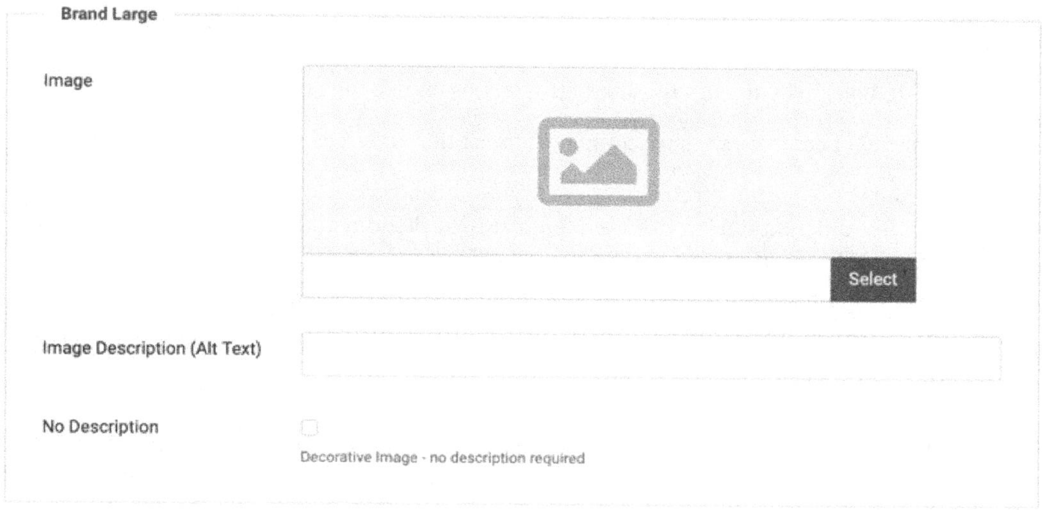

Figure 12.19 – Atum backend template | Image Settings | Brand Large logo settings

Image here logo replaces the Joomla logo in the website backend. It's useful to customize the logo for large websites and intranets so that you have a white-label system. Again, you can set up a description for the logo using **Image Description (Alt Text)** or disable the alternative text.

The options of the last group are related to **Brand Small**, as displayed in *Figure 12.20*.

Figure 12.20 – Atum backend template | Image Settings | Brand Small settings

Image in **Brand Small** replaces the Joomla logo on the website backend when the sidebar menu is collapsed with a small, square image. Also, in this case, it is possible to specify a description in **Image Description (Alt Text)** to be used as the alternative text or disable the description.

With this last group of controls, we have completed the options offered by the Atum template.

Going back to the list of administrator template styles, it is possible to duplicate, edit, and delete template styles. But differently from frontend templates, backend template styles can be set as the default for the whole backend and not assigned to specific pages or menu items.

In the next section, we will discover how to see the positions offered by a template.

Template positions

Each template offers several module positions, depending on its layout. You can find out which positions are available in a specific template by checking its developer's documentation or using the dedicated feature in the Joomla backend.

To preview the positions from the website backend, we need to enable the functionality first. In **System Dashboard**, click on the **Site Templates Styles** link, then on **Options**.

We need to enable the **Preview Module Positions** option, highlighted in *Figure 12.21*.

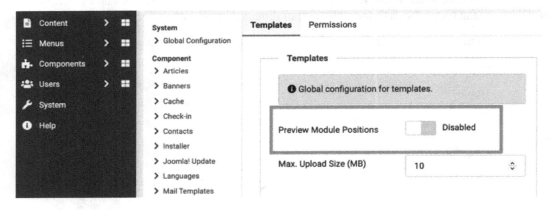

Figure 12.21 – Templates | Options

Click on **Save and Close** to go back to the styles page. You will now see an icon near each template style in the **Preview** column, as shown in *Figure 12.22*.

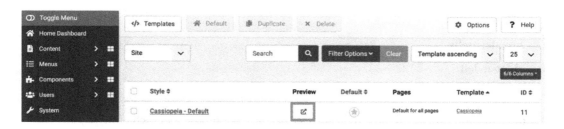

Figure 12.22 – Templates | Template Styles | Preview link

By clicking on the **Preview** link, you will see a page that shows all the module positions available in the template, as in *Figure 12.23*.

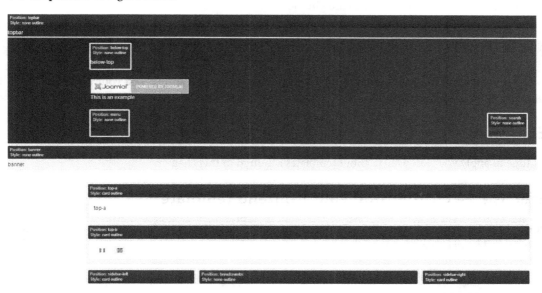

Figure 12.23 – Templates – module positions preview

As you can see in the screenshot, there are many module positions in the Cassiopeia template, as follows:

- **topbar**
- **below-top**
- **menu**
- **search**
- **banner**
- **top-a**

- **top-b**
- **breadcrumbs**
- **sidebar-left**
- **sidebar-right**

There are also many other positions. You can place one or more modules in each of those positions.

> **How to view module positions**
>
> You can check the module positions by adding the `?tp=1` string to the URL of your website or page, for example, `https://mysite.tld/?tp=1`, when the **Preview Module Positions** option is enabled in your website configuration.
>
> It's generally recommended to keep the **Preview Module Positions** preview option disabled, to prevent other people from discovering which positions are available in your template.

We have completed the exploration of the template management features. Test your knowledge of templates with the proposed exercises.

Exercises

It's time to apply your knowledge about templates acquired in this chapter.

Exercise 1 – customizing your frontend template

In this exercise, you are required to customize the default template style for your site, upload your logo, and add a personal tagline:

1. Open **System Dashboard** on your website.
2. Click on **Site Templates Styles** and open the **Cassiopeia – Default** style.
3. In the **Advanced** tab, enable the **Brand** option and upload an image in the **Logo** field.
4. Specify some text in the **Title** field. You may type your full name.
5. Type some text of your choice in the **Tagline** field. Remember that this text will be displayed right after the logo.
6. Enable the **Back-to-top Link** option and save your changes.
7. Now, look at the website frontend to check the result.

Exercise 2 – creating a new template style

In this exercise, you will create a new template style for the Cassiopeia template. Starting from the default one, you'll customize it and assign it to a specific page:

1. From the **Site Templates Style** page, select the **Cassiopeia – Default** style by checking the checkbox near the style name. Then click on the **Duplicate** button in the toolbar.

2. The new style will be automatically named **Cassiopeia – Default (2)**. Click on the style name and rename it, by typing `Cassiopeia - MyStyle` in the **Style** field.

3. In the **Advanced** tab, change the **Colour Theme** option to **Alternative**.

4. Now let's assign the template to the English home page of the website. Open the **Menu Assignment** tab and select the `English Home` menu item.

5. Now open the website frontend and navigate to the English version of the website. Then switch the language to Italian. You'll see that the template will look different between the two languages, based on the changes we've applied during the exercise.

Summary

In this chapter, we have explored the template management features of Joomla, focusing on templates and styles for both the frontend and the backend of the website. We have discovered the differences between a template and a template style. We have understood how to customize a template style, how to duplicate a style, and how to check and edit the template files.

In the next chapter, we'll go deeper into the template management functionalities, introducing overrides and how to deeply customize the style of the website.

13

Customize Everything with Overrides

In the previous chapter, we explored Joomla templates, the options to customize them, and the differences between template styles.

We'll now look at **overrides**, a feature that enhances the level of flexibility of Joomla, increasing the number of ways you can customize your website.

After reading this chapter, you will be able to do the following:

- Understand what overrides are
- Create an override for a module view
- Create an override for a component view
- Create a language override

> **Note**
> Creating overrides requires HTML, PHP, and CSS knowledge.

What is an override?

As we saw in the previous chapter, the appearance of your website highly relates to how the template is structured and styled. Sometimes you may want to customize how a specific part of the website looks, going beyond the options offered by the template style in use. Overrides help with that, allowing you to completely customize the appearance of your website through PHP, to make your website fit your styling requirements. Furthermore, overrides make you work on a copy of system files, without altering the original files, ensuring you have the opportunity to start from scratch in case of issues or when you change the template and, more importantly, preventing software updates from overwriting your changes.

Basically, with overrides, it's possible to completely rewrite all the **views** in Joomla, tailoring the appearance of any component or module output for your website.

> **What is a view?**
>
> A view is the PHP file that defines the appearance of the output of a component or a module. The view file includes the layout definition and all the page elements, such as tables, lists, and much more.

Overrides are heavily connected with templates, as for each template, it's possible to create specific overrides. When you create an override for a template, the original Joomla file for the specific view is copied to the /html folder under the template folder structure. The copy of the file under the template override folder is the one you need to edit at your convenience.

When loading a page, Joomla checks whether there is an override file for the specific layout in use and, if one exists, the override takes precedence over the standard layout.

The override system is heavily used in Joomla, in fact, most template producers distribute overrides for system standard views in their template packages so that they can provide customized layouts for core components such as articles, contacts, and categories.

In the next section, we'll discover where to use overrides and when they can be extremely helpful.

Where to use overrides

As displayed in *Figure 13.1*, Joomla provides the ability to create overrides for all elements that include a view:

- Modules
- Components
- Plugins
- Layouts

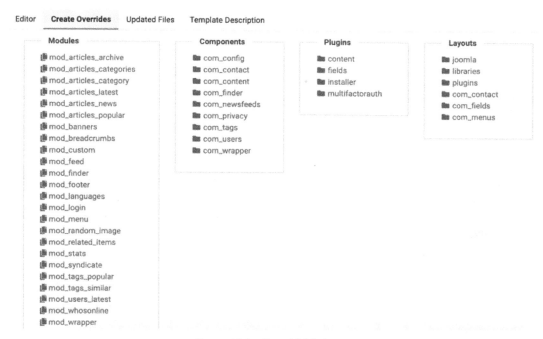

Figure 13.1 – Overridable items

This grants a high degree of flexibility, as each part visible on the public website is completely customizable.

Based on the item selected, there could be one or more views that can be customized; each view resides in a specific PHP file that will be added in the /html folder under the template in which you are creating the override.

If, on one hand, overrides increase the level of customization of your website's appearance; on the other, they can cause some files to not be up to date, as they were duplicated. To prevent missing updates, Joomla includes an interesting feature that checks automatically whether the original files of any of the overridden files have been updated, so that you can check and eventually apply changes to your files to ensure security and compatibility with the latest version of the CMS.

To check whether the files you have changed have been updated or not, on the template management screen, there is the **Updated Files** tab, as displayed in *Figure 13.2*.

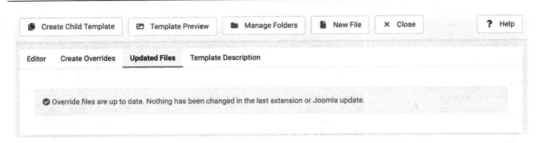

Figure 13.2 – Overrides | Updated Files

When a core or extension update involves any of the overridden files, then on the **Updated Files** screen, you can see the list of changed files. For each file, you can see the file path, the date when it was added to the list, the date the latest change occurred through updates, and the source of the update, as shown in *Figure 13.3*.

	Checked	Template File	Added to the list	Last change via Update	Update Source
☐	⊗	/html/com_contact/contact/default_form.php	2022-09-20 16:46:43	2022-10-13 11:09:45	Joomla Update
☐	⊗	/html/layouts/joomla/content/info_block.php	2022-09-20 16:46:43	2022-10-13 11:09:45	Joomla Update
☐	⊗	/html/com_contact/contact/default.php	2022-02-10 15:17:28	2022-09-20 16:46:43	Joomla Update
☐	⊗	/html/com_content/category/blog_children.php	2022-02-10 15:17:28	2022-09-20 16:46:43	Joomla Update
☐	⊗	/html/com_content/category/blog.php	2022-02-10 15:17:28	2022-09-20 16:46:43	Joomla Update
☐	⊗	/html/com_content/category/default_articles.php	2022-02-10 15:17:28	2022-09-20 16:46:43	Joomla Update
☐	⊗	/html/com_content/category/default_children.php	2022-02-10 15:17:28	2022-09-20 16:46:43	Joomla Update

Figure 13.3 – Overrides | Updated Files – List of changed files

You can check each file in the list by clicking on the file name.

If you enable the **Show Difference** toggle in the editing screen, you can see, in addition to the regular code editing box, a new box in which the changes to the file are highlighted. Removed content is highlighted in red, and added content is highlighted in green, as shown in *Figure 13.4*.

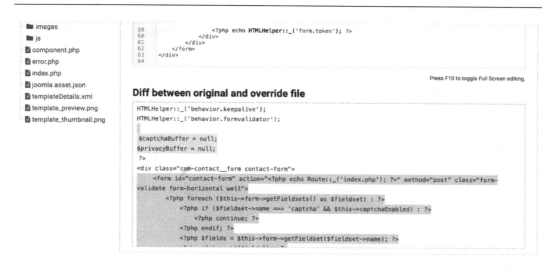

Figure 13.4 – Overrides | Updated Files | Show Difference

You can then verify each modified file to ensure it includes all the required code. After completing the operation, you can mark the file as checked by clicking on the symbol in the **Checked** column in the list of updated files. The file will be then marked as checked, as shown in *Figure 13.5*.

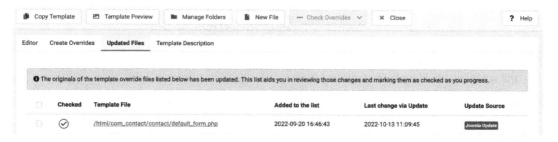

Figure 13.5 – Overrides | Updated Files | Checked file

In this way, your overrides are always up to date and kept in sync with the core updates. In the next section, we will create an override as an example.

Example – overriding the appearance of a single article

In this example, we will see overrides in action. We want to change the appearance of a single article, making our article titles rendered as an H2 header instead of H1.

Let's start creating our override:

1.   From **System Dashboard**, open **Site Templates**.

2. Since our website is using the Cassiopeia template, let's click on **Cassiopeia Details and Files**.

3. Open the **Create Overrides** tab – as shown in *Figure 13.1*.

4. In the **Components** group, click on the `com_content` folder. The list of overridable items in the group opens, as shown in *Figure 13.6*.

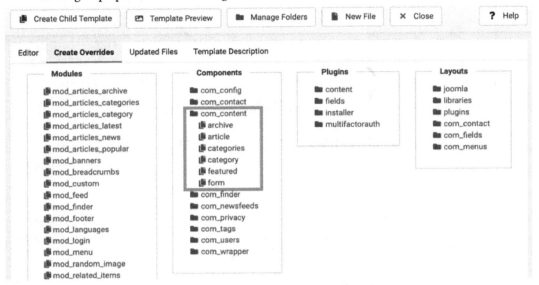

Figure 13.6 – Overrides | Create Overrides | com_content

5. From the list of overridable items in `com_content`, let's click on `article`. This represents the single article view in the frontend.

6. By clicking on `article`, the system confirms the creation of the override, displaying the path of the override files created, as in *Figure 13.7*.

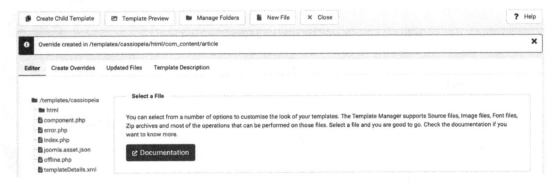

Figure 13.7 – Overrides | Create Overrides – Override creation confirmation

7. In fact, if we look at the /html/com_content/article folder of the Cassiopeia template in the **Editor** tab, we can see two files: default.php and default_links.php, as shown in *Figure 13.8*.

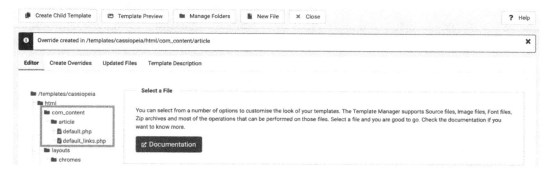

Figure 13.8 – Overrides | Override files

8. Let's open the default.php file by clicking on its name. The file opens in the code editor within the Template Manager. The code we want to edit resides in row 41 of the file, as highlighted in *Figure 13.9*.

Figure 13.9 – Overrides | File editing

9. At row 41, we replace the HTML <h1> tag with <h2> and click on the **Save & Close** button. We have created our first override – a very easy one – but that can be meaningful for SEO purposes, in certain cases.

10. Now open the website and check that the appearance of single article titles have changed to use H2 headers.

Overrides can also be used to add custom CSS class markers to page items in the template structure or to simplify the page view, removing non desired items.

> **Removing an override**
>
> If we have messed up the structure of the file or if we simply want to remove an override, we just need to delete the folder or the override file that is placed under the `html` folder of the template in use. For example, if we want to remove the override created in this tutorial, we can either remove the `/html/com_content` folder or the `/html/com_content/article/default.php` file.

In the next example, we will create an override of a module.

Example – overriding the style of a module

In this example, we want to override a module standard view. Let's work on the `mod_footer` module:

1. On the **Create Override** page (seen previously in *Figure 13.1*), let's click on **mod_footer** displayed in the **Modules** group.

2. The system will confirm the creation of the override, showing its path, as in *Figure 13.10*.

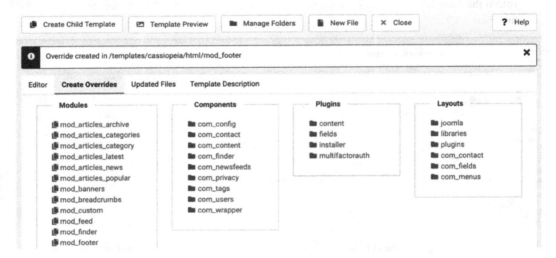

Figure 13.10 – Overrides | mod_footer override creation confirmation

3. Let's move to the **Editor** tab and navigate to the `/html/mod_footer` folder.

4. The only file in this folder is `default.php`, which we open by clicking on its name.

5. The file opens in the **Editor** tab, as shown in *Figure 13.11*.

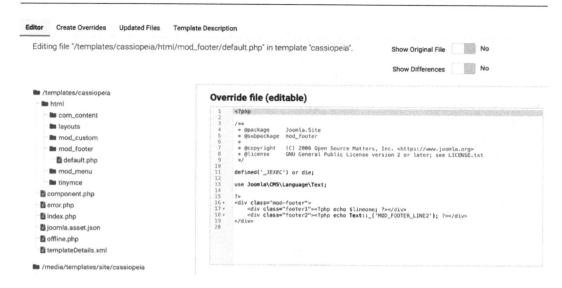

Figure 13.11 – Overrides | mod_footer override

6. Let's change the CSS class that is used to display the first line of the footer. Currently, by default, the CSS class used is `footer1`. We can change it to `myfooter` at row 17.

7. Click on **Save & Close** to save your override.

8. We now need to define our custom CSS class. To do so, in the template structure tree shown in the **Editor** tab, let's navigate to the `css` folder, as highlighted in *Figure 13.12*.

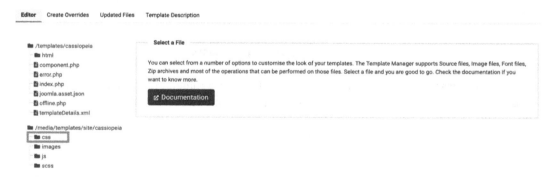

Figure 13.12 – Overrides | Template CSS folder

9. Click on the **New File** button in the toolbar. In the popup, select the `css` folder, type `custom` for **File Name** and select **.css** as **File Type**, as shown in *Figure 13.13*.

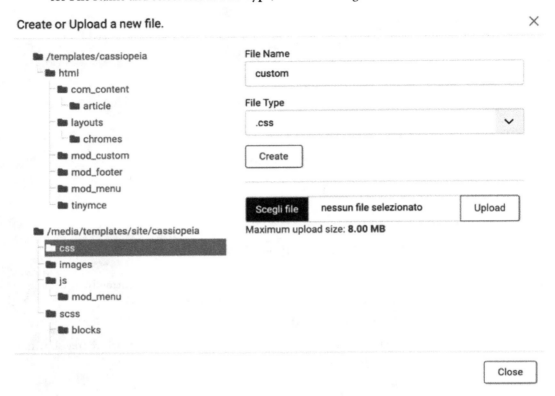

Figure 13.13 – Overrides | Creating a custom.css file

10. Click on **Create** and the file will be created in the `/css` folder. The system will open the `custom.css` file for editing right after its creation, as shown in *Figure 13.14*.

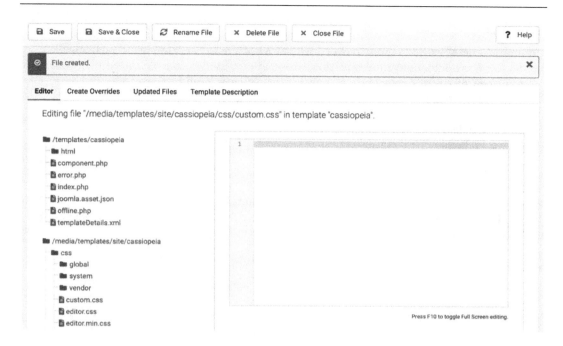

Figure 13.14 – Overrides | custom.css file editing window

11. Let's type the following rule in the custom.css file:

```
.myfooter {
  font-size: 13px;
  font-weight: 600;
  color: #1c77ba;
}
```

12. The CSS code will render the footer line that uses the myfooter CSS class in bold, 13-pixel font size and in blue. Click on **Save & Close** to apply changes and save the code.

13. Now open the website and check whether the footer is displayed with the style that we just defined. If the changes are not visible, clear your browser's cache.

> **Overriding your template CSS**
>
> In Joomla, there is a simple way to override the CSS of a template. Simply create a new file under the /css folder of your template called custom.css. Such a file can contain your customized CSS rules or completely new classes that you can recall from overrides and other Joomla items. Joomla automatically checks whether or not a custom.css file exists in the css folder of your template. If it exists, rules specified in it take priority over those of the standard template CSS files. The use of the custom.css file prevents your changes being lost while updating your templates.

In the previous examples, we explored the procedure to override a component output (single article view) and the style applied to a module (mod_footer), completing our basic overview on overrides. In the next section, we will explore another type of override that is applied to language strings: **language overrides**.

Language overrides

To complete this part about overrides, we should discuss language overrides. Sometimes you want to change some language strings to better fit your website needs. Language overrides help us with that, without the need to operate directly on original language pack files, preventing us from losing our changes while updating Joomla language files.

Language overrides allow us to modify a language string in the desired language simply from the Joomla backend.

Let's start creating our first language override:

1. From **System Dashboard**, click on the **Languages Overrides** link. The screen looks like *Figure 13.15*.

Figure 13.15 – Languages: Overrides

2. The **Languages: Overrides** page will look empty since there are no overrides that are applied generally to all languages and clients. To check active language overrides, we need to select the **Select Language & Client** option from the drop-down menu, as shown in *Figure 13.16*.

Figure 13.16 – Languages: Overrides | Select Language & Client

3. In this example, we want to change the word **Hits**, which is the visits counter shown for each article on the website frontend, as highlighted in *Figure 13.17*.

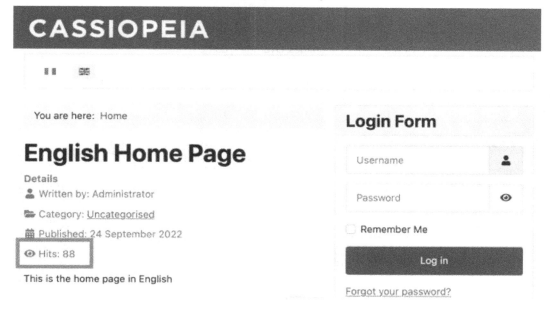

Figure 13.17 – Languages: Overrides | String to be overridden

4. To do so, let's click on **English (United Kingdom) – Site** in the **Select Language & Client** selection dropdown. Then click on the **New** button.

5. The edit override screen appears and looks like *Figure 13.18*.

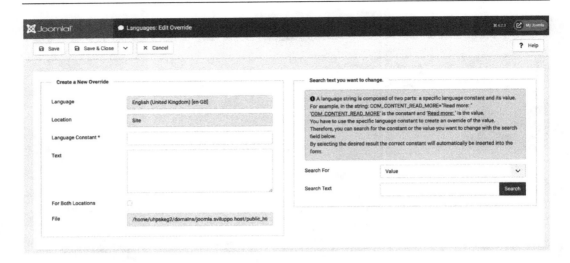

Figure 13.18 – Languages: Overrides | Edit Override

6. In the **Search Text** field, type `Hits` and click on the **Search** button. Results appear under the right column, as shown in *Figure 13.19*.

Figure 13.19 – Languages: Overrides | String search results

7. As you can see in the preceding screenshot, every language string is composed of text (that is the one shown on the website) and a constant. The constant is the unique string identifier in the system. You can search language strings either by **Value** (the visible text) or by **Constant** (the unique identifier). In this case, we select the first result, so the string identified by the constant `COM_CONTENT_ARTICLE_HITS`, by clicking on the result.

8. The left box is populated automatically with the corresponding **Language Constant** and the actual string **Text**.

9. Let's change **Text** from `Hits: %s` to `Page Views: %s`, as shown in *Figure 13.20*.

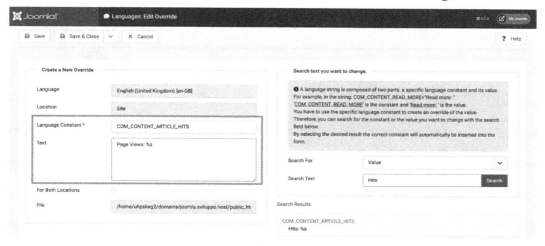

Figure 13.20 – Languages: Overrides | Create an override

10. Once done, click on the **Save & Close** button to create our override.

11. Now check the public website to see if the override is applied. Results should look like *Figure 13.21*.

Figure 13.21 – Language Overrides | A language override in action

Creating language overrides is simple and may be useful to customize how some of the strings are displayed in our website.

> **Special symbols and characters in strings**
>
> Some language strings may include special symbols and characters, such as the one we changed in the example above. The `%s` marker in a language string is replaced automatically on the website by a variable, in fact the original string was `Hits: %s` and on the website, we can see the number of hits. Be careful while creating overrides to keep all the special characters that represent variables or calculated values.

With language overrides we completed the exploration of overrides. Test your knowledge with the exercises proposed in the next section.

Exercises

It's time to apply the knowledge about overrides acquired in this chapter through the proposed exercises.

Exercise 1 – Create a module override

In this exercise, you are going to create a new override for the login module. We want to inject text into the login module once the users are logged in to warn them about the session expiration:

1. In the Cassiopeia template, create a new override for **mod_login**. In `/html/mod_login`, we can find two new files, named `default.php` and `default_logout.php`, respectively.

2. Since we want to edit the view of the module once users are logged in, we are going to edit only the `default_logout.php` file.

3. Delete the `default.php` file through the **Delete File** button.

4. Open the `default_logout.php` file and add the following code prior to line 36 of the file:

```
<p class="text-center">
Please note that your session will expire 15 minutes
after your last action.
</p>
```

5. Click on the **Save & Close** button to save your override, then open your website frontend and log in to see if your override works properly.

Exercise 2 – Create a language override

In this exercise, you are required to create a new language override.

In **Languages: Overrides**, create a new override for the **English (United Kingdom) – Site** language, changing the `Written by: %s` string to `Author: %s` on the website. To do so, you need to create an override for the string identified by the constant `COM_CONTENT_WRITTEN_BY`. Follow the steps seen in the preceding example to change the language string. Once done, save the override and check the results on the website frontend.

Summary

In this chapter, we have explored the override features of Joomla and understood how to create overrides for a component or a module view. We have also discovered a different type of override related to language files.

In the next chapter, we'll complete the presentation of the template-related features, introducing **child templates**.

Further reading

- Template Overrides – Joomla Documentation: `https://docs.joomla.org/J4.x:Template_Overrides`
- Case Study: A simplified version of Cassiopeia: `https://docs.joomla.org/J4.x:Cassiopeia_Template_Simplified_-_A_Case_Study`

14

Child Templates

In the previous chapter, we explored overrides, understanding how to customize the look of a website, as well as how to override language strings.

We'll now discover child templates, a brand-new feature introduced in Joomla 4.1 that allows you to create derived styles from a template.

After reading this chapter, you will be able to do the following:

- Understand what child templates are
- Understand the differences between child templates and overrides
- Understand the differences between child templates and duplicated templates
- Create a child template

What is a child template?

Child template management is a new feature of Joomla that allows you to create derived templates from your installed templates.

A child template is a template that uses all PHP, JavaScript, and CSS code of its parent template, inheriting all the parent template functionalities and characteristics.

The main purpose of using child templates is to prevent losing changes to the template while updating the original parent template. With a child template, you can customize the code of your template operating on the child's files, ensuring smooth updates to the parent templates.

It is also possible to amend the number and type of module positions in the child template differently from the parent template.

Does every template support child templates?

Not all Joomla templates support child templates yet. It is an optional characteristic for templates. You can check whether a template supports the creation of child templates by checking the `templateDetails.xml` manifest file, ensuring that it has the following code in it: `<inheritable>1</inheritable>`. If this string is present in the manifest file, then you can create child templates. It's also important that the template uses the `/media` folder for all static assets (images, CSS, SCSS, and JavaScript files).

A child template can be used as a normal template, but it inherits all the code from the parent template. Every part can be modified as needed using overrides. As usual, overrides take precedence over inherited code, even in child templates.

When created, a child template has only one file, called `templateDetails.xml`, which includes a reference to the parent template – for example, `<parent>cassiopeia</parent>` – indicating the parent template to which it's connected to the system. Additional files may be added through overrides as needed.

Child templates help you keep the original template files untouched. A template that supports this feature can have unlimited child templates.

Child templates are a great resource to be used when you want to do the following:

- Massively apply overrides to your template
- Differentiate your template between languages

Child templates also allow you to avoid duplicating templates when you just want to edit some files of the template, reducing the number of files to maintain.

In the next section, we'll see how to create a child template in your Joomla installation.

Creating a child template

To create a child template, open **System Dashboard** and click on **Site Templates**.

You can see whether your template supports child templates thanks to the **Parent** label next to the name of the template, as in *Figure 14.1*.

Figure 14.1 – Child templates | Support for child templates

From the list of templates, open your current frontend template. In our example, we'll use **Cassiopeia**, which supports child templates.

Click on the **Create Child Template** button in the toolbar, as highlighted in *Figure 14.2*.

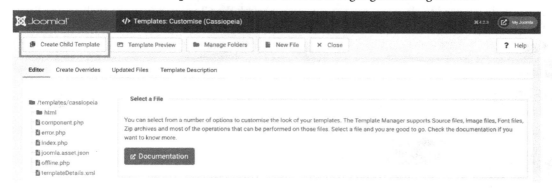

Figure 14.2 – Child templates | Create Child Template

In the pop-up window, you are requested to insert the name of the child template and to select one or more styles to be included in your child, as in *Figure 14.3*.

Figure 14.3 – Child templates | Create Child Template | Name and styles

Click on the **Create Child Template** button in the pop-up window to complete the procedure.

A message is displayed to confirm the creation of the new child template. To check the child template just created, you need to close the current template through the **Close** button in the toolbar. The list of available templates, including child templates, is displayed in *Figure 14.4*.

Figure 14.4 – Child templates | A child template

As you can see in the previous figure, the child template includes the name of the parent template in its name – in our example, where the child is called mychild, the child template is called Cassiopeia_mychild. Furthermore, under the name of the template, you can see that there is a label that marks it as **Child of Cassiopeia**, highlighting the fact that it's a child template derived from Cassiopeia.

By clicking on the name of the child template, we can explore the options and the file structure of our child template, as shown in *Figure 14.5.*

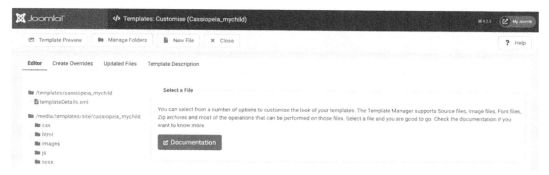

Figure 14.5 – Child templates | Manage a child template

The structure of files and folders of the child template is much simpler than the one of the parent template. In fact, it only contains `templateDetails.xml` in the `/templates/cassiopeia_mychild` folder. There is also a media folder to contain all the static assets: `/media/templates/site/cassiopeia_mychild`. This folder and its subfolders are empty – this will make our child template inherit original files from the parent template.

> **What are assets?**
>
> With assets are intended all static files: CSS, images, JavaScript, and SCSS. From Joomla 4.1 onward, assets are saved under the media folder. Older templates, which don't support child templates, have static assets saved under the main template folder.

We can add files and assets to our child template, as well as operate changes to the child definition file, by simply editing the `templateDetails.xml` file.

For example, if you want to add a new module position in your child template, just open the `templateDetails.xml` file and define your desired position, simply adding the `<position>my-position-name</position>` string in the position definition block, as highlighted in *Figure 14.6*:

Figure 14.6 – Child templates | Adding a module position to a child template

With this XML code, we added a module position called my-position-name in our child template. The position can be then used for modules of our website.

With child templates, you can also override the original template's index.php file or CSS files. Just copy them from the parent template to the child's folder and customize them as per your needs.

While creating a child template, the system also creates one or more template styles connected to the child template, according to the number of styles selected during the creation of the child, as in *Figure 14.7*.

Figure 14.7 – Child templates | Child template style

Template styles can be customized through the available options, as can be done with the parent template style, as well as set as the default template style for the website or assigned to one or more menu items, as with normal template styles.

Child templates for the backend

Child templates can also be created for backend templates that support them. Atum, the default Joomla 4 backend template, supports child templates. You can create a child template for your backend in case you want to operate massive changes and overrides so that you can benefit from the other advantages of child templates. With the child template, you create a new template style for Atum that is connected to your child template, and you can set it up as the default template for the backend of your website. Remember that in the backend, you can only assign a default template style for the whole backend interface, unlike with the frontend – you cannot assign a specific template style on a menu item basis.

In the next section, we'll talk about child templates and overrides.

Child templates and overrides

Child templates are the greatest example of overrides, and they are even more powerful than them. This is because many third-party templates include already overrides of some standard parts in the template's /html folder, and these overrides may be modified by template updates. Overrides made in child templates, instead, are safe from template and system updates, as they are in a separate position and are not altered.

In a child template, you can make all the desired overrides with all the features that we discovered in *Chapter 13, Customize Everything with Overrides*. Also, in this case, we can create overrides for **Modules**, **Components**, **Plugins**, and **Layouts**.

When you create an override in a child template, the /html folder is created automatically in the child's folder structure and, as usual, it contains all the overrides created for the child template, as in *Figure 14.8*.

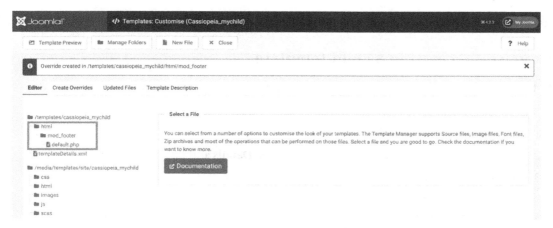

Figure 14.8 – Child templates | Overriding a child template

Overrides can be modified directly in the template manager, as we expect.

Also, in this case, you can override everything, creating a unique template for your website, and, if you don't need an override anymore, just remove the override folder. For each file that is not present in the child template, the parent template's corresponding one will be used as a fallback.

In the next section, we will explore a comparison between child templates and the option to duplicate templates.

Child templates or duplicated templates

Prior to the availability of the child templates in Joomla 4, it was a common practice to duplicate a template when you needed to heavily edit it.

Duplicating a template means creating a new template, simply copying files, folders, and assets from a template. This, however, makes the duplicated template stop receiving updates.

Furthermore, duplicating a template means having all the template files twice on the filesystem: one copy for the original template and the other copy for the duplicated template. This approach makes maintenance more difficult and time-consuming, as well as increasing the risks of leaving duplicated templates without updates applied due to fear of losing all the changes made.

Child templates, instead, host just the needed files, those files that are changed from the parent template, re-using all the other files. This is a great plus for maintenance, ensuring your website is more up-to-date and secure.

With this comparison of child templates and duplicated templates, we have completed our exploration of the child template feature. Put into practice what you have discovered with the proposed exercises.

Exercises

It's time to apply the knowledge about child templates acquired in this chapter.

Exercise 1 – creating a child template

In this exercise, you are required to create a child template in your Joomla 4 installation, using Cassiopeia as the default frontend template.

1. Open **System Dashboard** in your backend.
2. Click on **Site Templates**, and then on **Cassiopeia Details and Files**.
3. Click on **Create Child Template**, set the name to MyChild, and then click on **Create Child Template** in the popup.
4. The child template has been created. Click on the **Close** button to go back to the list of templates, and then click on **Cassiopeia_MyChild Details and Files** to open it.
5. Create a file called custom.css in the /media/templates/site/cassiopeia_mychild/css/ folder.

6. In the file, type the following CSS code (we're going to change the color of the footer that we set in *Exercise 1* of *Chapter 13*):

```
.myfooter {
  font-size: 13px;
    font-weight: 600;
  color: #FF4500;
}
```

7. Click on **Save & Close** to save the changes. Then, click on **Close**.

8. From the list of templates, click on the **Styles** button to move to the **Site Template Styles** page.

9. Set **Cassiopeia_mychild – Default** as the default template style for your website.

10. Open the website preview to check the changes. The footer text should be red.

Summary

In this chapter, we explored the **Child Templates** functionality included in Joomla. We compared child templates to template overrides and copies of the same templates.

In the next chapter, we'll explore **template frameworks** and their options.

Further reading

A deep dive into Joomla child templates – `https://magazine.joomla.org/all-issues/may-2022/a-deep-dive-into-joomla-child-templates`

15
Template Frameworks

In the previous chapter, we explored **child templates**, one of the newest features included in Joomla.

We'll now complete the discovery of template-related features presenting some of the major template frameworks available for Joomla.

Template frameworks are special frontend templates that include a layout builder and offer a wide series of customization options, including color palettes, fonts, module styles, and much more. They allow you to build rich and complex layouts without advanced coding skills.

After reading this chapter, you will be able to do the following:

- Understand what a template framework is
- Understand how to build a custom layout in Joomla
- Know the most used template frameworks

What is a template framework?

As mentioned in the introduction of this chapter, template frameworks allow you to build rich layouts for your website, offering many options and controls, and making the customization completely visual. With a template framework, almost no CSS/JS/PHP coding skills are required.

From a technical perspective, template frameworks are distributed as normal templates that can be installed through the extension installer feature of the Joomla backend. Sometimes, they are distributed in bundles with additional plugins or as a **package** that includes the template installation files, together with the plugin or module installation files.

Template frameworks generally offer a **layout builder** that implements the 12-column Bootstrap grid, so that you can create new module positions and reallocate all the other module positions everywhere in the layout grid, visually, simply by moving and resizing positions.

Template frameworks provide multiple default configuration sets that allow you to change the website color palette or font type. They also provide options to customize font type and size, colors, menu type, site logo, and much more.

Many template frameworks also offer the possibility to inject custom JavaScript and CSS code, through specific fields in their configuration panel. They also provide options to integrate third-party services such as comments, social networks, and analytics services.

Furthermore, template frameworks often include options to optimize the website, compress CSS and JS files, minify assets, optimize images, and much more.

In the next section, we'll analyze the advantages of using a template framework.

Why use a template framework

Using a template framework brings many benefits, allowing normal users to create stunning layouts and frontend experiences. Let's explore the major advantages of using one:

- Build a completely custom frontend layout with ease
- Add and resize module positions everywhere
- Customize colors, fonts, backgrounds, logos, and favicons
- Enable/disable advanced features with a few clicks
- Customize the whole template starting from a solid and fully responsive base
- No need to write complex PHP/JavaScript/CSS code
- Compatible with all major browsers out of the box
- Build a custom multi-level mega menu in a visual way (where supported)

Some template frameworks implemented their version of child templates, far before Joomla's core implementation, which we explored in *Chapter 14, Child Templates*.

Other template frameworks also implement some additional features, such as blocks that allow you to insert specific features, for example, slideshows, accordions, media galleries, maps, social media icons, and so on.

At the same time, using a template framework may bring some side effects in terms of performance and additional dependencies, and may not support all the Joomla extensions.

> **Consider potential vendor lock-in**
>
> Even though predefined blocks can be useful to build a wonderful template with ease, pay attention that vehiculating most of your website structure or content through these template-specific blocks may require additional efforts in case you want to change the template at some point. The use of modules and module positions in the template layout allows you to change the template more easily, as you can reuse modules and positions in other templates.

Let's now get to know which are the most used template frameworks for Joomla.

Most used template frameworks

Template frameworks are often embedded into commercial templates. It's very common to find commercial templates that are based on and include one of the most used template frameworks.

This is also because major template studios have developed their own template frameworks, on which they based their template production.

Furthermore, template frameworks providers also developed page builder extensions, which allow you to build pages in Joomla without even using articles and other components, customizing the whole page visually.

> **Template frameworks versus page builders**
>
> Template frameworks are special types of templates that allow you to completely customize your website layout and appearance with ease. Once configured, the template shows the contents of your website: articles, categories, component output, and much more.
>
> A page builder, instead, allows you to build and design a single page. With a page builder, you can define the layout of a page, placing modules, contents, and pieces that are predesigned and available in the extension, such as media galleries, accordions and tabs controls, embedded maps, and so on. Some template frameworks include a page builder, as well as some others that support one or more page builders. A page builder can also be used when using a regular template not based on any specific framework.

There are many template frameworks available for Joomla 4 and they offer a wide set of features and options. Among others, the most known and used are as follows:

- Helix Ultimate by JoomShaper
- T4 Framework by JoomlArt
- Gantry by RocketTheme

In the next sections, we'll see some of these template frameworks in action, starting with JoomShaper's Helix Ultimate.

Example – Helix Ultimate

Helix Ultimate is the second generation of template frameworks developed by JoomShaper, a leading extension and template provider.

Helix Ultimate is a fully responsive, mobile-first template, based on Bootstrap 5. It allows you to design your website in a visual way, presenting a real-time preview of the website while configuring it, so that you can easily check the impact of your actions.

Helix Ultimate offers a *drag and drop* layout builder so that you can create your custom layout, defining rows and column sizes and properties, granting you granular control over all the aspects of your website structure. It allows you to set the font size and colors, upload and adjust logo and website headers with a few clicks, and test your website preview at the different view sizes by simulating different device screen sizes.

It provides you with several predefined style options that you can activate or change as you wish, offering unlimited design combinations.

Helix Ultimate integrates a mega-menu builder, with which you can create a multi-level and composite navigation system for your website. Furthermore, you can enrich your mega menu by adding modules (e.g., the Login module or custom modules) to make your website's menu unique.

It also implements an off-canvas menu, which is used on mobile screens and is completely customizable so that you can provide a rich navigation experience to your mobile users.

Helix Ultimate offers a wide number of options to choose your desired font face, size, and color. It implements advanced blog styling tools, such as image resizing features and comment management functionalities. It also supports the import/export of the configuration of the template, making it easy to replicate the design on another website.

Helix Ultimate is available free of charge from the JoomShaper website and integrates complete support for SP Page Builder, which is the page builder extension developed by the same company.

In the next section, we'll see how to install Helix Ultimate.

Installing Helix Ultimate

Helix Ultimate is made up of two installation packages:

- A template
- A system plugin

To install it, download the latest version from the developer website, then install the template through **System Dashboard | Install – Extensions | Upload Package File**, simply by dragging and dropping the installation file. Repeat the procedure for the Helix system plugin. The system plugin is active by default after the installation. Let's now explore the Helix Ultimate template.

Customizing with Helix Ultimate

To start customizing your website using Helix Ultimate, open the **Site Template Style** page from **System Dashboard**, then click on the **shaper_helixultimate – Default** template style. The main page, as shown in *Figure 15.1*, shows a big green button (**Template Options**), which opens the framework configuration page, and the **Menu Assignment** tab, from which you can assign the template style to the menu items:

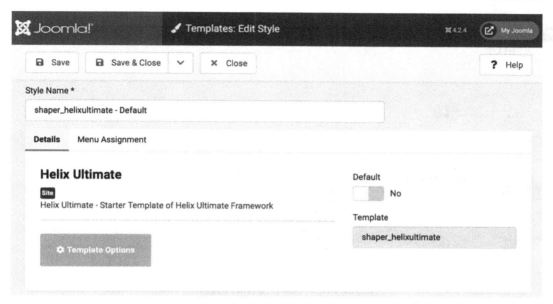

Figure 15.1 – Helix Ultimate | Templates: Edit Style

Let's click on the **Template Options** button to see all the customization controls offered by Helix Ultimate. The website preview is opened with a floating menu from which you can access all the commands.

The **Basic** menu item – shown in *Figure 15.2* – allows you to do the following:

- Specify your website logo
- Choose a structure layout for your website header
- Decide whether to use a fluid or boxed layout
- Implement social media icons
- Display copyright and a link to the top in the footer
- Customize the error page
- Enable the Coming Soon mode

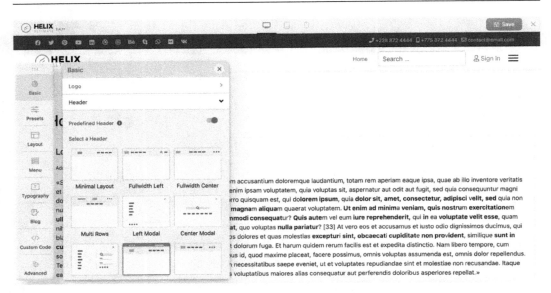

Figure 15.2 – Helix Ultimate | Basic

At the top of the page, there is a toolbar that shows the logo of Helix Ultimate and the version in use, the controls to emulate different screen sizes (desktop, tablet, and mobile), and the buttons to save and close the screen.

The main part of the screen is occupied by the preview of the website with the Helix Ultimate template style applied.

The **Presets** menu item opens the color palette options. From the page, you can pick one of the default predefined sets of colors or enable the **Custom Style** option, which allows you to pick your desired color for each of the styled elements, as shown in *Figure 15.3*:

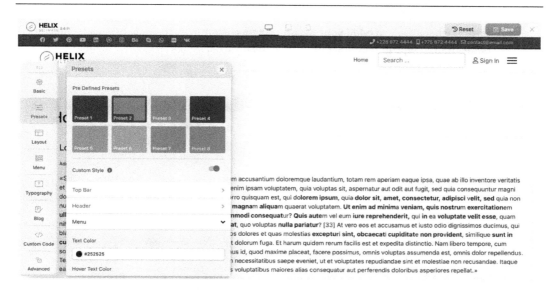

Figure 15.3 – Helix Ultimate | Presets

The **Layout** screen allows you to build your custom layout for your website, as shown in *Figure 15.4*. Here, you can create and change the rows and columns where to place module positions, as per your needs. The layout builder is based on the 12-column Bootstrap grid and allows you to specify custom CSS IDs and classes for each part:

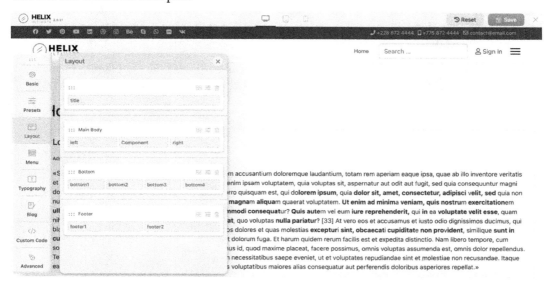

Figure 15.4 – Helix Ultimate | Layout

The **Menu** screen is where you can build your website menu, customizing the style of each menu item. You can select the desired type of menu, set the size of the drop-down menu (for submenus), and the animation, as shown in *Figure 15.5*:

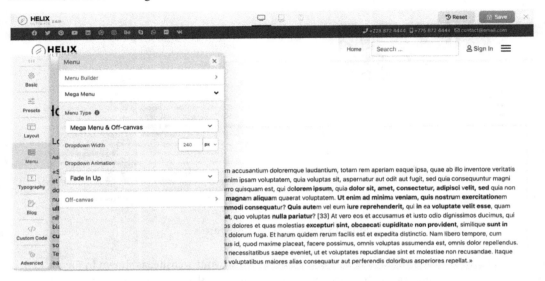

Figure 15.5 – Helix Ultimate | Menu

From the same screen, you can also set the options for the **Off-canvas** menu that is shown on mobile screens. Furthermore, Helix Ultimate allows you to build a rich mobile menu, integrating login features, social icons, contact details, and much more.

From the **Typography** page, as shown in *Figure 15.6*, you can customize the **Font** family, including the size and weight of the text of your website, having the chance to set options independently for each type of text – headers, menu items, and contents:

Figure 15.6 – Helix Ultimate | Typography

The **Blog** screen, among others, offers options to enrich your articles defining different image sizes and the ability to crop them to a specific size, as shown in *Figure 15.7*:

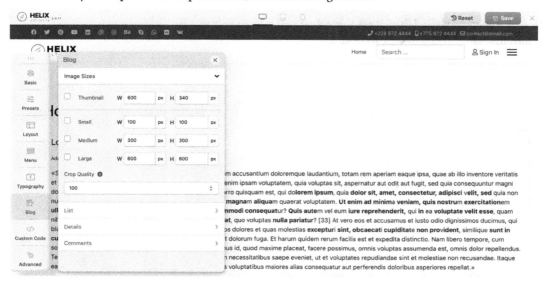

Figure 15.7 – Helix Ultimate | Blog

The **List** and **Details** tabs on the same page allow you to set the size of the image to be shown in the different article layouts. Helix Ultimate also integrates with some external comment services, such as Disqus, IntenseDebate, and Facebook.

The **Custom Code** page allows you to insert custom code in your template in a different place of the page code markup, as shown in *Figure 15.8*:

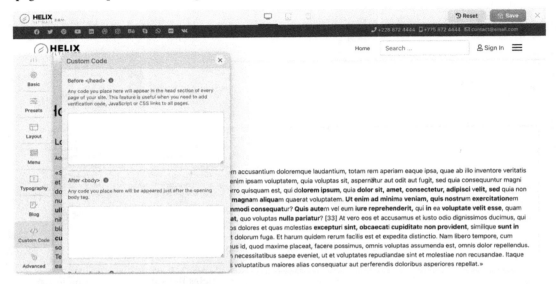

Figure 15.8 – Helix Ultimate | Custom Code

The last screen of Helix Ultimate is the **Advanced** page, as shown in *Figure 15.9*, which includes options that allow you to do the following:

- Compress CSS and JS files
- Compile CSS as SCSS
- Enable/disable FontAwesome and Google Fonts
- Enable/disable image lazy loading
- Import/export the configuration
- Specify your Google Analytics 4 tracking code

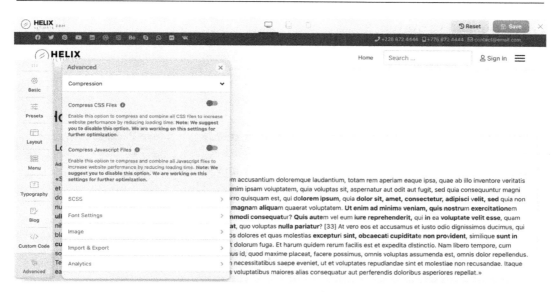

Figure 15.9 – Helix Ultimate | Advanced

Once you have completed all the desired changes to the template, you need to save them by clicking on **Save** in the toolbar, then close it by clicking on the **X** symbol. To check your website with the Helix Ultimate framework, mark it as the default template style for your website and open your website frontend.

With all these options and the real-time preview, Helix Ultimate is one of the most used template frameworks and it's also used as the base for many commercial templates.

In the next section, we'll explore the T4 Framework by JoomlArt.

Example – T4 Framework

T4 Framework is a template framework developed by JoomlArt, one of the largest Joomla template and extension development companies. T4 Framework is a complete template framework that includes a layout builder, a mega-menu designer, and a wide range of controls to customize your website appearance.

It's available in two releases, a Bootstrap 4 version and a Bootstrap 5 one. It integrates FontAwesome and Google Fonts and allows you to work on any page item, from text style to colors, from module positions, names, and sizes to their background options.

T4 Framework offers tools to optimize your template speed, combining and minifying JavaScript and CSS files, as well as editors to work on CSS and SCSS.

In the next section, we'll explore how to install and use T4 Framework.

Installing T4 Framework

T4 Framework is distributed through two packages:

- The template
- The system plugin installation files

Install the template through **System Dashboard | Install – Extensions | Upload Package File**, simply by dragging and dropping the installation file. Repeat the procedure for the T4 system plugin. The system plugin is active by default after the installation. Let's now work on our template.

Customizing with T4 Framework

To start customizing your website using T4 Framework, open the **Site Template Style** page from **System Dashboard**, then click on **t4_bs5_blank – Default** (which is the name of the T4 blank template based on Bootstrap 5).

The T4 Framework management screen will look like *Figure 15.10*:

Figure 15.10 – T4 Framework | Overview

As displayed in the previous figure, the Framework page differs from the regular Joomla backend for its setup and offers specific options and configuration panels. The **Overview** page shows the style name and some information about the template and shows a preview of the website with the template applied on the right side of the page.

On the top bar, there are buttons to preview the website at different sizes (desktop, tablet, and mobile), save the changes, open the public website, and close the page.

On the left side, we can find the menu to go through all the options offered by the framework: **Site Settings**, **Navigation**, **Theme Color**, **Layout Settings**, **Global Settings**, **Menu Assignment**, and **Tools**. T4 Framework is also available with a Dark Mode to save energy and reduce eye fatigue.

On the **Site Settings** page, as shown in *Figure 15.11*, you can find controls to do the following:

- Set the site name

- Set the site slogan (or subtitle)

- Upload the site logo for desktop and mobile

- Customize the website's typography: font style, color, and size

- Customize page appearance, through background color or images

- Set up author configuration for articles, set whether to show a link to the **Author** page or not, and avatar settings

- Implement a website favicon

Figure 15.11 – T4 Framework | Site Settings

The **Navigation** page shows a series of options to configure your website's main menu, offering a flexible mega menu, as shown in *Figure 15.12*.

There are also controls to set up the **Offcanvas** menu for mobile devices and act on menu breakpoints, making your design respond to your needs:

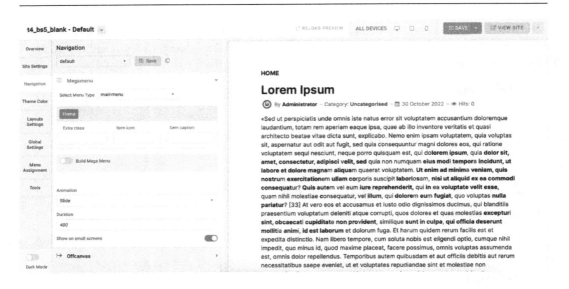

Figure 15.12 – T4 Framework | Navigation

The **Theme Color** page collects all the color-related controls, allowing you to choose the desired color for the background, text, links, menu items, and much more, as shown in *Figure 15.13*:

Figure 15.13 – T4 Framework | Theme Color

On the **Layout Settings** page, as shown in *Figure 15.14*, you can build your page layout by customizing rows and columns, creating and modifying module positions, adding new sections, and much more:

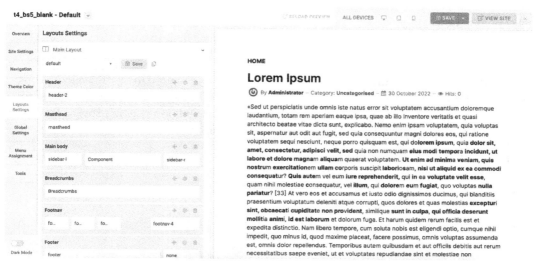

Figure 15.14 – T4 Framework | Layout Settings

On the **Global Settings** page, as shown in *Figure 15.15*, you can find controls to do the following:

- Choose the frontend template editor style
- Enable/disable the CSS and JS optimization features with any eventual exclusion
- Inject custom PHP/CSS/JS code in your template in different positions
- Enable/disable template add-ons, such as FontAwesome and **IcoMoon**
- Enable/disable **OpenGraph**

Figure 15.15 – T4 Framework | Global Settings

The **Menu Assignment** page, as with all the other Joomla templates, allows you to choose which menu the template style should be assigned to. The **Tools** page includes a built-in editor to operate on CSS and SCSS template files, directly from your website backend.

Once you have completed all the desired changes to the template, you need to save them by clicking on **Save and Close** in the toolbar. To check your website with the T4 Framework, mark it as the default template style for your website and open your website frontend. Building a custom template for your website using T4 Framework is very easy thanks to all the visual controls and options.

In the next section, we'll explore the Gantry template framework.

Example – Gantry

The last template framework we'll get to know in this chapter is Gantry, developed by one of the most known Joomla template studios: RocketTheme.

Gantry is an open source, fast, and lightweight template framework that integrates an easy-to-use layout manager, mega-menu support with a visual editor, and a powerful particle system. Particles are simple blocks that can be imported and placed anywhere in your template.

Gantry implements a built-in way to handle overrides and allows you to have template styles derived from a base template. It's a similar implementation to child templates, which we explored in *Chapter 14, Child Templates*, but it's template specific.

Let's see how to install the Gantry template framework.

Installing the Gantry framework

Gantry is distributed through three packages:

- The Gantry component
- Two template installation files: Helium theme and Hydrogen theme

Install the component first through **System Dashboard | Install – Extensions | Upload Package File**, simply by dragging and dropping the installation file. Then, repeat the procedure for the two template installation files.

Customizing with Gantry

To start customizing your website using the Gantry framework, click on **Gantry 5 Themes** from the **Components** menu, then on **Available Themes**. There, you can find the two themes installed: **Helium** and **Hydrogen**, as shown in *Figure 15.16*:

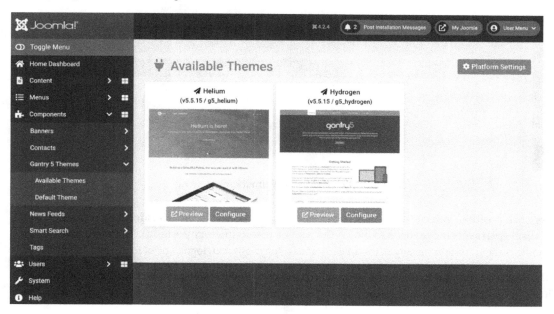

Figure 15.16 – Gantry | Available Themes

In this example, we will explore the Helium theme. Let's click on **Configure** to see the template configuration screen.

The setup screen shows the **Base Outline** style of the Helium theme. This represents the master style for the template, serving as the parent template, which is inherited by the child styles. The **Layout** tab shows the page, as shown in *Figure 15.17*, allowing you to build your template layout acting on module positions, rows, and columns of the page:

Figure 15.17 – Gantry | Helium theme | Layout

For each position, you can define the name, options, and styles. In the left sidebar, you can find the available particles (the predefined blocks that can be placed in every position). There are particles to handle content, system messages, module instances, copyright text, logos, social icons, and much more.

The **Styles** tab allows you to choose between color presets and to customize the color of each template item: body, titles, links, background, and so on, as shown in *Figure 15.18*:

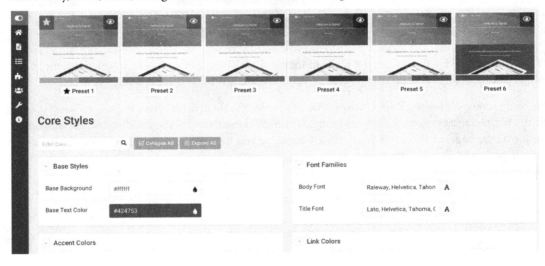

Figure 15.18 – Gantry | Helium theme | Styles

The **Page Settings** tab, shown in *Figure 15.19*, allows you to enable some services like Font Awesome, and customize the favicon, page meta tags, and page attributes, among other options:

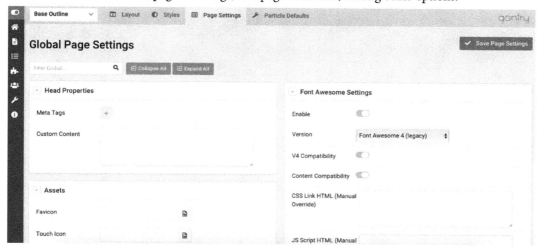

Figure 15.19 – Gantry | Helium theme | Page Settings

From the **Particle Defaults** page, you can set the default values for some particles, such as the copyright text, the logo, and some options that are applied globally throughout the template, as shown in *Figure 15.20*:

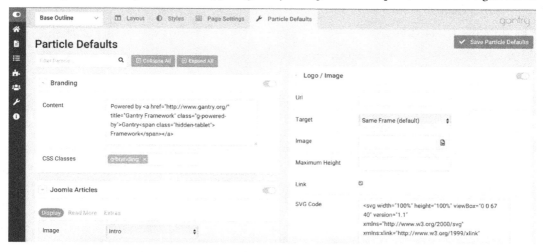

Figure 15.20 – Gantry | Helium theme | Particle Defaults

Once you have completed the setup of **Base Outline**, you can work on the specific styles, which Gantry calls **theme outlines**. Theme outlines are like child templates: they inherit everything from the base outline and allow you to customize any aspect, including layout, styles, page settings, and particle values. Theme outlines can be assigned to menu items, as we normally do with template styles.

Gantry also includes a menu editor, which is available by clicking on the **Menu** button in the toolbar, as highlighted in *Figure 15.21*:

Figure 15.21 – Gantry | Helium theme | Menu

The Gantry menu editor allows you to easily build your custom mega menu for your website by simply dragging and dropping menu items as well as particles, as shown in *Figure 15.22*:

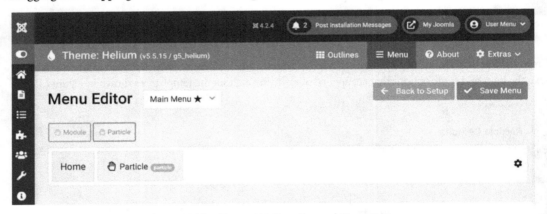

Figure 15.22 – Gantry | Helium theme | Menu Editor

When you insert a particle in the menu, you can choose which particle you want to add from a pop-up window, as shown in *Figure 15.23*:

Figure 15.23 – Gantry | Helium theme | Menu Editor | Particle selection

Once completed, save the menu and the work on the template. It's time to assign a theme outline to one or more menu items – or as site default – and check your website frontend. Gantry is very powerful with its rich configuration features and built-in particles.

With Gantry, we have completed the exploration of three of the most used Joomla template frameworks. Test your knowledge with the exercises contained in the next section.

Exercises

It's time to apply the knowledge you acquired in this chapter about template frameworks.

Exercise 1 – Use a template framework

In this exercise, you are required to install the Helix Ultimate template framework and build a simple layout with it:

1. Download and install the latest version of Helix Ultimate (template and plugin) from this page: https://www.joomshaper.com/downloads/template/helixultimate.

2. Install the template first, then the plugin from your website's backend.

3. From **System Dashboard** | **Site Template Styles**, open the **shaper_helixultimate – Default** style.

4. Click on **Template Options**.

5. Upload your logo and favicon from the **Basic** page.

6. Enable **Boxed Layout** from **Basic** | **Body**.

7. On the **Typography** page, enable the **Body** option and choose **Georgia** as the font, set the weight to **Normal**, and the font size to **12px**.

8. Save the changes and close the page.

9. On the **Site Template Styles** page, select **shaper_helixultimate – Default** and mark it as the default template style for your website by clicking on the **Default** button in the toolbar.

10. Now, open the website frontend and check the template you created.

Summary

In this chapter, we understood what a template framework is in Joomla and how it can help build a custom design for a website, without having coding and development skills. We've explored three of the most used template frameworks – Helix Ultimate, T4 Framework, and Gantry – getting to know their setup and configuration options.

In the next chapter, we'll explore some advanced security features, including **multifactor authentication**, and other functionalities to increase your website security.

Resources

- Helix Ultimate framework: `https://www.joomshaper.com/helix`
- T4 Framework: `https://www.joomlart.com/t4-framework`
- Gantry template framework: `https://gantry.org`

16
Advanced Features – Access and Security

In the previous chapter, we explored **template frameworks** for Joomla, understanding the ways to easily build a custom design for our website, without the need for coding skills.

We'll now look at some advanced features of Joomla dedicated to website access and security. We'll explore the multi-factor authentication functionality, the **WebAuthn** authentication option, and the HTTP headers management feature.

After reading this chapter, you will be able to do the following:

- Strengthen the security of your website through HTTP headers
- Enable multi-factor authentication for your website's users
- Set up webAuthn authentication for your website

Let's start by exploring WebAuthn authentication.

Setting up passwordless authentication for your website

Joomla 4 introduced the possibility to log in to your website through **WebAuthn** authentication. WebAuthn is the **W3C Web Authentication** method and allows you to implement a passwordless login using a FIDO2 or FIDO U2F authenticator, which can be either physical or virtual. Examples of authenticators that are supported include Windows Hello, Apple TouchID, Apple FaceID, and others.

Let's learn how to enable passwordless authentication in Joomla:

1. From the **System Dashboard** area, click on **Plugins**.
2. In the search box, type WebAuthn; then, press *Enter*.
3. Click on the **System – WebAuthn Passwordless Login** plugin.

4. Enable the plugin by changing its **Status** to **Enabled**, as shown in *Figure 16.1*, and click on **Save & Close**:

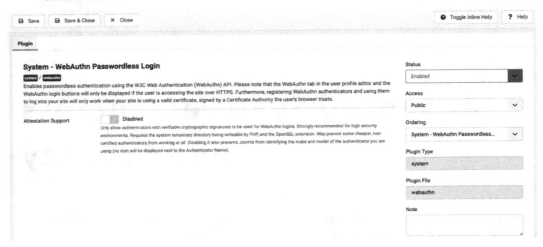

Figure 16.1 – System – WebAuthn Passwordless Login

As you can see, the plugin has an option – disabled by default – to increase the security of the website, allowing additional verification of the HTTPS certificate in use.

5. Click on **User Menu** (at the top right of the screen), then on **Edit Account**.

6. You will see a new tab called **W3C Web Authentication (WebAuthn) Login** on the user account page, as displayed in *Figure 16.2*. From this page, you can complete the WebAuthn onboarding process:

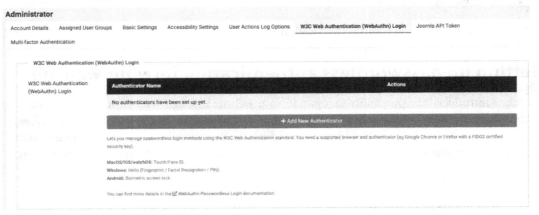

Figure 16.2 – User Edit | W3C Web Authentication (WebAuthn) Login

7. To start the onboarding process, click on the **Add New Authenticator** button.

8. Then, if you are using a device that supports **FIDO2** or **FIDO U2F**, your system will prompt the authentication setup screen. For example, on a macOS that supports TouchID, you will be requested to authenticate with your fingerprint to continue with the setup.

9. Once done, the authenticator will be listed on the WebAuthn page, as shown in *Figure 16.3*:

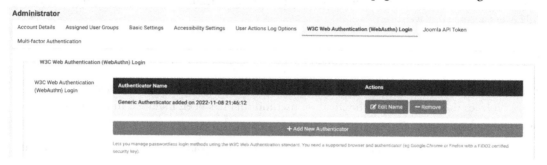

Figure 16.3 – User Edit | WebAuthn | Authenticator Saved

10. To test our new passwordless authentication, let's log out from the backend. Then, on the login screen, only type your username and click on the **Web Authentication** button, as shown in *Figure 16.4*:

Figure 16.4 – Login screen | Web Authentication button

11. The system will now prompt the authentication request through a fingerprint or other means, based on the authenticator configured.

With these few steps, we set up passwordless authentication on our website. Each user may set up their WebAuthn authentication on their user profile, regardless of whether they are backend or frontend users.

In the next section, we'll explore the multi-factor authentication features that help strengthen security while users access your website.

Multi-factor authentication

Since Joomla 4.2, the CMS offers out-of-the-box support for multi-factor authentication. This new feature replaces the two-factor authentication method that has been included in Joomla for years since version 3.x.

Multi-factor authentication is a way to strengthen the security of your website, allowing an additional level of verification while users log in to the website.

Multi-factor authentication occurs in two separate steps: the users insert their login credentials (username and password) and then they are requested to execute the additional validation via one of the supported methods.

Natively, Joomla offers multiple authentication validation methods:

- Verification code
- YubiKey
- Web authentication
- Email verification
- Fixed code

For each login validation method, there is a specific plugin that can be enabled or disabled. Enabling the corresponding plugin means that the validation method can be used in multi-factor authentication.

You can find all the plugins related to multi-factor authentication by going to **System Dashboard | Plugins**, filtering by **Type**, and selecting **multifactorauth**, as shown in *Figure 16.5*.

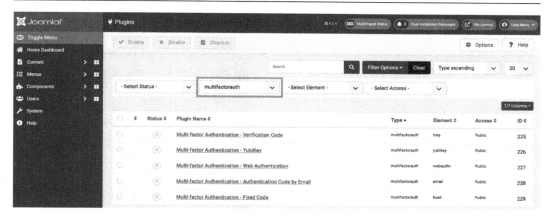

Figure 16.5 – Multi-factor authentication plugins

Let's explore such methods, one by one, starting with **Verification Code**.

Verification Code

The **Verification Code** validation method is offered through the **Multi-factor Authentication – Verification Code** plugin and is the evolution of the previous two-factor authentication plugin that's been available in Joomla for years. It is a TOTP authentication system, which allows you to connect a code-generator app such as Google Authenticator, Authy, or similar software. Once enabled, to must log in to your website. After typing in your username and password, you will be required to enter a 6-digit code generated through the authentication app.

> **TOTP authentication**
>
> **TOTP** means **Time-Based One-Time Password**. It's an authentication method that makes you use a code that is generated automatically and expires after a certain number of seconds; it can only be used once. TOTP is one of the most used multi-factor authentication methods.

This plugin doesn't have any options. To start using it, just enable it.

YubiKey

The YubiKey authentication method is offered through the **Multi-factor Authentication – YubiKey** plugin. This authentication method uses a hardware key connected to the user's device through a USB port to allow the user to log in to the website. Login would be impossible without the hardware key, so people who use this authentication method generally bring such small keys with them.

This plugin also doesn't have any options. Enabling it is enough to offer your users the opportunity to use such an authentication method.

Web Authentication

The **Web Authentication** method is offered through the **Multi-factor Authentication – Web Authentication** plugin. This method allows users to log in using W3C **Web Authentication (WebAuthn)**, a passwordless way to access the website. It implements the use of an authenticator, which can be physical or virtual. Some of the most used authenticators are Windows Hello, fingerprint readers, Apple TouchID, and FaceID, but any FIDO2 or FIDO U2F authenticators can be used.

Enabling this plugin allows your users to set up WebAuthn as their multi-factor authentication method.

Email Verification

The **Email Verification** method is offered by the **Multi-factor Authentication – Authentication Code by Email** plugin. This method allows users to receive a one-time code via their email address, with which they can complete the authentication process.

This code is valid for a limited time. The plugin offers a few options, as displayed in *Figure 16.6*:

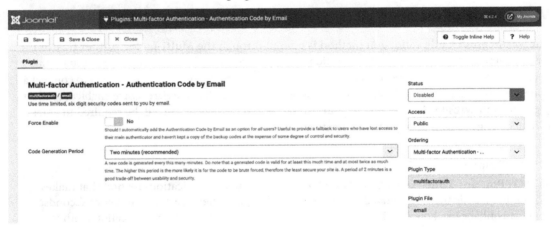

Figure 16.6 – Multi-factor Authentication | Authentication Code by Email

Let's explore the options offered by the plugin:

- **Force Enable**: This is activated by default and provided an additional level of verification for all users. As the hint under the option says, it's very useful if users have issues with any other multi-factor authentication methods.

- **Code Generation Period**: Here, you can choose the interval between code generation.

Next, let's look at the last of the multi-factor authentication method, the fixed code.

Fixed Code

The **Multi-factor Authentication – Fixed Code** plugin is a sample plugin for developers that helps them develop new multi-factor authentication plugins. It should not be used on live websites.

In the next section, we'll learn how to activate multi-factor authentication on our website.

Enabling multi-factor authentication

In this example, we'll enable multi-factor authentication via email verification. To enable multi-factor authentication via email, we need to enable the related plugin and activate the method in the user account. Let's proceed step by step:

1. From the **System Dashboard** area, click on **Plugins** and filter by **Type**, selecting **multifactorauth** from the dropdown.

2. Locate the **Multi-factor Authentication – Authentication Code by Email** plugin and enable it.

3. Click on **User Menu** (the top right of the screen), then **Edit Account**.

4. You will see a new tab called **Multi-factor Authentication** on the user account page, as displayed in *Figure 16.7*. Such pages will show all the validation methods available (enabled) on the website:

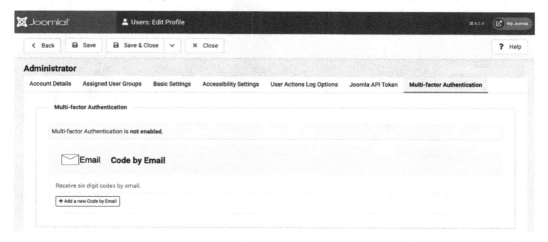

Figure 16.7 – Users: Edit Profile | Multi-factor Authentication

5. To enable the **Code by Email** option, click on the **Add a new Code by Email** button.

6. Once done, the method setup page will open, as shown in *Figure 16.8*. Here, you have the chance to specify a custom title for the validation method and set it as the default multi-factor authentication method for the user account:

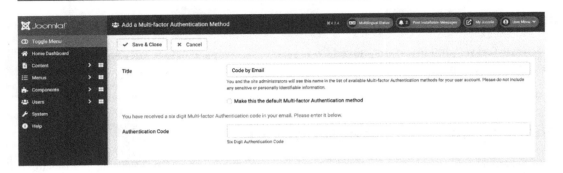

Figure 16.8 – Add a Multi-factor Authentication Method | Code by Email

7. To activate **Code by Email** as a multi-factor authentication method for the user, you need to insert the 6-digit code you received via email in the **Authentication Code** field. Remember that the code is valid only for a few minutes, as per the plugin's options.

8. Congratulations! You've enabled **Code by Email** as a multi-factor authentication method for your account. Due to this, the **Multi-factor Authentication** tab will have updated to show the enabled methods, as shown in *Figure 16.9*:

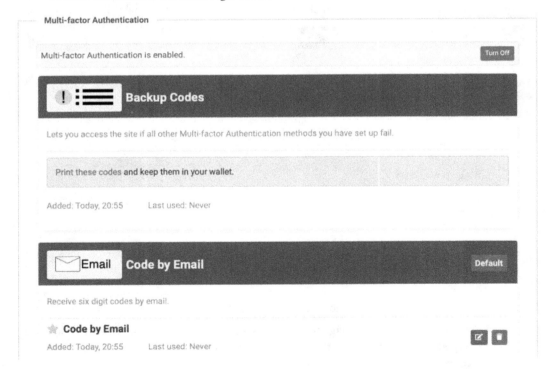

Figure 16.9 – Multi-factor Authentication status for the account

From this page, you can also download **Backup Codes** for the account. Backup codes should be used in case the selected validation method that's been enabled for multi-factor authentication is not available.

By clicking on the **Print these codes** link, you can see and print the available backup codes, as displayed in *Figure 16.10*:

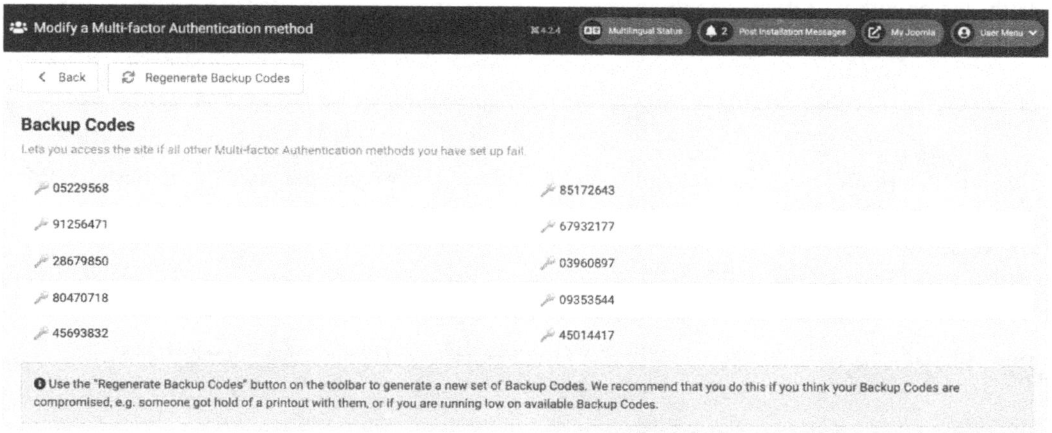

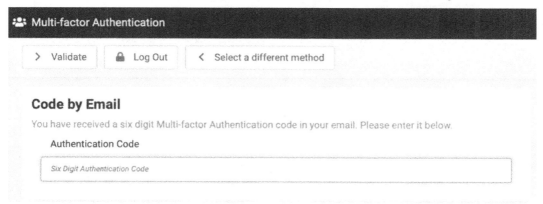

Figure 16.10 – Multi-factor Authentication | Backup Codes

Backup codes can be regenerated by clicking on the related button. Each backup code can be used just once. To see your multi-factor authentication in action, just log out from your website backend and log in again.

After typing in your username and password, a second validation screen will appear, requesting login validation through the multi-factor authentication method selected, as shown in *Figure 16.11*:

Figure 16.11 – Multi-factor Authentication | Login validation

After inserting the authentication code you received via email, the login process will be completed, and you will see the **Home Dashboard** area.

> **Multi-factor authentication is personal**
>
> Multi-factor authentication is configured on a per-account basis. Each user can enable one or more than one authentication method among those available. When multiple authentication methods are enabled, the user may select one of them to be the default, which will be the first one to be shown when logging in, though they can select another one from those configured.

It's also possible to disable or enforce multi-factor authentication on a per-user group basis, in the **Users** component's **Options** area, you can find two options that allow you to do so, as displayed in *Figure 16.12*:

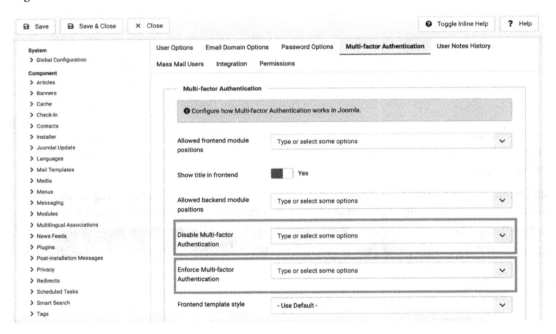

Figure 16.12 – Users | Options | Multi-factor Authentication

It's recommended to enforce multi-factor authentication for user groups that have backend access or administrative permissions on your website so that you can increase the security level of your website.

In the next section, we'll explore the HTTP header security options.

Increasing your website security with HTTP headers

In this section, we'll explore an integrated feature that allows you to increase the security of your website, thereby controlling the HTTP headers that are provided as a response from your server. Well-configured HTTP headers are useful for preventing and reducing the risk of certain types of attacks, such as **Cross-Site Scripting** (**XSS**) and data injection attacks.

Joomla offers a system plugin that allows you to define HTTP headers to configure a **Content Security Policy** (**CSP**) and **HTTP Strict Transfer Security** (**HSTS**).

You can act on these advanced settings from the dedicated plugin, called **System - HTTP Headers**, which you can find by going to **System Dashboard | Plugins**, filtering by **Type**, and selecting **System**.

The plugin offers several options, as displayed in *Figure 16.13*:

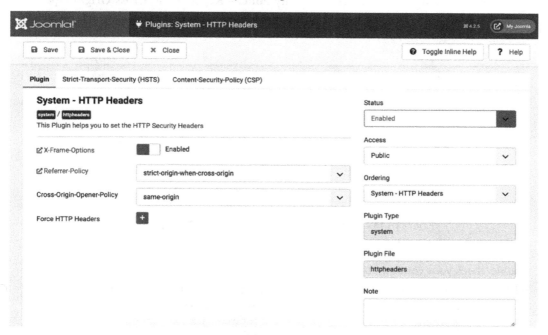

Figure 16.13 – System – HTTP Headers | Plugin

On the mail screen, you can act on the following options:

- Enable or disable the **X-Frame-Options** tag. This tag is useful for preventing pages from being rendered within the `<iframe>`, `<frame>`, `<embed>`, or `<object>` tags.

- Specify a **Referrer-Policy**. Define which and how much information should be passed to referrers. This is an advanced configuration option that can be used to prevent the potential disclosure of information to referred websites.

- Specify a **Cross-Origin-Opener-Policy**. This parameter is useful for isolating your document object when a new window is opened.

- The **Force HTTP Headers** option allows you to specify custom HTTP headers for your website, as displayed in *Figure 16.14*. From this option, you can specify several types of headers: **Content=Security-Policy, Content-Security-Policy – Report-Only, Cross-Origin-Opener-Policy, Expect-CT, Feature-Policy, Permissions-Policy, Referrer-Policy, Report-To, Strict-Transport-Security**, and **X-Frame-Options**:

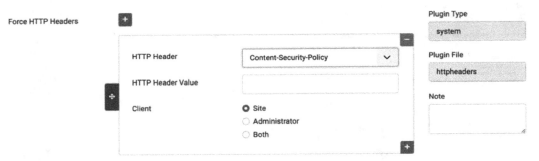

Figure 16.14 – System – HTTP Headers | Force HTTP Headers

> **Double-check your configuration**
>
> HTTP headers control the way your web server responds to requests for your website. Pay attention while configuring headers, as wrong configurations may cause your website to not work properly. In the case of a wrong setup, you can disable the header you specified in the plugin to reinstate the regular functionalities. It's highly recommended that you review the documentation related to each type of HTTP header to find out the most suitable configuration for your use case.

From the second tab, **Strict-Transport-Security (HSTS)**, you can enable or disable HSTS, as shown in *Figure 16.15*:

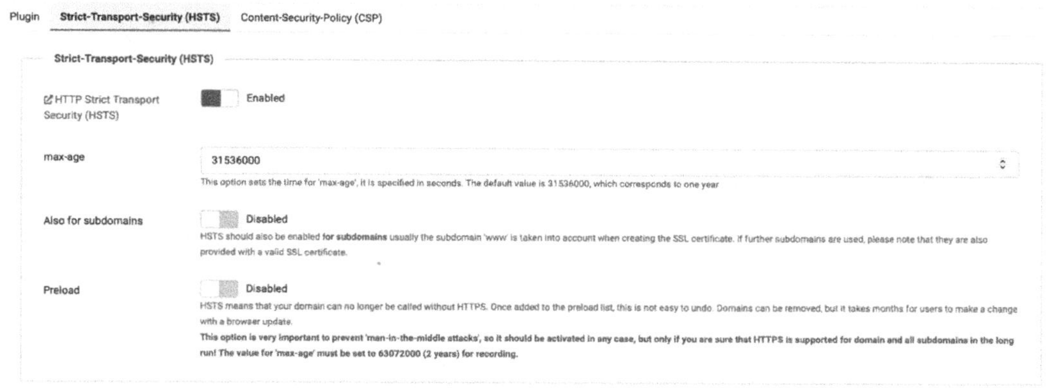

Figure 16.15 – System – HTTP Headers | Strict-Transport-Security (HSTS)

Strict-Transport-Security can be enabled when there is a valid SSL certificate for your websites. It will enforce the use of HTTPS for your website's domain and all its subdomains.

From the same tab, you can specify **max-age** (how long the header will be valid for), decide whether you want to enforce HSTS **Also for subdomains**, and if you want to include your website in the **Preload** list. This last option may only be suitable if you don't want to make your website available in HTTP anymore, but only in HTTPS.

In the last tab, **Content-Security-Policy (CSP)**, as the name suggests, you can specify a CSP for your website. This setting can heavily help prevent XSS attacks, harden the security of the website, and define from which websites you allow various types of resources to be loaded: scripts, frames, images, fonts, and much more.

There are several parameters to configure on the CSP screen, as shown in *Figure 16.16*:

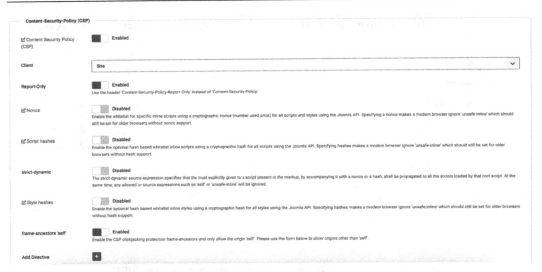

Figure 16.16 – System – HTTP Headers | Content-Security-Policy (CSP)

Let's explore the options for setting up CSP:

- **Content Security Policy (CSP)**: Enable or disable CSP for your website.

- **Client**: Specify if you want to enable the policy for your website's frontend (**Site**), backend (**Administrator**), or both sites (**Both**).

- **Report-Only**: Enable the policy without enforcing any rules. All the violations will be reported in the browser console but not effectively blocked. This setting is helpful while you're working on your CSP, before making it effective.

- **Nonce**: Use a cryptographic nonce (a unique number that's used just once) for all scripts and styles.

- **Script hashes**: Use a whitelist that includes a cryptographic hash for each script used by the website.

- **Strict-dynamic**: Extends trust given to scripts that are explicitly included in the page markup, as well as to scripts loaded by such root scripts.

- **Style hashes**: Use a whitelist that includes a cryptographic hash for each style used by the website.

- **Frame-ancestors 'self'**: Enables protection against clickjacking attacks.

- **Add Directive**: This allows you to specify the directives of your CSP, as shown in *Figure 16.17*:

Figure 16.17 – System – HTTP Headers | Content-Security-Policy (CSP) | Add Directive

In the group of fields, you can specify the parameters for your directives, select a **Policy Directive**, write the rule syntax in the **Value** field, and select a **Client**.

An example of a rule is as follows:

- **Policy Directive**: `font-src`
- **Value**: `'self' example.com *.example.com`
- **Client**: `Site`

The rule we reported in this example allows your website to load fonts files from its domain, such as `example.com`, and any subdomain of `example.com`. A common scenario when you want to enable Google Fonts would require implementing the following CSP:

```
Content-Security-Policy: default-src 'self';font-src fonts.
gstatic.com;style-src 'self' fonts.googleapis.com
```

As you can see, this would require three rules:

- A `default-src` directive with a **Value** of `'self'`
- A `font-src` directive with a **Value** of `fonts.gstatic.com`
- A `style-src` directive with a **Value** of `'self' fonts.googleapis.com`

This set of rules will allow your website to load style files (CSS) and font files (TTF, OTF, and so on) from the Google Fonts service.

A well-configured CSP would mitigate the risk of XSS, clickjacking, and other types of attacks. Note that mistakes in the policy could lead to broken functionalities or some parts of the website not being displayed. It's recommended to test your settings using **Report-Only** mode to ensure all the functionalities work as expected, before enabling your CSP in production environments.

Now that we've covered CSPs, we've finished exploring HTTP headers.

Exercises

It's time to apply the knowledge you've acquired in this chapter with the proposed exercises.

Exercise 1 – WebAuthn authentication

In this exercise, you will enable WebAuthn authentication on your account, as described in the first part of this chapter. Please note that you will need a device that supports FIDO2 or FIDO U2F authenticators such as TouchID, FaceID, Windows Hello, or similar technologies.

> **Requirements**
> Please note that to enable and use WebAuthn authentication, your website must be configured to use HTTPS with a valid/trusted SSL certificate (such as Let's Encrypt or another valid certification authority).

After enabling the WebAuthn authentication method for your account, log out from your website backend and try to log in again, typing your username and clicking on the **Web Authentication** button, then using the authenticator you configured.

Exercise 2 – multi-factor authentication

In this exercise, you will configure multi-factor authentication for your account. Follow the instructions included in the dedicated section of this chapter, *Email verification*, to enable the **Authentication Code by Email** method for your account.

Summary

In this chapter, we explored some advanced features dedicated to website access and security. We got to know the WebAuthn functionality and explored the multi-factor authentication methods available in the Joomla core. We also learned how to set up multi-factor authentication using the **Code by Email** method.

Then, we introduced HTTP headers and how they can help increase a website's security level. From here, we explored how to configure HTTP headers and their related options and introduced some basic concepts of CSP. It's recommended that you deepen your knowledge about HTTP headers and configuration with the links provided in the *Further reading* section.

In the next chapter, we'll go through a case study of a corporate website built with Joomla 4.

Further reading

To learn more about the topics that were covered in this chapter, take a look at the following resources:

- **Time-based One-Time Password** (**TOTP**): https://en.wikipedia.org/wiki/Time-based_one-time_password
- Joomla WebAuthn authentication documentation: https://docs.joomla.org/WebAuthn_Passwordless_Login
- Web Authentication: https://en.wikipedia.org/wiki/WebAuthn
- X-Frame-Options: https://developer.mozilla.org/en-US/docs/Web/HTTP/Headers/X-Frame-Options
- Referrer-Policy: https://developer.mozilla.org/en-US/docs/Web/HTTP/Headers/Referrer-Policy
- **Strict-Transport-Security** (**HSTS**): https://en.wikipedia.org/wiki/HTTP_Strict_Transport_Security
- Content Security Policy: https://developer.mozilla.org/en-US/docs/Web/HTTP/CSP

Part 4: Case Studies

In this part, you will see some real-life examples of how Joomla has been implemented to build successful websites in different scenarios.

Three case studies will show you how powerful and versatile Joomla is. You'll see how Joomla helped a company to increase effectiveness and reduce time-to-market for new pages, empowering its marketing department. In the second case study, you'll see how to build a full-featured e-learning portal with Joomla, sell and manage subscriptions through the website, grant access to online classes, and allow learners to track their progress. In the last case study, you'll see how to develop an accommodation booking system, allowing visitors to book an apartment through the website; you'll also see how to integrate and sync the website's availability calendar with third-party booking portals.

This part has the following chapters:

- *Chapter 17, Case Study – A Corporate Website in Joomla*
- *Chapter 18, Case Study – An Online Academy with Joomla*
- *Chapter 19, Case Study – A B&B Booking System with Joomla*

17

Case Study – A Corporate Website in Joomla

In the previous chapter, we explored some of Joomla's advanced features dedicated to access and security.

In this chapter, we'll explore a case study, showing how Joomla has been deployed and used in a specific corporate scenario.

After reading this chapter, you will understand the following:

- How Joomla has been deployed in a corporate environment
- How Joomla has helped the company reach its goals
- How Joomla helps reduce the time to market for new pages

Introduction

In this case study, we'll analyze the experience of Host.it, an Italian hosting service provider that was an early adopter of Joomla 4 for its corporate website.

Host.it has been involved with Joomla since its inception – in fact, it acted as a supporter and sponsor of the Italian Joomla community, providing it with free hosting infrastructure, co-organizing JoomlaDay Italy, and sponsoring localization activities.

The company offered a Joomla-compatible hosting service when other major hosting companies didn't, and this allowed it to conquer an important market share among Joomla hosting services.

The Host.it website was originally built in 2017 during the company rebranding, and it was released as a monolith Java application that included the company **Customer Relationship Management (CRM)** system, the web shop, the client panel, and the public website. This was the natural choice since the core systems of the company were developed using Java and **Java Server Page (JSP)**.

Over the years, the company realized that the marketing team was struggling to be more Agile and effective in publishing new web pages or changing existing ones given that each change to the public website needed a full release of the whole monolith software. This made the company less reactive in updating its website and increased the effort necessary to create marketing initiatives and campaigns.

Furthermore, the website was not brilliant in terms of performance, as it included many unused parts and styles inherited from previous releases.

During 2021, the company decided to rebuild its website – let's see what the goals of the project were.

> **Note**
> The website analyzed in this case study is available in the Italian language only.

Project goals

The company launched the project to rebuild its website from scratch and established several goals that the new website should meet:

- Reduce the time to market when building new pages
- Reduce the time required to change or update the website
- Increase the website speed
- Increase the **Search Engine Optimization** (**SEO**) of the website
- Reproduce the same layout and look and feel of the previous website

The project wanted to decouple the public website from the monolith Java application, leaving the CRM and the e-commerce part untouched. The website mostly included product pages with information and comparative tables, service description pages, product comparison modules, and configurators to provide real-time quotations to customers.

Furthermore, the new website needed to integrate the company's blog, which was built in WordPress and held over 300 articles. In the next section, we'll see why the company chose Joomla to create its website.

Why Joomla?

Having been the patron of the Italian Joomla community for years and one of the most used hosting services for Joomla in the country, the company had great expertise on Joomla. Furthermore, Joomla was already in use for other public and internal websites in the company, since it powered Host Academy, an e-learning portal; several company landing pages used by the marketing team; and an intranet portal used by customer service to handle work shifts, vacation plans, and requests.

Besides the internal expertise, Joomla offered several advantages that influenced the decision:

- A brand-new stable version approaching (Joomla 4)
- A lightweight, powerful, and fast core
- Built-in multilanguage support
- A modular structure

Joomla 4, which was still in the Beta phase at the time the decision was made, looked future proof in the eyes of the company, allowing the use of cutting-edge technology, being based on a modern graphic framework such as Bootstrap 5, and supporting the future internationalization path of the company.

Let's now see how the project reached its goals.

Reproducing the previous website using another technology

The first challenge was to reproduce the previous website's look and feel. The company management wanted to make the release of the new website unnoticeable to visitors, so the whole website layout, navigation system, graphics, and color palette were reproduced in a Bootstrap 5 template for Joomla 4.

The development of this custom template, based on Cassiopeia, required a few weeks of work on the part of two experienced Joomla developers, **Marco Biagioni** and **Alessandro Chessari**.

The result was identical, as you can see in *Figure 17.1* and *Figure 17.2*.

Figure 17.1 – Host.it home page developed in JSP

As you can see in the following screenshot, there are just small spacing and sizing differences between the two versions:

Figure 17.2 – Host.it home page developed with Joomla 4

Replicating the whole layout required the development of a series of custom modules, such as the customizable cards on the home page (visible in *Figure 17.2*), which show the product lines and their prices.

These cards are completely configurable in the backend as a specific type of module, as shown in *Figure 17.3*.

Figure 17.3 – Home page card module | Card details

The cards module, developed specifically for the website, allowed the creation of cards with information about the product, using the **subform** field to handle multiple items. Each card handles multiple fields, such as the title, icon, and price, and allows the style to be customized, setting the font size, the anchor text for links, and much more.

Another custom module that has been developed is the service configurator, a module that allows the website visitor to configure the product as desired and get the price in real time, as displayed in *Figure 17.4*.

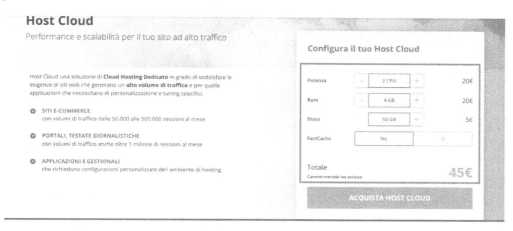

Figure 17.4 – Service configurator module

The team also developed a module to look up for domain names. This module interacts with the e-commerce APIs to show the status of a domain name and allows the user to register or transfer it. The module includes a JSON import feature that allows administrator to load the list of managed **Top Level Domains** (TLDs) and their prices. The domain lookup module is shown in *Figure 17.5*.

Figure 17.5 – Domain lookup domain

There were also other modules developed, such as another card module to show the reasons to buy a certain product or service, a module to show calls to action, a customized breadcrumb module, and much more.

This approach, based on modules, allowed the team to build a completely customized layout and re-use some parts; in fact, the domain lookup module is implemented for two pages, and the card modules were deployed for multiple pages and places.

The use of modules avoided the use of page builders or layout builders, ensuring clean and lightweight code, which was directly reflected by the website's performance, as we'll analyze in the next section.

A fast and modern website

As mentioned earlier, one of the main goals of the project was to provide the company with a fast and modern website that was decoupled from the monolith Java application.

Joomla 4, since the tests conducted during the early Beta phase, achieved great results in terms of performance, with reduced response and loading times. Furthermore, performance was crucial for the company, which sells fast hosting services, and it couldn't have a slow-loading website.

Starting from a lightweight frontend such as Cassiopeia, the use of modern standards for images, such as **WEBP**, and the minification of CSS and JavaScript allowed the website to be reactive and ensured fast loading times.

To check whether the goal was fulfilled, the company tested the old website and the new one with **GTMetrix**, simulating an unthrottled connection from London that was closer to their data centers.

The previous website (JSP) was graded C, with 66% as result for performance, as displayed in *Figure 17.6*.

Figure 17.6 – GTMetrix Results | Old website in JSP

Instead, the new website achieved an A grade, with 98% in terms of performance, as depicted in *Figure 17.7.*

Figure 17.7 – GTMetrix Results | New website in Joomla 4

All the fundamental performance metrics were improved, especially **Core Web Vitals**, which are appreciated by search engines and users.

The test on the new website was made right after the release of the website to ensure a fair condition and consistency with the previous test. The current website includes several new sections that might have altered the performance results.

In the next section, we'll analyze how the technology change has been managed to retain the SEO position.

Keeping the position

A major challenge was minimizing the impact of the migration on the company's current search engine position, considering that all the URLs of the website also changed due to the technological transition, moving from URLs that included the `.jsp` extension to URLs without any extension. This purpose requested the team to extensively map all the URLs of the old website using **Screaming Frog** and prepare an `.htaccess` file with all the redirects from the old URL to the new URL.

The hardest part was represented by the blog since there was the need to import – almost automatically – all the contents from the WordPress instance. This was handled using the **CMigrator** extension, which allowed the team to import all the articles and their images and categories. Again, all the URLs were mapped, and the redirects were setup in the `.htaccess` file.

After publishing the new website, the team still detected certain 404 errors, which were triggered by certain pages or resources that were almost hidden. The team then used the **Redirect** component of Joomla, which allowed the team to identify and address all the remaining errors.

All these activities allowed the website to keep its search engine position and minimized the impacts of the whole migration.

In the next section, we'll see which extensions have been used in the project.

Extensions used

Besides the custom modules developed specifically for the project, there were a few extensions used on the website:

- **CMigrator by CompoJoom**: Used temporarily to migrate content from the WordPress blog
- **Akeeba Backup**: To quickly create backups on the fly while working on the website
- **GDPR by J! Extensions Store**: Used to manage cookie mapping and classification, displaying a cookie bar and complying with privacy regulations
- **OSMap by JoomlaShack**: Used to create and maintain an XML sitemap to be sent to search engines
- **Phoca OpenGraph**: Used to manage OpenGraph tags for the contents
- **LiteSpeed Cache**: Used to unleash the benefits of caching functionalities offered by the server

Overall, the team tried to keep the number of extensions used to the bare minimum to reduce security risks and the impact on the website's performance.

With the list of extensions used on the website, we have completed this case study.

Summary

In this chapter, we went through a case study that demonstrated an implementation of Joomla 4 in a corporate environment, where the CMS was used to build a brand-new corporate website that needed to match some specific requirements in term of look, feel, and performance.

In the next chapter, we'll analyze another case study – creating a learning portal with Joomla.

18

Case Study – Online Academy with Joomla

In the previous chapter, we explored a case study in which Joomla was serving as a content management system for a corporate website.

In this chapter, we'll explore another case study, showing how Joomla has been used to build and manage an online academy.

After reading this chapter, you will be able to do the following:

- Understand how Joomla could manage a subscription-based website
- Understand how Joomla is serving online learning materials to thousands of learners.

Introduction

In this case study, we'll see how Joomla can be used to build a complete online learning portal, providing access to courses, lessons, and related tests for its subscribers.

An online academy has several requirements, especially when access to the learning material needs to be limited to subscribed users.

The academy website existed for years and used standard Joomla articles to render the courses' materials. A new development was needed to improve the user experience and increase the engagement of learners. Let's see the goals of the project.

> **Note**
> The website analyzed in this case study is available in the Italian language only.

Project goals

The company started a project to rebuild the website of the academy, defining the following requirements in terms of functionalities and goals:

- Allow users to access content only with a valid subscription
- Provide subscriptions with different subscription duration
- Allow subscribers to track their progress in a specific course
- Automatically release a completion certificate when a student completes a course

The website features a series of pages that present each of the available classes, describing the course structure, the number of lessons, and an introductory video.

Furthermore, it includes a private area dedicated to subscribers in which users would be able to manage their subscriptions, access courses, and learning paths, and download their certificates.

In the next section, we'll see why the company chose Joomla to create its website.

Why Joomla?

The company had already used the previous version of Joomla to build several internal and client-facing websites. Furthermore, the academy website itself was built in Joomla 3.x; therefore, choosing Joomla 4 was a natural choice.

The adoption of Joomla 4 represented the perfect moment to reimagine the user experience and build a completely new subscriber area and improved course pages.

In the next section, we'll analyze the solution implemented by the company.

The solution

The website was to include two main features:

- Sell subscriptions
- Allow users to view learning materials once they have a valid subscription

To manage the subscriptions, the company decided to continue using **Membership Pro**, an extension that allowed the team to create subscription plans and set several options based on the status of the subscription.

For example, when the subscription is valid, the user gets added to a specific user group in Joomla, linked to a specific access level, allowing them to access contents restricted to such an access level.

At the same time, whenever the subscription expires, the user gets removed from such user group and the access to content is automatically removed.

The academy offers three types of subscriptions, with duration as the only difference between them, so the configuration for all the subscriptions is nearly the same. With any subscription, in fact, the user can access all the contents of the academy for 1 month, 3 months, or 12 months.

Membership Pro allowed the team to handle the whole sales process, including the payment methods, thanks to the integration with PayPal and many other offline and online payment plugins. With PayPal integration, the company was able to collect payments through credit and debit cards and PayPal accounts. For a specific subscription plan, the company set the automatic renewal of the subscription through PayPal automated payments.

As mentioned earlier, the **ACL** controls of Joomla have been crucial in the setup of this website, since **access levels** and **user groups** were widely used in connection with the subscription plans and their status. In fact, a custom access level and a user group have been created and assigned to users when subscribing, as well as removed once the subscription elapsed.

Once the subscription part was defined, the team focused on improving the learning experience. In fact, the previous version of the website used standard Joomla articles and categories to propose the course contents to subscribers. This resulted in several limitations, including the lack of learning progress tracking and the need to create complex custom layouts to display the courses.

The team, after thorough research, decided to adopt **OSCampus Pro** as the **Learning Management System (LMS)**. OSCampus was selected due to its simple structure and its features. In fact, it allows you to do the following:

- Organize lessons in courses and courses in learning paths
- Track the progress of lessons in each course
- Handle exams/tests at the end of each course
- Automatically issue a certificate when a test is passed

All these features were identified in the list of project goals, so the extension resulted in the right choice for the website.

In OSCampus, the team organized the courses in learning paths by topic and loaded all the lessons of each course. To host videos for the lessons, the team decided to use **Vimeo** to reduce server workload and benefit from a professional video streaming platform. The team also produced a short evaluation test for each of the courses, which required a score above 70% to pass it and obtain the certificate.

In each lesson, most of the screen area is dedicated to the video player. The page also shows the commands to navigate between lessons or to go back to the course index, as shown in *Figure 18.1*.

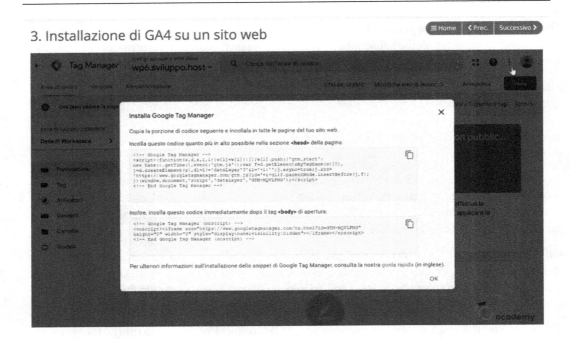

Figure 18.1 – Online academy – single lesson

For each course, a recap page is available in which there is a list of lessons, as shown in *Figure 18.2.*

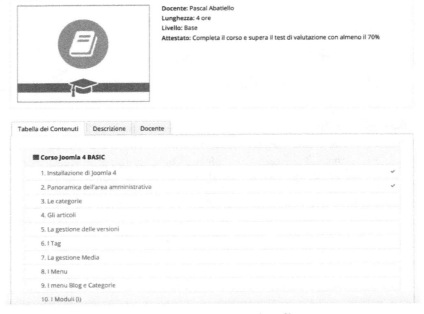

Figure 18.2 – Online academy – list of lessons

All the courses and lessons have been assigned to a specific access level so that they are accessible only to users with a valid subscription.

At the time of writing, the academy hosts more than 1,200 video lessons, in more than 100 courses, and manages more than 8,000 subscribers.

Another important goal was to improve the user experience for subscribers. To do so, the team created a user dashboard using **SP Page Builder**, as shown in *Figure 18.3*.

Figure 18.3 – Online academy – user dashboard

From the dashboard, the subscriber can access the available courses, check their progress, download their certificates, check their subscription, manage their subscription, manage their account, access additional services and materials, and log out from the reserved area.

One of the most requested features was the one that allows subscribers to track their progress. This has been accomplished thanks to a specific view of the OSCampus component that creates a page displaying the completion status of each course started by the subscriber, as shown in *Figure 18.4*.

I miei corsi

Tieni traccia dei tuoi progressi e riprendi le lezioni dal punto in cui avevi interrotto

I miei corsi

☰ Titolo del Corso	🗓 Ultima visita	▣ Progresso
Corso Bing Webmaster Tools	Luglio 2,	
Corso Fondamenti di CSS3	Novembre 28, 2022	
Corso Fondamenti di HTML5	Novembre 28, 2022	
Corso Joomla 3.x Basic	Novembre 28, 2022	37%
Corso Joomla 3.x Plus	Novembre 28, 2022	
Corso Joomla 3.x Security	Novembre 28, 2022	100%
Corso Joomla 3.x SEO	Novembre 28, 2022	
Corso Joomla 4 BASIC	Novembre 28, 2022	
Corso Joomla 4 SEO	Novembre 28, 2022	

Figure 18.4 – Online academy – course progress

When all the lessons are completed and the test is passed with a grade above 70%, a completion certificate is issued automatically and is available for download on the specific page of the user dashboard.

Beyond the new user dashboard and all the features dedicated to subscribers, the team also worked heavily on the public website, creating new pages for each course. To simplify the design process, the team adopted **Helix Ultimate** as a template framework and SP Page Builder to easily create stunning pages.

For each course, the team built a page that displayed the course title, a preview of the first video lesson, and a description of the course, as shown in *Figure 18.5*.

Figure 18.5 – Online academy – course presentation

Furthermore, for each course, the team created a table of contents, shown on the course presentation page, as displayed in *Figure 18.6*.

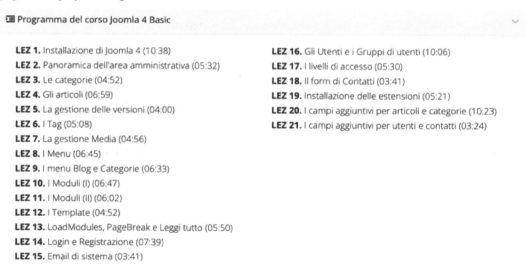

Figure 18.6 – Online academy – course table of contents

This new website structure and the improved user experience offered by the user dashboard allowed the academy to increase its subscription and engagement rates. This was because users could now find more information about the academy and its courses on the public website and could easily track their progress and download their certificates.

In the next section, we'll discover which extensions have been used for the project.

Extensions used

Besides the custom modules developed specifically for the project, there were a few extensions used on the website:

- **Akeeba Backup**: Used to quickly create backups on the fly, while working on the website
- **GDPR by J!Extensions Store**: Used to manage cookie mapping and classification, display a cookie bar, and comply with privacy regulations
- **Membership Pro by JoomDonation**: Used to sell and manage subscriptions
- **OSCampus Pro by JoomlaShack**: Used to manage courses, lessons, and learning paths
- **LiteSpeed Cache**: Used to unleash the benefits of caching functionalities offered by the server
- **SP Page Builder**: Used to build pages quickly

Overall, the team tried to keep the number of extensions used to the bare minimum, to reduce security risks and the footprint on website performance.

With the list of extensions used on the website, we have completed this case study.

Summary

In this chapter, we went through a case study that shows the implementation of Joomla 4 to manage an e-learning portal. Joomla has been used to handle the subscription sales and, thanks to ACL, grant proper access to learning resources.

In the next chapter, we'll analyze another case study, creating a **Bed and Breakfast** (**B&B**) website with Joomla.

19

Case Study – A B&B Booking System with Joomla

In the previous chapter, we explored a case study in which Joomla was powering an online academy.

In this chapter, we'll explore another case study, showing how Joomla has been used to build a **Bed & Breakfast (B&B)** website and handle bookings.

After reading this chapter, you will be able to do the following:

- Understand how Joomla can manage an accommodation booking website
- Understand how to integrate the bookings calendar with third-party services

Introduction

In this case study, we'll learn how Joomla can be used to develop a website for a B&B/tourist rental, to show the apartment and allow potential guests to book their stay.

The website was a brand-new development, to be done right after the renovation of the apartment, with the start of renting activities. Let's look at the goals of the project.

> **Note**
> The website analyzed in this case study is available in the Italian language only.

Project goals

The apartment owner wanted to have a website for his tourist rental and set the following requirements:

- Allow potential guests to see the apartment with presentation pages that included pictures
- Allow guests to book their stay through a professional reservation system that shows apartment availability in real time

- Keep the availability calendar in sync with third-party specialized portals

The website was meant to be very simple with a couple of pages to present the apartment, the booking system, and a contact page.

The most complex feature would have been the booking system, integrated with external services.

In the next section, we'll see why Joomla was selected to create the website.

Why Joomla?

The owner already had a Joomla 3.x website for another of his properties, where the same features were already deployed successfully. The adoption of Joomla 4 was the evolution of an already reliable technical solution, which we'll analyze in the next section.

The solution

The website was to have two main purposes:

- Exhibit the apartment
- Manage bookings and availability

To quickly build layouts and customize the graphics, the team chose to use **Helix Ultimate** as a template framework, together with **SP Page Builder**. Thanks to the visual layout builder offered by the page builder, the page structure was created easily, as shown in *Figure 19.1*:

Figure 19.1 – SP Page Builder | page layout builder

The page builder, together with the template framework, gave the website a modern and clean design, highlighting the images of the apartment thanks to carousels, alternated with text descriptions, as shown in *Figure 19.2*:

Figure 19.2 – Home page | layout with text and images

SP Page Builder also offers some graphics effects that can be applied to images, such as the parallax effect, which was deployed for large images at the bottom of the home page and on other pages, making the image scroll with the mouse.

The **Open Street Maps** technology has been integrated into the contact page to show the position of the apartment on an interactive map. This is draggable and zoomable and perfectly integrated into the layout of the website, as shown in *Figure 19.3*:

Figure 19.3 – Contact page | interactive map

Another page has been built with SP Page Builder to illustrate details of the entire apartment. On this page, each room of the apartment has been described, accompanied by the related photos, which can be zoomed out in a popup after they've been clicked, as shown in *Figure 19.4*:

Figure 19.4 – The apartment | layout text with thumbnails

To manage bookings and apartment availability, the team used **Solidres**, an online booking and reservation system for Joomla. **Solidres** allows you to create and manage one or multiple properties, as well as define the characteristics, pricing, and availability of each property.

A property in **Solidres** is used to manage general rules, addresses, and tax setup, describe the property, set the payment methods, and much more.

Within a property, it's possible to create one or more accommodation solutions, such as rooms. A room is a rentable unit, in which it's possible to set up occupancy numbers and limits, price plans, and specific fields, such as equipment and facilities. The availability calendar is tied to the room, as a property may have additional rooms to rent and each of them has a different availability, as shown in *Figure 19.5*:

Figure 19.5 – Solidres | availability calendar

In this case, there's only one apartment so the apartment has been set up both as a property and as a room within the property.

Solidres also allows you to close rooms to block bookings in certain periods. This may be useful when the room is not available due to maintenance or landlord unavailability. The system also allows you to manage discounts and coupons and accommodate promotional initiatives, and can also handle complex configurations in terms of stay length and periods.

Through a dedicated plugin, **Complex Tariff**, the system can manage special offers and composite calculation methods for the rental fee based on the number of guests, nights, and eventual options.

Solidres is also able to calculate taxes, such as VAT and tourist tax, which is mandatory in many cities in Italy. For example, in this case, *Tourist Tax* gets calculated for each stay, based on the number of guests and number of nights.

Nowadays, apartments for tourist rentals should also be published on dedicated portals such as Airbnb and Booking.com to increase the number of reservations received and maximize occupancy rates. Being published on these websites requires the owner to manage multiple availability calendars, with the risk of overbooking or missing reservations. To solve these issues, **Solidres** offers a plugin, **iCal**, that allows the owner to keep the availability calendar of the website synchronized with the ones on Booking.com and Airbnb.

This plugin regularly pushes changes in availability in both ways, so in case a reservation is made in any of the three endpoints, the availability is updated across the three websites. This resulted in increased efficiency, removing the need to manually check and updates calendars, and maximized the room occupancy rates, thanks to the additional exposures. This sync is done through the **iCal** export and import features offered by the **iCal** plugin, given that portals such as Booking.com and Airbnb also offer calendar sync features through the **iCal** format, as shown in *Figure 19.6*:

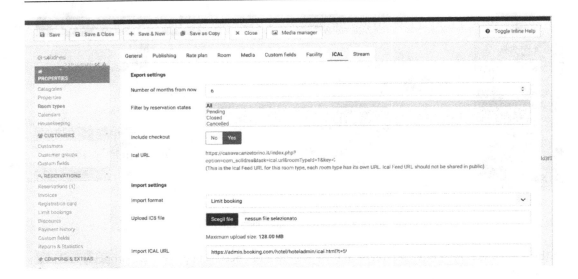

Figure 19.6 – Solidres | iCal import and export features

To manage the sync activity, a cron was created in the Joomla **Scheduled Task** feature, which we explored in *Chapter 9, Planning Operations with Scheduled Tasks*. A **GET Request** type of task that's executed regularly every 10 minutes ensures the sync between booking systems, as shown in *Figure 19.7*:

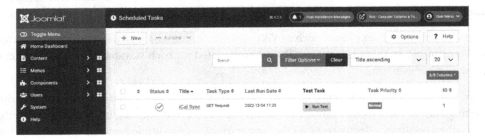

Figure 19.7 – Scheduled Tasks | task to sync iCal endpoints

Even though **Solidres** can manage multiple payment methods, including payments by credit/debit cards, the owner decided to only implement offline payments with bank transfers. At the end of the booking, the system shows the user how to make the payment by bank transfer, including the details in the confirmation email. The owner can track the payment status of each reservation, adding notes and registering the date and the amount received by each guest, as shown in *Figure 19.8*:

Figure 19.8 – Reservation payment tracking and notes

The system can generate receipts and invoices, as well as customizable email notifications to landlords and guests. Furthermore, it's available as a mobile app for Android and iOS, with which the landlord can view and manage reservations from a mobile device thanks to QR codes added to reservation confirmation emails, as shown in *Figure 19.9*:

Figure 19.9 – Preview of a reservation confirmation email

In the frontend, the booking system proposes a few steps to allow guests to select the room, the desired period of stay, and the offer, as shown in *Figure 19.10*:

Figure 19.10 – Frontend booking flow

The system offered all the needed features to handle reservations professionally and keep the availability in sync with external booking websites, reducing the amount of effort needed by the landlord.

In the next section, we'll discover which extensions were used for the project.

Extensions used

For this website, the list of extensions that were used is very short:

- **Solidres**: Used to manage reservations, with plugins such as **iCal** and **Complex Tariff**
- **SP Page Builder**: Used to build pages quickly

Now that we've looked at the list of extensions used on the website, we have completed this case study.

Summary

In this chapter, we went through a case study that showed how to implement Joomla 4 to manage a tourist rental solution and its reservations.

With this case study, we have completed our journey of learning Joomla. There are still a few more topics, which can be explored at `https://docs.joomla.org`. Joomla has a rich roadmap ahead with many interesting new features planned for the next versions.

I hope you found this book interesting and that you learned the basics of Joomla.

Index

Symbols

Packt.com

Subscribe to our online digital library for full access to over 7,000 books and videos, as well as industry leading tools to help you plan your personal development and advance your career. For more information, please visit our website.

Why subscribe?

- Spend less time learning and more time coding with practical eBooks and Videos from over 4,000 industry professionals

- Improve your learning with Skill Plans built especially for you

- Get a free eBook or video every month

- Fully searchable for easy access to vital information

- Copy and paste, print, and bookmark content

Did you know that Packt offers eBook versions of every book published, with PDF and ePub files available? You can upgrade to the eBook version at packt.com and as a print book customer, you are entitled to a discount on the eBook copy. Get in touch with us at customercare@packtpub.com for more details.

At www.packt.com, you can also read a collection of free technical articles, sign up for a range of free newsletters, and receive exclusive discounts and offers on Packt books and eBooks.

Other Books You May Enjoy

If you enjoyed this book, you may be interested in these other books by Packt:

Modernizing Enterprise CMS Using Pimcore

Daniele Fontani, Marco Guiducci, Francesco Minà

ISBN: 9781801075404

- Create, edit, and manage Pimcore documents for your web pages
- Manage web assets in Pimcore using the digital asset management (DAM) feature
- Discover how to create layouts, templates, and custom widgets for your web pages
- Administer third-party add-ons for your Pimcore site using the admin UI
- Discover practices to use Pimcore as a product information management (PIM) system
- Explore Pimcore's master data management (MDM) for enterprise CMS development
- Build reusable website components and save time using effective tips and tricks

WordPress Plugin Development Cookbook - Third Edition

Yannick Lefebvre

ISBN: 9781801810777

- Discover action and filter hooks, which form the basis of plugin creation
- Explore the creation of administration pages and add new content management sections through custom post types and custom fields
- Add new components to the block editor library
- Fetch, cache, and regularly update data from external sources
- Bring in external data sources to enhance your content
- Make your pages dynamic by using JavaScript, jQuery, and AJAX and adding new widgets to the platform
- Add support for plugin translation and distributing your work to the WordPress community

Packt is searching for authors like you

If you're interested in becoming an author for Packt, please visit `authors.packtpub.com` and apply today. We have worked with thousands of developers and tech professionals, just like you, to help them share their insight with the global tech community. You can make a general application, apply for a specific hot topic that we are recruiting an author for, or submit your own idea.

Share Your Thoughts

Now you've finished *Joomla! 4 Masterclass*, we'd love to hear your thoughts! Scan the QR code below to go straight to the Amazon review page for this book and share your feedback or leave a review on the site that you purchased it from.

`https://packt.link/r/1803238976`

Your review is important to us and the tech community and will help us make sure we're delivering excellent quality content.

Download a free PDF copy of this book

Thanks for purchasing this book!

Do you like to read on the go but are unable to carry your print books everywhere?

Is your eBook purchase not compatible with the device of your choice?

Don't worry, now with every Packt book you get a DRM-free PDF version of that book at no cost.

Read anywhere, any place, on any device. Search, copy, and paste code from your favorite technical books directly into your application.

The perks don't stop there, you can get exclusive access to discounts, newsletters, and great free content in your inbox daily

Follow these simple steps to get the benefits:

1. Scan the QR code or visit the link below

https://packt.link/free-ebook/9781803238975

2. Submit your proof of purchase
3. That's it! We'll send your free PDF and other benefits to your email directly